"Baad Bitches" and
Sassy Supermamas

THE NEW BLACK STUDIES SERIES

Edited by Darlene Clark Hine
and Dwight A. McBride

*A list of books in the series
appears at the end of this book.*

"Baad Bitches" and Sassy Supermamas

BLACK POWER ACTION FILMS

STEPHANE DUNN

UNIVERSITY OF ILLINOIS PRESS

Urbana and Chicago

Library of Congress Cataloging-in-Publication Data
Dunn, Stephane, 1967–
"Baad bitches" and sassy supermamas : Black power
action films / Stephane Dunn.
p.   cm. — (The new Black studies series)
Includes bibliographical references and index.
ISBN-13 978-0-252-03340-7 (cloth : alk. paper)
ISBN-10 0-252-03340-X (cloth : alk. paper)
ISBN-13 978-0-252-07548-3 (pbk. : alk. paper)
ISBN-10 978-0-252-07548-X (pbk. : alk. paper)
1. Blaxploitation films—United States—History and criticism.
2. Adventure films—United States—History and criticism.
3. African American women heroes in motion pictures.
I. Title.
PN1995.9.N4D86   2008
791.43'652996073—dc22   2007048113

In love, dedication, and memory
to the toughest woman I ever knew,
my grandmother, Mrs. Idene Ward.

Word Revolution vs. World

Bitch/Ho/Nigga/ Nigger
Baaad Bitch 'scuse me   no offense meant
I coulda   woulda   shoulda
bleep bleep bleep
politically correct myself
You know the N-word   B-word
mama said she'd wash yr mouth out with soap
cuss words   fightin' words   Who you callin'
bleep
Fill in the blanks with blank words
Erase 300 plus yrs   Jim Crow   & all isms
magic ease away
N-words and B-words   Not call the lover I love
my niggaaaaa
Or sadly   or   cleverly   rename & flip 'em
baaad brotha'   tough sista' handlin' her shit
thoughts into words   words into matter
revolutions of the soul
mind meeting spirit meeting
thoughts meeting words meeting transformation
so it's been said   spoken   sang
free yr mind
body   will   follow

Contents

Preface

In 1973, when I was seven years old, *Get Christy Love* premiered on television. It lasted only one brief season, but I never forgot Christy, played by pretty Teresa Graves. I was an avid television watcher who, like a lot of other kids, knew the theme song to *The Brady Bunch* by heart and loved action series like *Police Woman* and later *The Six Million Dollar Man* and *Charlie's Angels.* Yet, as much as I loved the groovy, blonde- and brown-haired, perfect-looking Brady family, I had a bit of Claudia in me—the Shirley-Temple-and-Barbie-doll-hating narrator in Toni Morrison's *The Bluest Eye.*

As a young black girl consuming popular media imagery and internalizing cultural thinking about the relationship between skin color and perceptions of feminine beauty, I wasn't hip to the historical implications of whitened aesthetics of beauty and glamour or to the power signified by the control of representations. However, I was hungry, like many black folk, to see more of an array of blackness, black people and black culture, to *see me,* vivid and central on that screen that so held my attention. My television-watching childhood was punctuated by the relatively few significant black TV presences—the sitcom *Good Times,* the miniseries *Roots,* and the rare movies where young black girls were the center of the story, such as the book-based *I Know Why the Caged Bird Sings* and *Roll of Thunder, Hear My Cry.*

Going to the movies, especially the drive-in, was a unique family event. The big screen presented such intense color, animation, and thrilling action that I sat terrified, gleefully so, in the backseat of our Pontiac, watching *Jaws* and *King Kong.* I saw that whether beast or human, bodies within that huge screen space became intense visual spectacles, often through the intensifying inscriptions of masculinity and femininity, whiteness and blackness, "sameness" and "otherness." Since the days of Christy, I've been enthralled by the heightened sense of entertainment that action films offer. I can still see pretty, chocolate-skinned Christy smiling and kicking butt. I remember one episode in particular where Christy went to a park disguised as a prostitute to catch a serial killer. Sure enough, the rapist-killer showed up and was soon martial arts–whipped by Christy: "You under arrest, Suugah." Of course, now through the prism of my developing critical spectatorship, I see that while the character signified the public visibility of a feminist and black liberation aesthetic, Christy's sexy, tough black woman cop role also demonstrated the continued influence of historical dominant inscriptions of black femininity.

Throughout the era of the technologically advanced action blockbuster, from *Rambo* and *The Terminator* to the racial buddy *Die Hard*–type movies, action cinema has remained a distinctly white masculine power–oriented fantasy arena. Looking at turn-of-the-twenty-first-century action film, we see the emergence of black male action stars like Will Smith and Wesley Snipes, crossover martial arts action heroes such as Jackie Chan and Jet Li, and a new generation of tough women in television and film, including Xena the Warrior Princess, Buffy the Vampire Slayer, Sydney of *Alias,* Tomb Raider Angelina Jolie, and *Kill Bill's* female assassins. Perennially cast in secondary roles or not at all, black women are virtually unheard of in the arena of action film stars.

In the summer of 2004, Oscar winner Halle Berry—the preeminent "black" Hollywood movie actress, beauty icon, and rare black woman costar of mainstream dramatic and action films (the James Bond movie *Die Another Day* and *X-Men* and its two sequels)—starred in *Catwoman,* a critical and commercial flop. Action film is predominantly still a fantasy arena in which black people—both men and women, but especially women—are too often absent, peripheral, symbolic signifiers, comedic relief, and/or exotic objects. Such a presence reveals much about the operation of racial, gender, and economic power within the cultural fabric of the United States.

The last period when there was a noticeable black female action hero presence on-screen occurred during that 1973 Christy Love era when blaxploitation films were being churned out by Hollywood. The birth of sassy supermama heroines Cleopatra Jones and Foxy Brown came into being because radical political activism—the Black Power and feminist movements especially—helped to disturb the American cultural sense of the stability of traditional racial and gender power relations. The issue of black film imagery may seem a subject that has been fairly exhaustive. Yet, the relationship between power and the image must continue to be vigorously engaged, for representations continue to be historically rooted, politicized cultural signs that evolve and shift according to the contemporary moment. Despite the critical and popular attention that has been accorded to the blaxploitation genre and black film history, the racial, gender, and sexual politics that shaped the fantasy of power through, in part, the differently inscribed bodies of women, black women in particular, require more attention.

I am still almost as avid a television and film watcher today as I am a reader. I hasten to add that now my pleasure in being engaged by this media is bound up with the pleasure of the interrogating gaze that I direct toward it. My critical spectatorship, then, as astute cultural critic, bell hooks might say, involves the pleasure in being entertained in part by actively viewing and deconstructing representational strategies, in interrogating the politics shaping the "power of the image," to paraphrase visual studies feminist Annette Kuhn. What fascinates me about television and film culture is the power of these media to present appealing versions of realities and fictions, to perpetuate and create consumer desires, and to veil the reality of their political implications through the allure of the entertainment mask. Particularly interesting as well is the relationship they suggest between the political and cultural environment, specifically how television and film create, fictionalize, reconstruct, and/or presume to record contemporary social realities.

During my writing of this book very much concerned with the representation of sexual, racial, and gender power and the problematic imagery of black femaleness in big screen action narratives, the issue of female sexual objectification in popular media and our voyeuristic pleasure in it has been hotly debated. Hip-hop-tinged, white pop icon Justin Timberlake's (accidental?) brief exposure of Janet Jackson's nipple during the halftime show of Super Bowl XXXVIII fueled a backlash against the taken-for-granted cultural consumption of sexual objectification that has been especially linked to the exhibition of female bodies. While various political figureheads, parent groups, and social commentators decried this "perverse" spectacle, the outcry itself became a spectacle cast as a narrative about the degeneration of culture mores, the exploitation of sex, the corruption of children, and so on. It is almost comical that a second of bared breast missed by most viewers during a long-sacred gendered and eroticized American ritual was treated as the height of inappropriate, public pornographic exhibition.

We live engaged by media where the soft pornographic objectification of women's bodies with its racial and class subtexts has long been playing out for popular consumption. While breasts spill out of bikini-tight tops on televi-sion twenty-four hours a day—and not just on movie channels and X-rated stations—Jackson's nipple suddenly became the embodiment of our society's curious historical relationship with the alternately glorified and puritanic-like discomfort with the sexualized female body in the public sphere. It seems that despite the constant display and emphasis on breasts in popular culture and media, the nipple occupies some mystically sacred bodily space, the public revealing of which signifies some sort of taboo social disruption, much like the general veiling of the penis even in films where female nudity is plentiful.

The publicly unspoken racial implications of the Justin-Janet fiasco height-ened the outrageousness of it all. The media glare on the flash of a black wom-an's breast and the subsequent backlash eerily reverberates with the historical hypervisibility and problematic treatment of the black female sexual body. We can consider black women stars during different cultural periods and geographical settings and observe a see-sawing racist sexual glamorization of the breasts on one hand and the demonization of them as signs of sexual wildness and racial difference on the other. Always there are the haunting questions for the black woman public figure associated with a sexual or sex symbol persona: How much power and control can/does she possess over the boundaries of her commodified body for economic and social gain? Is it possible to forge an autonomous public sexual imagery that is a radical departure from the stereotypical inscriptions that have for so long shaped it? What would such imagery look like?

As I think of the Janet Jackson breast furor, I think of the graphic over-focus on Pam Grier's breasts in her 1970s blaxploitation films and on women's breasts generally in cinema, and I think back to the celebrated Josephine Baker in Paris, forever captured in black and white, sassily nude-breasted in her famous banana skirt, and back to Sojourner Truth baring her breast in the face of racist sexism to affirm her black woman's identity, and back further still to the public confiscation of Sarah Bartman's butt, genitalia, and breasts when she was "sold" as the infamous Venus Hottentot to European audiences in the nineteenth century.

In continuing to study and interrogate representations produced during distinct cultural and political eras, we can understand further the connection between cultural production, politics, power, and imagery. Through looking at action film texts that emerged out of a unique black cultural period shaped by feminist, civil rights, and Black Power liberation struggles, I attempt to unpack the complex dynamics that generated radical and conservative fan-tasies of the status quo. My hope, however, is not to provide just a window into the time but to emphasize the need to understand the operation of race, gender, and sexual politics that purposefully masquerades as mere entertainment before our very eyes. It is my desire then to suggest the power of cinema imagery and how possible it is to utilize this power for truly transformative representations wherein pleasure is derived from the mutual engagement of viewing and critical interrogation.

Acknowledgments

I give thanks to the Creator for strength and grace. In the course of working on this book, I was blessed to receive grants from Ohio State University (Mansfield) and to engage in invaluable research in archives at Indiana University, Berkeley University, and UCLA. I thank Joan Catapano and the University of Illinois Press community, including Darlene Clark Hine, Dwight A. McBride, and Angela Burton. My sincerest appreciation goes to the following individuals: Linda Mizejewski, Mark Anthony Neal (especially you, New Black Man), Michael Eric Dyson, Sherrie Inness, Valerie Lee, and many invaluable professors along the way, including Ewa Ziarek, Samuel Longmire, and the late Esrkine Peters. Much love and more thanks than words can express go to Zina B (for the group and the positive energy) and to my special soul sisters April Langley and Tyeta Beattie—you are my very own "sheroes." I especially thank my folk: my sexy, sassy aunts; my sisters, Katina and Risa, for always believing this would come to pass and for being some tough, accomplished women; brothers Bryant and Steve; Jerry Watson; and most of all my mother, Mrs. Earnestine Watson, for being my steady compass throughout this life. N. M., I'm so glad to be sharing the moment with you. To all of my intellectual sister warrior-writers for the example and the brilliance, I am eternally indebted: bell hooks, Patricia Hill Collins, Barbara Christian, Barbara Smith, Michelle Wallace, June Jordan, Audre Lorde, Toni Morrison, Angela Davis, Toni Cade Bambara, Alice Walker, Paula Giddings—there are unfortunately far too many to name. My appreciation overflows for those baad, beautiful screen sistas and real-life tough women who gave me and so many black women the pleasure of watching them be larger than life on-screen, especially Tamara Dobson, Pam Grier, and Teresa Graves.

"Baad Bitches" and
Sassy Supermamas

Race, Gender, and Black Action Fantasy

> Popular culture, commodified and stereotyped as it often
> is, is not at all, as we sometimes think of it, the arena where
> we find who we really are, the truth of our experience.
> It is an arena that is *profoundly* mythic. It is a theater of
> popular desires, a theater of popular fantasies. It is where
> we discover and play with the identifications of ourselves,
> where we are imagined, where we are represented, not only
> to the audiences out there who do not get the message, but
> to ourselves for the first time.
>
> —Stuart Hall, "What Is This 'Black' in
> Black Popular Culture?"

"Black" Fantasy, "Baad Nigger" Heroes, and Supermama Goddesses

"Girl, my daddy used to take us over there—where was that place? Oh yeah, right. Anyways, girl, we went to see all of them. Seem like everybody and they mama was there. Sometimes you could see two or three of 'em at a time at the drive-in. *Shaft, Super Fly, Coffy* . . . girl, yeah. I can't even remember the names of some of them, but we used to go to see those movies all the time." I love to ask grown-up black folk about blaxploitation films, then sit back and listen as they start to smile and laugh and then go into remembrances. Through historical criticism, we know that the cycle of studio-supported 1970s ghetto action films referred to as blaxploitation became a hotly contested site over the proliferation of negative black imagery and Hollywood exploitation. Contemporary black cultural remembrances from 1970s moviegoers about experiencing these productions provide another filter, for the nostalgic favor of black consumers toward films like *Shaft, Super Fly,* and *Foxy Brown* fills in another part of that history.

Thirty years after the early 1970s, the black action film genre born out of the political vitality of the late 1960s and early '70s enjoys a cultlike status in the popular imagination. Contemporary youth culture defined by hip hop suggests this love, for it has continuously recycled specific elements of the superfly, "baad Nigger" model so implicitly associated with the genre.[1] These two cultural explosions provide intriguing parallels, particularly in the relationship between visual representation and sound. The black heroic action narratives of the '70s spawned soul music with searing social critique and urban-edged, gritty lyrics as well as fashion and language trends. The rebellious and at times radically critical, ghettocentric style of hip hop and rap music generated what some called a wave of contemporary blaxploitation action dramas in the 1990s.

In Isaac Julien's 2002 documentary *BaadAssss Cinema*, Afeni Shakur, mother of the legendary late rap icon Tupac, relates that the young rapper devoured those early-'70s ghetto action flicks. The self-styled public imagery of Tupac's peer and collaborator Snoop Dogg is a study in the continuing glamorization of the black urban pimp or mack's masculine persona, which films like *Sweet Sweetback's Baadasssss Song* (1971) and *Super Fly* (1972) brought to new heights of cultural fame. Young black female entertainers are not left out of this affection for blaxploitation film culture. Rapper Foxy Brown, for example, named herself after the screen character that remains most definitive of actress Pam Grier's queen of blaxploitation fame. Rapper Lil' Kim has exuded a male-defined idea of black female baadness that owes some of its contemporary manifestations to the few "baad bitch" heroines of blaxploitation who were shown using traditional masculine tools and feminine sexual power to enter and survive in racist, patriarchal worlds.

One of the most striking and disturbing legacies of the ghetto action film explosion of the early 1970s is the hypermasculine machismo at the center of the genre. Patriarchal power and masculine bravado were envisioned in part through the accepted naming and treatment of women, black women in particular, as "bitches" and "hos." This book is a cultural exploration that seeks to unpack the intersecting racial, sexual, and gender politics in several major early-1970s black action fantasies. I explore the implications of the new baad black heroes who were configured to no small degree through representations of black femaleness. "Bitches" signifies on the general demonized portrait of women as phallus-adoring, catty whores in most blaxploitation vehicles. It is by now a taken-for-granted note in black film histories and criticism that women in major Hollywood studio–controlled productions as well as black male–produced independent films—for example, *Sweet Sweetback's Baadasssss*

Song, The Spook Who Sat by the Door (1973), *Shaft* (1971), and *Super Fly*—are primarily confined to the position of the cool hero's subordinate sex object.

"Baad bitches" and "sassy supermamas" is a way of signifying those soul diva characters—sassy, attractive, stylish black heroines with plenty of 'tude—who seemingly and problematically flip this positioning in the few male-produced black female action vehicles such as *Cleopatra Jones* (1973), *Coffy* (1973), and *Foxy Brown* (1974). Here, the black female protagonist is a sexy, streetwise, tough woman who shows no fear, takes on powerful whites and men, and, according to the genre's expectations, wins. White female enemies pitted against the heroine also exemplify empowered women who especially threaten white patriarchal power.

The general critical commentary on these "macho goddesses,"[2] "phallic black women,"[3] or "supermama" heroines by largely black male film critics primarily notes the sexualized treatment of them, a signal of the films' patriarchal orientation. Coffy, Foxy, and Cleopatra have been mentioned in feminist film studies, but generally, black female representation and spectatorship are treated peripherally. Since they have been largely dismissed as merely overly sexualized female hero flicks and subsumed under the masculine criticism of the genre, there has been little in-depth attention given to the myriad implications of the representational codes that structure the characters and action as well as to the films' importance as revealing cultural artifacts. The lack of relatively intensive black feminist exploration of the texts and their implications over the years have contributed to the dismissal of the films as so obviously cheap and exploitative of women that the politics therein do not warrant intense scrutiny.

I want to expand this scarce critical treatment by considering the distinct elements and implications of these supermama characters and films that generalized discussions of blaxploitation, focused on the "baad nigger" hero films, have not yet adequately addressed. In addition, I want to explore the crucial differences between the politics evident in *Cleopatra Jones, Coffy,* and *Foxy Brown* and give them and black women's engagement of these unique character icons much needed deeper consideration. In chapter 1, I explore the legacy of the major supermama film characters and address black female spectatorship in part through discussing the influence of these icons on the contemporary personas of such hip-hop divas as Foxy Brown and Lil' Kim.

The cultural meaning and/or significance attached to these characters by black women consumers vary across generations, from those who were teenagers or young adults during the time of the films' original release and those coming of age in the hip-hop generation. Those of the latter generation continue to draw on the cultural styles associated with the heroic figures of blaxploitation film. Criticism addressing the blaxploitation genre by and large dismisses or ignores issues of black female spectatorial desire—how these fantasy narratives and character icons might both repel and appeal to generations of black female audiences given the films' patriarchal structure but unique "fantasy" of baad black female action heroes. This book is thus my shout out to these unique, lingering, inadequately explored black super-woman icons.

Despite their marginalized status in film culture studies, Coffy, Foxy Brown, and Cleopatra Jones offer much for consideration. These revealing character representations acknowledge the impact of feminism and black feminism and, at the same time, the anxieties they provoked. We can glimpse these contrary strains through considering how they became a space where competing notions about traditional gender roles, femininity and masculinity, and white and black male phallic power struggles could be safely and fantastically engaged. This legacy provokes several questions: How do the representations of racially inscribed female figures in the roles of heroes and/or bad guys and their positioning in relation to men indicate such concerns? In what ways do they then both revise and/or fail to re-imagine the traditional gender and racial power hierarchy?

Several key thoughts motivate my exploration of a film culture of which I admittedly remain both affectionate spectator and staunch critic. First, while watching these films again, many years after my childhood introduction to most of them and through a preoccupation with the differing ways that women appear in cinema, I was struck by their distinct *racialized* patriarchal structure. While the naked array of breasts and parade of phallus-worshiping women is certainly a taken-for-granted staple of such '70s exploitation cinema, reading beyond acknowledgment of this problematic sexualization is not. What I am drawn to are the many political implications of these fantasy spectacles, which hinge on the bold romp of contrasting, extreme depictions of racialized feminine and masculine identities. Thus, second, I am interested in how these fantasy revisions of traditional racial, gender, and sexual power suggest the very real and imagined social disturbances provoked by the political radicalism of the late 1960s through the early 1970s, especially Black Power and feminism. In chapter 2, I explore these dynamics and address the Black Power movement's impact on the development of the popular black film era and its politics.

The male filmmakers of the black revolt–themed action narratives and the supermama flicks rely on historic and contemporary race, gender, and sexual mythologies to affect exhilaratingly sensationalist racial dramas. In my interrogation of films that re-imagine a historical era's diverse political consciousness and its meanings and consequences, I highlight the representations of raced bodies and social and political identities—the Black Power revolutionary and black jezebel, for example—which are made visible by manipulating racial and gender difference at the site of the body. I hope to emphasize how the phallic or patriarchal orientation of B-grade film productions reveals the ways popular cinema entertainment acts out racialized patriarchal power through artistically confiscating the imagined bodies and social identities of women and the racial contrasts ascribed to them.

The fantasy that these films marketed to black moviegoers was the spectacular reversal of the racial and/or patriarchal status quo, tapping into the social reality of racial oppression and racial tensions. So, by investing in a lot of relatively cheaply made vehicles, Hollywood studios made a great deal of money while their films never radically upset either the racial patriarchal politics implicit in their making—the actual idea of white supremacy and patriarchy as the natural order—nor popular contemporary and historical notions about race. Black men like Melvin Van Peebles made money too by offering a black masculine fantasy that accessed the lingering aura of the popular Black Power masculine image.

That the films were driven by the desire to make money of course is no surprise, but they were driven too by a host of unconscious and intentional political aims shaped by ideas of race, sex, and gender. Few of these productions, save perhaps texts like *The Spook* and *Sweetback,* were intended by the creators to function as spaces to articulate authentic representations of black political discourses and identities. In the Hollywood studio productions of black action films, political radicalism is refashioned or recreated, alternately ridiculed or problematically affirmed in deeply heterosexist, male-produced action fantasies; the films thus embody the appropriation of aspects of and anxieties about the political interrogation of established boundaries of racial, gender, and sexual power in the late 1960s and early 1970s. Yet, they offer a phantasmagoria of simultaneously radical and conservative visions of social power relations.

My use of the word "fantasy" is a way of invoking the desire of black audiences for depictions of black agency in action thrillers where white supremacy would be contested outside the perimeters of dominant film perspectives about black identity. It refers to the spectatorial desire of a diverse black moviegoing audience that yearned for the pleasure of viewing black characters who looked, talked, and acted "black," operated in an identifiable black geographical and cultural domain, and who defied and won against white authority. The films testify to the cultural legacy of the civil rights struggle and the impact of Black Power, though they came to personify movement away from serious black political treatment, the distortion of the political meanings of "Black Power," and a troubling exploitation of black consumer desire and soul culture.

"Fantasy" is meant to suggest too, then, the distance between the serious orientation and potential of feminist and Black Power politics that advocated the radical transformation of traditional power structures and the film representations of lone black heroes who topple singular corrupt white figures rather than systematic power. As fantasy, cinema is involved in the social production of desire and as such appeals to the perceived yearnings of specific audiences and draws disparate viewers to the screen by manipulating those desires, images, and aspects of social realities. This speaks to the power implicit in being able to manipulate political discourse and imagery on the big screen.

The phallus—that is, a masculine signifier of patriarchal power—is crucial to the representation of fantasies about social power structures, something that the films' prominent themes of castration and emasculation indicate. These are heavily racialized, gendered themes that reveal the historical order of racial patriarchy, including the emasculation of black men and the fantasy of white male castration as a metaphor for black male (and black female) revenge and triumph. Images of white and black female bodies occupy a crucial role in such fantasies; in differing ways, they trigger castration anxiety and emphasize the fight for patriarchal supremacy between white and black men. Hence, it is no surprise that such screen fantasies of blaxploitation "baad nigger" heroes revolve around a plot in which the white patriarchal authority that dominates the social world is being disturbed by black heroes and white women in atypical power roles.

In chapter 3, I explore two major black male–produced revolution-themed action films that offer radical critiques of white male supremacy but fail to interrogate the gender politics underlining the masculine vision of black revolution; instead, they indulge in the fantasy of black male ascension to phallic power. Though distinct from the other films that became exemplary of the blaxploitation genre, they do not radically upset the relegation of women to male-controlled "bitch" and "ho" status. *Sweetback* and *The Spook* instead use such female figures as symbolic signifiers of their black male protagonists' sexuality and masculine power. They preeminently construct women as the subordinates of black men; their role, if any, in black revolutionary rebellion is defined by the black phallic hero's access to their sexual bodies and desires.

These hypermasculine versions of rebellion and Black Nationalist revolution are telling cultural artifacts, for they manifest the particular obsession with racial masculinities that dominated the politicized cultural ethos of the Black Power era. *Sweetback* and *The Spook* reverberate with the problem of sexism and with the neglect of addressing sexism radically enough in black liberation struggle, as indicated by the public representation of masculine-imbued Black Power nationalist discourse. The two films' sensational version of masculine-oriented black revolution ignores the reality of black men and women working actively together under the Black Power politic and beyond the narrow sexual perimeter that they suggest.

A similar structuring perspective informs representations in black female blaxploitation fantasies as well, for they too, as I have said, reveal the political and cultural era's obsession with competing versions of white and black patriarchal power and with the threat of female empowerment. The treatment of black and white women by the male filmmakers suggests a somewhat scary specter of female power, even though the films were intended to capitalize on the feminist impact by offering strong women who embody the traditional masculine power possessed by their male peers. In the narratives that I examine, both the imagery of women and of black male power indicate a devaluation of the era's radical politicization through the grotesque terms in which they are presented.

White female enemies of the black female protagonist, for instance, are often cast as lesbian "bad" bitches who indicate the terrors of phallic power when displaced onto the white female, whereas black male characters are frequently aspiring corrupt figures who meet their end in racial violence— lynching and castration. Yet, the positioning of a black female character as the hero of an action film is unique in that it revises, albeit not unproblematically, the marginal positioning of black women and their regular exclusion from action film hero status. As I discuss in chapter 4, the representation of a black female heroine like Cleopatra Jones embodies contradictory strains—a (black) feminist potential and, at the same time, on other levels, the reassertion of some traditional racial and gender boundaries. The latter is more prominent in *Coffy* and *Foxy Brown,* which I address in chapter 5.

My readings of film representations have been shaped by many theoretical discourses, including feminist film criticism, black cultural criticism, and black feminist discourse. The black feminist theorization of "racial patriarchy," for example, is significant for my focus on how intersecting racial and gender politics structure the films and the representations of racial and gender hierarchies within the films. Racial patriarchy acknowledges the historical hierarchy of race and gender, which places social groups in specific power relations to one another: black women share an alliance with black men in a racist society, but at the same time, they need to confront black male sexism.

Black feminist intervention in film and cultural criticism enlarges contemporary feminist film criticism, which, despite its departures from the psychoanalytic theory exclusivity, still tends to make gender rather than other categories and (white) female representation implicitly stated (or not) the center of feminist film studies. Film critic Jane Gaines insightfully points out that if gender is the beginning focal point in a feminist analysis of oppression, then it "helps to reinforce white middle-class values, and to the extent that it works to keep women from seeing other structures of oppression, it functions ideologically."[4]

My search for ways to articulate the multiple politics that I address throughout this project led me to think of the film texts, their historical political background, and the politics that inform representations in them as an interrogation of the controlling heterosexist, racialized patriarchal gaze. Together, these words personify the politics defining the films' orientation, that is, their racially inscribed, male-defined, heterosexual perspective and the power dynamics suggested by who could create, direct, and decide the narrative style and vision for fantasies of Black Power–era heroes. Hence, they also signify on Hollywood's appropriation of political representations and its manipulation of black consumer desire through the allure of the "new" black empowerment confined within the safe boundaries of texts that reinforced traditional notions about the patriarchal and racial status quo.

I must also, of course, think of commercial film in terms of its capitalist functions and aims. Cultural theorist bell hooks has conceptualized a meaningful way of thinking about the interacting issues of white supremacy, patriarchy, capitalism, and nationalism. Her term "white supremacist capitalist patriarchy" allows for a way of seeing and speaking to the interconnected operation of these politics, which is particularly important in a study dealing with the racial and gender implications of a genre such as blaxploitation in which economic exploitation is such a relevant factor. Keeping such a concept in mind, hooks opines, helps keep prominent the interlocking systems of domination that "determine our reality" and their simultaneous functionality.[5]

Race, Gender, and the Spectacle of Melodrama

How can we critically posit 1970s black B-grade action cinema, besides its distinct blaxploitation categorization in black film history, in order to place it within the dominant historical style of popular Hollywood film? Black-oriented action films of the '70s actually exemplify popular cinema's tendency toward melodrama forged through the spectacle of race, class, sex, and gender representation. Sharon Willis calls attention to the commitment of cinema to spectacle because it amplifies what we think of as the visibility of gender and race:

> So powerful is our cultural wish to believe that differences give themselves to sight that the cinema is able to capitalize, both ideologically and financially, on the fascination that dazzling visual contrasts exercise upon us. At the same time, as films read our social field, they may both mobilize and contain the conflict, uneasiness, and overwrought affect that so often accompany the confrontation of everyday practices. Cinema seems to borrow and channel those energies through a volatile affective range, from terror, fascination, pleasure, and comfort, while it proliferates representations of social difference as central or peripheral spectacle.[6]

The point Willis makes here is that cinema plays on our belief that we can *see* and on our desire to see the racial and gender identities that we think of as concrete and "obvious." The representations of bodies on-screen signal a multitude of social differences that we are conditioned to recognize. The body thus functions as an "aesthetic and ideological sign" that will be associated with specific socially constructed identities.[7] Thus, it produces a "what you see is what you get" evaluation, a feature that defines what film scholar Anna Everett has called the "transparent" segregated text that has significant racial and gender ideologies and the "ability to smuggle racist values into the narrative transaction without censure."[8]

The black-versus-white and man-versus-woman plots of 1970s black action films unfold against a canvas that marries stunning visual effects and sound. We are offered the contrasting images of ultra-macho men, phallic women, ultra-feminine women, feminized men, and lesbian butches; as such, they rely heavily on the visual display of social difference that we can imagine we *see* through representations of role reversals and actual physical bodies. Whereas race prevalently "functions to constitute concrete individuals as white and black," gender operates to inscribe the exhibition of racial and gender archetypes such as the macho man or excessively sexualized woman.[9]

Action cinema is particularly aligned with the display of the body as a visual spectacle more than with dialogue, a point Yvonne Tasker highlights in *Spectacular Bodies*. Tasker offers the key observation that action film hinges on the "complex articulation of both belonging and exclusion" that is tied to the body of the hero and the masculinity that it personifies.[10] Spectacle then does not merely refer to special effects, stunts, and an over-the-top sequence of events but to the intersecting "visual qualities" that "define cinematic experience." Spectacle, furthermore, constitutes "sensuous" experience, in which the awesome visuals and hence "feelings of exhilaration" are provoked by landscape, bodies, action, and other elements. Form and content make up the "action" of action film, Tasker explains. Spectacle elicits the desire of spectators to want to follow the film's development to the end by effecting a visual pleasure that makes us want to "stop and stare."[11] With its gleeful exhibition of outrageous violent action, exoticized landscapes, and exaggerated characters affecting comedic spectacle, exploitation action cinema of the 1970s offered fantasy escape that played on the obviousness of its exploitative visual effects.

The '70s black action film cycle ushered in the unique visibility of black superheroes who appeared as colorful comic book–like protagonists against the backdrop of black urban ghetto scenes and gritty soundtracks. Their bodies became spectacle in the melodrama of cool black heroes at war with evil white enemies. Black Power–themed films such as *Sweetback* provide filmic examples of a politicized manipulation of spectacle as a tool to capture public attention and space; the film emerged amid the Black Panthers' and others' use of racialized spectacle to fight "historic invisibility" and to seize public space to provoke national attention on the black liberation struggle.[12]

Linda Williams's discussion of the connection between film, race, and melodrama in *Playing the Race Card* reminds us that though race is "a fiction," it is also true that it "constructs 'racialized subjects' in the political imagination."[13] Racialization "gives meaning to the visible signs of difference and that meaning has long been embedded in popular culture in such icons as the beaten black man or the endangered white woman."[14] The historical reality of American racial drama is brought to life through bad white characters and black heroes who live outside mainstream middle-class authority.

No matter how surreal and fictional the plot, action, and characterizations, the versions of white villainy, racial victimization, and black heroism in the films obviously draw on the very real racial tensions of the day.[15] The presence of political and social issues from the contemporary moment is a significant feature of both literary and cinema melodrama. *Sweetback, The Spook, Coffy, Cleopatra Jones,* and other 1970s black films acknowledge such social realities as black poverty, drugs, and racial oppression. The ways that they exemplify the melodramatic tradition is further illuminated, Williams argues, if we consider melodrama in one of its major functions—as a method of representation that contains a "particular moralizing function" and that encompasses many genres. Understood as a "cultural mode," melodrama serves as a way to conceptualize various types of cinema, including "western melodrama, crime melodrama, sex melodrama, backwoods melodrama, romantic melodrama, and so on."[16]

Though melodrama has been inscribed with a gendered tradition that associates it with the feminine, it is so only in some of its "manifestations." It more aptly suggests a mode of drama that centralizes pathos and action or "the sufferings of innocent victims and the exploits of brave heroes or monstrous criminals."[17] Indeed, viewing '70s black fantasy action films as a unique manifestation of cinema's melodramatic tradition makes sense when we consider how these narratives share staple features of traditional masculine action cinema in their exhibition of black victimization, revenge, and triumph: "We have only to look at what is playing at the local multiplex to realize that the familiar Hollywood feature of prolonged climactic action is, and I would argue has always been, a melodramatic spectacle. . . . Indeed nothing is more sensational in American cinema than the infinite varieties of rescues, accidents, chases, and fights. These 'masculine' action-centered climaxes may be scrupulously motivated or wildly implausible depending on the film."[18] The B-grade categorization of 1970s black action flicks, with their racially and sexually overt representations, contrived dialogue, and outrageous plots, does not negate their cultural significance but rather cements the genre as a unique entry in the melodramatic tradition. In the spirit of indulging further in the pleasures and problems of these black action fantasies, I explore what roles women and their imagery played in creating the exhilaratingly sensational culture that continues to attract our gaze.

1

The Pleasure of Looking

Black Female Spectatorship and the Supermama Heroine

She's the Godmother . . . The baddest
One-Chick Hit-Squad that ever hit the town!
—*Coffy* ad

I am the baddest chick. . . . I'll show you magic.
—Lil' Kim, "Magic Stick"

Black Seeing: Going to the Movies While Black

"The thing about Cleopatra is that she was sharp, you know?"

"I liked the way she looked. And talked. Just the way she spoke was so sophisticated and cool."

"I like her look, the way she carried herself; her whole vibe is sharp to me. And she was a dark-skinned, strong, beautiful woman. That's what I like." That from my friend Zina B, a postmodern, Manolo Blahnik–wearing, majestic chocolate Cleopatra diva herself.

I was in Atlanta at Zina B's house with her mother and sister, my sister, and several other women between thirty and forty-five. We had gathered to watch *Cleopatra Jones* and one of Pam Grier's films, *Coffy*. Two of the ladies remembered seeing *Cleopatra Jones* back in the day, two more had seen it on video, and for the rest it was a first viewing of the film starring a nevertheless familiar screen character. We had just finished watching it—which was an experience of communal bonding and interactive spectating. We laughed in glee when Cleopatra kicked some so-called tough guy's or chick's butt, shared and yelled our appreciation at her high chic appearance—"We ain't mad at you, girl"—and held a running conversation about her animal print fur coats, high-brimmed hats, tailored man suits, and majestic, ebony physique. At the end of the movie, we were feeling good and talking about how bad Tamara Dobson as Cleopatra was and wondering who in the world could play that role now. Only a Grace Jones–like diva, we agreed, but who?

The conversation became a little less enthused as I slipped in *Coffy*—we'd all seen it at least once. Zina B volunteered that she liked Grier—who was really beautiful—but hated the Coffy-type roles "'cause they were too degrading." Another one of the sisters who had seen many of the blaxploitation films at the movies as a teen offered that at least Coffy and Foxy won. Back in a 1974 *Ms.* article, "Keeping the Black Woman in Her Place," Margaret Sloan, a founder and chairwoman of the National Black Feminist Organization, appreciated the rarity of a fighting black woman action movie character like Coffy, saying she loved her despite the limitations of the narrative.[1] In a 1975 interview with Grier, Jamaica Kincaid echoes Sloan, describing *Coffy, Foxy Brown,* and *Sheba Baby* (1975) as technically flawed and violent films with one "outstanding redeeming value": the films offered the rare Hollywood showing of an "independent, resourceful, self-confident, strong, and courageous" woman. "Above all," Kincaid stresses, "they are the only films to show us a woman who triumphs!"[2]

Grier has said that her roles "exemplified women's independence." She projected shades of her African American women relatives' tough attitudes and no-nonsense business personas into her portrayal of Foxy Brown. "I based my screen characters," Grier reveals, "on my mother, aunts, and grandmothers. They were the kind of women who would fight to their last breath before they'd give their purse to some punk robber."[3] Grier herself came up with a few of the resourceful survival maneuvers in both *Coffy* and *Foxy Brown.* For example, in the first film, Coffy escapes a violent encounter with some other women by pulling out a switchblade that she's hidden in her Afro. In the latter, Foxy uses her car to rescue her brother, and in another scene, the infamous lesbian brawl, Foxy artfully uses a chair to fend off some hostile Amazon-sized women.

I queried various black women viewers by distributing a survey that posed several key questions: Did you like these black female heroines and their films (*Coffy, Foxy Brown, Cleopatra Jones*)? How would you describe any or all of these films and roles (Grier's or Dobson's)? What do you remember about them? What did or do you like about them? Dislike? The most oft-repeated sentiment by the respondents was that they liked that the characters were strong women, but their appreciation of black female heroines who fought back didn't negate what many black women referred to as the over-sexualization, even degradation, of Grier in the films.

The women I surveyed varied in age from twenty-two to sixty, with the majority between thirty-five and fifty-five. While most were professional women, about a fourth were working-class. Their introduction to and historical relationship with the films also varied. Some were young adults and adolescents at the time of the films' release and had viewed them first at the movies and over the years at least once again through cable television or video. A handful of the respondents were hip-hop-generation viewers who knew *Coffy* and *Foxy Brown* through videos and the confiscation of blaxploitation in hip-hop culture—fashion, music, film references, and movie remakes. I had several small-group movie sessions with a handful of women who were viewing the films for the first time since seeing them at the time of their release. While all of the women were familiar with Pam Grier, *Foxy Brown,* and Grier's blaxploitation film roots, several had never viewed *Cleopatra Jones* or heard of the film or Tamara Dobson.

While the younger generation viewers tended to demonstrate less antagonism toward the explicit relationship of sex and female power drawn in the films, black women across class and age were quite savvy about recognizing how the character representations of the superheroines were shaped by, as one sister wrote, a "white man's fantasy vision" that somewhat celebrated stereotypes of black female sexuality. Quite a few women, of the seventy-five or so who replied, also noted the difference between the overt exploitative aspects of Coffy and Foxy Brown and the rather sophisticated presentation of a black superwoman in *Cleopatra Jones.* Of course, more than to the filmmakers' radical vision, we owe the considerably softened sexual representation of Cleopatra Jones in part due to the effort of the male producers to achieve a PG rating, thus maximizing its box office potential.[4]

In her review of *Cleopatra Jones,* Sloan finds more empowerment in the tough woman presented by Dobson's character. While that narrative too fell below "art," Sloan applauds Cleopatra Jones for at least being "her own woman." At the end of her review, Sloan calls for more black women on the screen and throughout the film industry as producers, directors, and editors in order to present the fullness of black female experience. But for that moment, she suggests, Cleopatra Jones spoke to the yearning of many black women for more complex and empowered black woman representations. As a sister sitting behind Sloan at the movie's end declared, "Damn. That movie felt good."[5]

Film critics such as Ed Guerrero and Jesse Rhines have noted that blaxploitation films were geared toward a young urban black male audience. Yet, we know that through theater screenings, video and DVD rentals, and cable television that in the thirty years since the films' emergence, a few generations of black women culture and film consumers have been part of the blaxploitation audience. When it was released back in 1973, *Cleopatra Jones* made over $3.25 million in commercial release and spawned a successful soundtrack that sold over half a million copies. *Coffy*, produced that same year for $500,000, made $2 million. In domestic film rentals, *Foxy Brown* made $2.46 million.[6] Guerrero concurs with black film historian Donald Bogle and other black male critics that "black women could find little in their adolescent-male-fantasy-oriented roles to identify with."[7] The problem with this dismissive reading is that it obscures how black women may negotiate the racial and gender politics underlying the narrative but still find various types of pleasure in viewing action cinema generally and the rare fantasies of a baad black woman heroine, especially one headlining a Hollywood film.

Film theorist Judith Mayne points out that textual theories of the spectator have offered that cinema structure "assigns a position of coherence to the implied spectator,"[8] yet we must recognize that various real viewers may see the films in far more diverse ways than that intended by filmmakers and marketers. The crucial feat is not to view the texts as having complete or dominant control over viewing positions, though the film controllers may have intended spectators and their expectations in mind. We must also avoid the other extreme of viewing movies as only offering positions created by viewers. A more appropriate approach would be to address the complex ways that "meanings are both assigned and created."[9] There is a distance between the "cinematic address," or how a text presumes specific spectator responses, and "cinematic reception," the actual responses of viewers and the conditions surrounding them.[10]

It is especially challenging to attempt to shed light on black female spectatorial desire, since it has been largely ignored in mainstream and feminist film criticism. Fortunately, black cultural and film critics such as bell hooks, Jacqueline Bobo, and Manthia Diawara, among others, have offered the beginnings of a developing body of black film criticism highlighting race and gender and offering some particular focus on black women viewers. By directing critical focus to black women's responses to such key African American women–oriented films as the film adaptation of Alice Walker's *The Color Purple* and filmmaker Julie Dash's *Daughters of the Dust,* hooks and Bobo have helped to challenge the gender and racial exclusiveness of such early psychoanalytic feminist readings as Laura Mulvey's pioneering 1971 essay "Visual Pleasure and Narrative Cinema." In it, Mulvey ignores the racial implications of patriarchal film structure and possible viewing positions.

Trying to study black female viewers in relation to the 1970s supermama action flicks—the missing link in popular film studies—is additionally challenging because of the lack of attention, then and now, in contrast to more well-documented public responses to films like *Shaft, Super Fly,* and *Sweetback,* primarily by black male viewers and critics. In addition, the familiar question arises of what strategies are appropriate and adequate for gaining a valid enough sense of a specific viewing audience without seeming to offer a definitive accounting—which is, of course, an impossibility.

The historical problems of stereotypical black film imagery and black exclusion in dominant cinema has unsurprisingly meant that the critical address of black film spectatorship has tended to revolve around how black viewers have negotiated and continue to negotiate the politics of dominant cinema ideologies. Recognizing that the position of the spectator in cinematic apparatus is socially, historically, and "psychically constituted," Diawara has offered a way of interrogating African American spectating of dominant cinema through "resisting spectatorship." Here, Diawara reads D. W. Griffith's pioneering film *The Birth of a Nation* (1915), discussing how the dominant politics of the narrative "compels the Black spectator to identify with the racial inscription of the Black character" and observing at the same time the resistance of the black spectator to this fantasy version of United States history. Thus, "resisting spectatorship" denotes a resistance to the racist encoding of the text. The dominant cinema positions black characters largely for the "pleasure" of white viewers. In contrast to the denial of spectatorial identification with black characters in narratives where they lose, *Coffy, Foxy Brown,* and black male hero flicks like *Shaft* and *Super Fly* offer this sort of potential identification for black male and female viewers. Diawara's discussion raises the pivotal question of how various black spectators might identify with dominant cinema representations of blacks and addresses issues of "passive identification."[11]

bell hooks has offered helpful analyses of black spectatorship and black female spectatorship in particular. She suggests the existence of an interrogating gaze that challenges dominant construction. Echoing cultural theorist Stuart Hall, hooks argues that spaces for agency are possible for black people who can "both interrogate the gaze of the Other but also look back, and at one another, naming what we see." She offers a crucial reading of the politics of gender infusing the black male gaze as well as the dominant racist and gendered gaze. In their role as spectators, she argues, black men could engage phallocentric power that "mediated racial negation" in this imaginary zone.[12] Such a reading exemplifies the phallocentric gaze structuring *Sweetback, The*

Spook, and many blaxploitation films that overtly offer sexualized fantasies of black phallic power that were intended to appeal particularly to a black heterosexual male viewership.

Given these gendered politics, black female spectators have had to navigate a cinematic apparatus that situates their presence as "absence" and denies the black female body in order to reinforce or support white supremacy and the phallocentric gaze. Black women movie lovers have mediated their moviegoing amid dominant constructions of black women as Sapphire—the "black bitch." Referring to the movie classic *The Birth of a Nation* too, hooks observes that black women spectators have been very conscious of how the politics of race have underlined gender representation. However, many black women spectators have looked with an oppositional gaze that enables them to interrogate critically the positioning of white womanhood as the "object of the phallocentric gaze" and then decide not to "identify with either the victim or the perpetrator." In this way, a critical space is opened up for the deconstruction of the phallocentric gaze and the positioning of women.[13]

It has been unfortunate that mainstream feminist film criticism has neglected black female spectatorship. Looking at this subject requires acknowledging and understanding the role and impact of the historical mainstream devaluation of black womanhood in media on black women's looking and movie experience. Black women's ways of resistance to the dominant cinematic apparatus is essential for the emergence of a critical black female spectatorship.[14]

There is still much to be explored about how black viewers navigate mainstream cinema, black-oriented commercially produced films, black independent cinema, and the activity of going to the movies. One of the aspects of black moviegoing that has been little explored relates to black audiences' collective experience of looking at or viewing film within various public spaces. Black viewers prior to the modern legal (as well as social) breakdown of Jim Crow very often saw movies collectively at theaters from the balcony—that is, in segregated spaces that positioned them as secondary viewers. Black viewers have had to negotiate not only looking but also the actual act of seeing movies in the public sphere.[15] In spaces that did not cater to a black clientele and in those that did, as was often the case with the theater showings of such black films as *Sweetback* and *Shaft,* an important part of the experience was watching films in collectivity and as part of smaller gendered and classed groups within the larger black audience.

Addressing black spectatorship in ways that acknowledge these aspects can enlarge the important consideration of the ways black audiences navigate the racist gaze of dominant cinema. Film theorist Jacqueline Stewart offers an approach that embodies this effort with her conceptualization of "reconstructive spectatorship." Here, Stewart addresses the diverse manner in which "black viewers attempted to reconstitute and assert themselves in relation to the classical cinema's racist social and textual operations." By giving important attention to the "public dimension of spectatorship" or "the public context of exhibition," Stewart encompasses the "collective, the contextual, and the physical dimensions of black spectatorship," thus moving beyond the stress, in her words, on the "individual, the textual, and the psychic." Stewart's approach enlarges hooks's and Diawara's crucial work by in part encompassing black cinema scholar Mark Reid's idea of "'polyphonic' spectatorship," which allows for viewers' readings of "black-oriented" films from various multiple "social and psychic (and not simply racial) positions."[16] Stewart explains that her reconstructive spectatorship aims to address the viewer as part of a viewing public rather than as just the individual viewer.

Stewart explores black spectatorship in the context of black migrant viewers from the South going to the movies in American urban areas amid early-twentieth-century racial "de jure and de facto" segregation. Black viewers attended movies in second-run theaters as part of audiences in the Black Belt, or in theaters that might have served white and black audiences at different times. Black moviegoers, who were not the cinema's "imagined audience," had to contend with dominant stereotypes of the black body that demonized the very smell, sound, and physicality of blackness when attending theaters outside the Black Belt in such cities as Chicago. However, in theaters catering more exclusively to a black clientele, black spectators could feel a sense of "ownership, comfort, and control."[17]

In such an environment, Stewart argues, we can imagine that the pleasures of the cinema went further than spectators' ability to resist or "lose her- or himself" in the screen. Responses are shaped by viewers' "experience of inhabiting and interacting with others within the space of the theatre." Stewart reminds us that some historians have proposed that the cinema provided a space in which "marginalized, alienated, fragmented social groups could reconstitute themselves in(to) new public formations."[18]

Stewart's study on the impact of urban living on the social aspects of black life in the public arena and on the collective experience of going to the movies is quite relevant for considering the 1970s actions films, which were particularly marketed in cities with significant black populations. These productions, and subsequently the sensibilities of the viewers, exemplified a distinctly urbanized black cultural consciousness in turn shaped by upheaval and a Black Power movement that was itself increasingly identifiable with the urban site and the poor and working-class folk who populated city ghettos. In certain public movie spaces, diverse behaviors might be enabled as well as various modes of interactive movie watching that mediated problematic representations or enhanced the viewing of more radical or nontraditional black imagery.

The social space of theater, aside from the "imaginary space of the screen," suggests a range of possible cinematic pleasures, from individual identification and resistance and/or embrace to collective "rejection" of screen imagery. This acknowledges the impact of black viewers' sense of public self on spectatorial pleasure. Within this social space, the black audience could be very diverse across age, class, and gender: "Youth audiences might feel licensed to be boisterous; the presence of 'ladies' might curtail crude behavior."[19]

The experience of collectively seeing '70s black action films enhanced the pleasure of moviegoing for black viewers. One of the features of this experience appears to have been the call and response nature of interaction between audience members and the screen. That the theater space here provided a site enabling experiences of racial solidarity that went across class and gender lines is clear. At such theaters as New York City's Art & Cinerama, the Victoria, the Penthouse and 86th Street Twin theaters, De Mille and 34th Street East theaters, and the Apollo on 125th, Chicago's State Street Theatre and Wood's Theatre, and Palace and State Theatres in Gary, Indiana, black moviegoers talked back to the screen, rooting for their superfly anti-heroes or superwoman heroines, dissing the heroes' losses, and roaring loud approval at the conclusion's show of black triumph. Various spectators shouted responses to one another, to anonymous other spectators, and to members of their own group within the larger audience before the movie's beginning, during the showing, and afterward. They did so with a certain freedom of expression, using various black speechisms, including the profane, without being policed by dominant social mores or institutional restrictions.

In my conversations with black folk who were old enough to experience the films at drive-ins and various theaters during the 1970s, I have been struck by how seeing the films with family and friends and among primarily black audiences stands as a key part of their remembrances. As one California lady in her fifties put it to me, "It was just wild, you know. Me and my girlfriends went to see them together a lot. Snuck to see some of 'em 'cause some of our parents didn't exactly see them as films for young girls to see. There'd be a bunch of black people laughing and talking, both to each other and the people on screen. We hollered right along with them and had a good time." Several of my aunts continue to launch into a litany of "Remember when we went to see . . ." whenever I bring up Pam Grier, *Coffy*, or *Foxy Brown*.

In histories and recent documentaries that explore the black action film explosion, black viewers' remembrances of such films as the legendary *Sweetback* offer glimpses into the popular reception by black viewers. There are accounts about the lines of people waiting to get in to see *Sweetback* and *Super Fly* and about these films' impact on audiences who hungered for new visions of black heroism. One famous story related by Melvin Van Peebles relates how an old black woman seeing the film prayed aloud that the Lord wouldn't let Sweetback get caught.

Quentin Tarantino, the popular white filmmaker whose uniquely styled film work has fetishized '70s kung fu cinema and blaxploitation film culture, positions himself as a young white voyeur of not just the film texts but of the spectatorial responses and interaction of collective black viewing audiences. His comments reveal the possible distinct dynamics of social interaction in theater spaces that showcased black-oriented commercial films:

> Downtown L.A., the Broadway area, was like a Black Hollywood. . . . All those old theaters, every film was a blaxploitation film. I felt like I was in a black world. Every theater was a blaxploitation film. So I go into this theater and everybody is talking through it, and they're making fun of everybody. "Awww, suck my dick" *[laughter]*. "Fuck you, motherfucka." All right, all this shit is going on. I had never been in a theater where this was going on before. . . . I'm in third grade, okay, maybe. I'm thinking, wow, this is really kind of cool.[20]

Similarly, Michael Mann, executive producer of *Baadasssss*, Mario Van Peebles's 2004 film dramatization of his father's making of *Sweetback*, reflects back on the social interaction of black viewers when he and his wife saw the pioneering film at the State Theatre in Chicago, an establishment serving a large black clientele. There was a riot in the theater, Mann remembers. The audience, which was 75 percent black, was so taken with *Sweetback*. "There was a dialogue," Mann explains, "between the screen and the audience."[21]

Part of the exhilaration experienced by various black viewers stemmed from the shared energy and pleasure invested in the fantasy unfolding on-screen and from the expectation of black triumph. And too, the gendered shaping of the text and characters—the masculine and raced bravado or power of the hero, the sexual presentation of women, or the tough, sexy black woman—appealed to the desires and/or expectations of diverse individual viewers and groups of viewers within that collective. The black cultural identification enabled via the soul music, vernacular language, black ghetto setting, and visibility of black characters positioned as anti–white power or "the Man" most certainly enhanced the collective experience of viewing pleasure.

Such moviegoing dynamics for black viewers continue in contemporary times. During the 1990s explosion of black ghetto films that frequently cast rap icons, such as *Boyz in the Hood, New Jack City,* and *Juice,* and the rise of black urban professional romance films, like *Waiting to Exhale, Love Jones, Love and Basketball,* and *The Best Man,* I observed how much black folks' pleasure in going to see such films was enhanced by collective viewing via small groups attending together and within audiences populated primarily with black spectators. Though black viewers flock to see many types of Hollywood films, especially big budget action releases, different movies attract various types of expectations among diversely gendered and classed groups of black folk. For instance, the rare instance of a group of black women headlining a major commercial release poses a unique pleasure for many black women viewers.

I can still remember the excitement that my black women friends and I felt in anticipation of going together to see the screen version of Terry McMillan's *Waiting to Exhale* (1995). For weeks leading up to its release, we planned for the event, determined to see it the first weekend it hit theaters. Regardless of the major critical flaws in the film, the experience of sitting there in the theater together, surrounded mostly by other black women, was exhilarating. We talked back to the screen and to each other, reveling in points of identification with the dilemmas of the women characters, alternately laughing and sympathizing aloud and loving the visual imagery of Angela Bassett, Lela Rochon, Whitney Houston, and Loretta Devine, so beautifully vivid and brown. The film also led to a commercially successful soundtrack produced by Babyface that we listened to during girlfriend get-togethers. In a similar manner, I can imagine black women viewing *Cleopatra Jones* on its release on July 4, 1973, and being particularly enthralled with the rare appearance of a celebrated, dark-skinned superwoman on-screen.

Of course, the contemporary era of black commercial films sees an increasingly diverse number of viewers go to see certain black-oriented films, especially white adolescents who consume rap music and who are coming of age in a cultural era shaped heavily by hip hop. Yet, the problems of inhabiting a black body—particularly, it seems, a youthful black male body—continue as black consumers go to movies during an age of super-multiplexes located in or near major shopping centers that attract a range of racial and class groups. Many of these integrated movie spaces carry out policies that have serious racial, gender, and class implications. Instances of violence or perceived bad behavior at inner city theater sites that especially draw young black male audiences become additional justification for constructing the poor and lower-class black male body as an icon of violence and incorrect social behavior. Thus, it is not uncommon for theaters in integrated, popular shopping sites to police the comings and goings of certain black moviegoers. One can especially observe an increased police and/or security presence during premieres of black, hip-hop-associated films, whether comedic or action.[22]

Black women moviegoers too confront racist and sexist stereotypes of their physical and social selves that they must negotiate as spectators in the public sphere. One-dimensional contemporary portraits of black femaleness, the historical imagery of the Sapphire-like bitch, the amoral jezebel, and subsequently the demonization of black women's bodies and cultural personality have created dominant notions of a loud, socially uncouth, and even dangerous or violent black female type that upsets public space. This creates a particularly tricky mediation for black women who often enter the public space of the theater and encounter these types of images of themselves, live and in color on the big screen. In the study *Check It While I Wreck It*, Gwendolyn Pough assesses the situation accurately: "Black women . . . cannot opt to leave their peculiarities at the door. They are physically marked as Black and female."[23] This determines the ways in which black femaleness is processed. Black female consumers and spectators must negotiate this reality as participants in the public sphere.

The Daughters of Foxy Brown and Cleopatra Jones

In 1996's *Set It Off*, a film about four poor black women who turn to bank robbing in order to achieve economic empowerment, rapper and movie actress Queen Latifah (née Dana Owens) plays the macho, ghetto butch Cleopatra (Cleo). Pam Grier starred as Jackie Brown in Quentin Tarantino's 1997 film of the same name, and Beyoncé, the current rising crossover sex symbol–entertainer, plays Foxxy Cleopatra in the 2002 Austin Powers film *Goldmember*. The collective cultural memory of popular fictionalized characters and period styles is extremely influential. Often, it ensures their survival far beyond the moment of their original appearance on the cultural scene and seals them in cultlike affection within the communities that claim ownership of them. The pervasiveness of the renewed critical interest in the blaxploitation genre and its continued stylistic influence in the current hip-hop/rap generation suggests that this is so. Those of the latter generation, a significant number of whom would have been too young or not yet born at the time the most enduring of the movies emerged between 1971 and 1974, experience the blaxploitation culture more in retrospect through videos, DVDs, and movie channels.

Blaxploitation movie culture, which spawned a black popular cultural phenomenon characterized by a distinctive soul style that encompassed everything from urban archetypes to fashion and urban-infused rhythm and blues music that mythologized the black ghetto, has maintained its appeal as popular culture inspiration. hooks observes that blaxploitation brought to the screen for the first time the "obsession of poor and working-class people with style."[24] The style, films, and character icons continue to be recycled. Samuel Jackson stars as Shaft in the 2000 remake. Halle Berry has long been entertaining a remake of *Foxy Brown,* and there may also be plans underway for a remake of *Cleopatra Jones.* The iconic popularity of the genre's stylistic elements also continues to be quite evident in hip-hop culture, particularly in rap music.[25]

For many 1970s African American movie fans, films like *Shaft* and *Super Fly* presented realistic facets of black urban ghetto life. The heroes who bucked "whitey" and "the system" appealingly represented a culture counter to mainstream society. In the focus on little-before-seen black urban communities and poor and working-class folk in Hollywood, the films gained a certain cultural affection as the predecessors of the "keepin' it real" aesthetic or a so-called authentic blackness associated with lower-class culture.

Unfortunately, in spite of its engagement with social realities, neither rap music culture nor the blaxploitation cultural phenomenon marks a radical departure from the sexist tendencies of the larger American society. The glorification of the stereotypical black male phallic reputation and of black male sexuality, along with the extreme sexual objectification of black women that pervaded blaxploitation movie culture, has found a kinship in rap music representation, especially in videos and stage performances. As rap music has gained a global commercial following and success, both recognition of its social and political radicalism as well as criticism of the misogyny, violence, sexism, and nihilism that infuse too much of it have increased.[26] Rap music's intersecting sexual and gender politics are glaringly demonstrated in the prolific use of the terms "bitch" and "ho" as synonyms for women in rap lyrics and music videos where the half-naked, sexually gesticulating bodies of women have become an accepted signature trademark. Like its cultural predecessor's identification of ghetto street life with real blackness, rap music culture has valorized thug life and the problematic masculinization of ghetto life as the core of "keepin' it real."

In the early 1990s, activist and former leader of the National Congress of Black Women Delores C. Tucker waged war against rap music's sexual explicitness and became a frequent target in the lyrics of some of hip hop's most visible artists like the late Tupac Shakur. Politicians, social activists, radical-minded hip-hop artists, authors, and intellectual cultural critics continue to interrogate the meanings and consequences of the "keepin' it real" aesthetic. The concept has come to encompass a host of references: the appreciation of hip hop's history, truth about the hardships of ghetto life, street credibility and thug status, the valorization of the social codes of the culture, and the location of one's rap music identity in the ghetto even after achieving commercial music success.

Yet, "keepin' it real" has problematically come to personify classed, gendered, and sexualized representations implicitly tied to notions of "real" blackness. A number of recent writings as well as public conversations have interrogated this dilemma. Johnathan L. Jackson Jr.'s 2005 sociological study *Real Black: Adventures in Racial Sincerity,* for instance, suggests that racial authenticity imposes stereotypes and argues instead for the concept of racial sincerity, which challenges the limitations authenticity imposes on identity. Paul Beatty's novel *The White Boy Shuffle* offers a fictional interrogation by satirizing contemporary notions of young black male identity within shifting cultural and geographical settings, and Adam Mansbach's 2005 novel *Angry Black White Boy* directs an impressive fictional critique of the racial and class dynamics implicit in the claim to racial and cultural authenticity that hip hop's "keepin' it real" model posits.

At a June 2001 summit organized by hip-hop mogul Russell Simmons, a gathering of black representatives and leaders, social activists, hip-hop entertainers, and scholars discussed hip hop and responsibility. In a review of the summit, hip-hop scholar Tricia Rose addresses the male-dominated structure of the panels, the relative silence of the actual hip-hop entertainers present, and the disturbing absence of discussion on the problem of sexism and misogyny. Rose highlights the critical historical significance of the "keepin' it real" aesthetic and at the same time the problems of its contemporary manifestations by noting that rap artists have avoided responsibility for their participation in producing and contributing to these problems under the rationale that they are merely speaking the truth about where they come from.

However, while rap importantly highlights the reality of poverty, violence, racism, and drugs that oppress black ghetto life, it has become a cop-out for taking responsibility for the harmful images and messages disseminated in rap music culture. Rose cites the mainstream's emphasis on the association of materialism and the consumption of women's bodies with male self-worth and social status as a serious influence on rap music culture but suggests that these realities are not a given "but are created ones. And if those have been created, is it possible to create new ones? Artists need to be challenged to think through the impact of their words and not be allowed to hide behind the shield of reality."[27]

In spite of its sexist nature and violent overtones, women have long begun to participate successfully in hardcore rap, proving that they can be "iller" (naughtier) or at least just as "ill" as their male counterparts. Two of the most commercially successful of these rappers, Lil' Kim and Foxy Brown, have come under the most critical scrutiny, especially from various black women cultural critics and feminists. Since Josephine Baker wowed Parisian audiences with her wild onstage and offstage antics as well as with her performance of black female exotic primitivism, the question of to what extent a controversial sexual black female performer is being exploited and/or subverting that exploitation has been raised.[28] It is crucial that we continue to interrogate representations of black female sexuality in popular culture, including global hip-hop culture and rap music: "Popular culture provides countless examples of black female appropriation and exploitation of 'negative stereotypes' to either assert control over the representation or at least reap the benefits of it. Since black female sexuality has been represented in racist/sexist iconography as more free and liberated, many black women singers, irrespective of the quality of their voices, cultivated an image which suggests they are sexually available and licentious."[29]

In rap music culture, "bitch" has also been revised as "Bitch" to signify a hardcore woman who makes money and proudly flaunts her sexual libido and sexuality. She is the "around the way sista" who can hold her own with the gangsta thugs of rap music. In her insightful discussion about this particular signification in *Black Sexual Politics*, Patricia Hill Collins observes that it has become a contested term fraught with racial as well as class implications, as her students argued: "All women potentially can be 'bitches' with a small 'b.' This was the negative evaluation of 'bitch.' But the students also identified a positive valuation of 'bitch' and argued . . . that only African American women can be 'Bitches' with a capital 'B.' Bitches with a capital 'B' or in their language, 'Black Bitches,' are super-tough, super-strong women who are often celebrated."[30] As Collins outlines, "bitch" links the historical constructions of black female sexual wildness, whereas "Bitch" suggests a woman who controls her own sexuality, manipulating it to her advantage. She further comments that it is this notion of a hip-hop diva that Sister Souljah presents in her 1999 best-selling novel *The Coldest Winter Ever.*[31] Here, the protagonist, Winter Santiago, daughter of a fallen drug king, attempts to survive and elevate her status in the ghetto community by adhering to the rules of "Bad Bitch" conduct. A "Bad Bitch," according to her, knows how to use her sexuality and sexual attractiveness to attain a high roller or baller—a man of some high monetary means.[32] However, Sister Souljah explodes this idea of female empowerment and the "Chickenhead" model of ghetto black femaleness through Winter's and her family's demise.[33]

Women's confiscation or revision of the "Bad Bitch" label to signify female empowerment has a long history. During the second-wave feminist fervor of the early '70s, Jo Freeman's "The Bitch Manifesto" (1971) critically reconfigured "Bitch" as a call to sisterhood and liberation struggle, declaring that the "true bitch" was self-determined, militant, and beautiful. Today, the "Bad Bitch" label and persona now function as a mode of expression; it is a way of participating in the braggadocio that remains such an important aesthetic element of rap music lyrical play and representation. Nevertheless, this is a risky proposition. It offers the allure of transgression, a seductive construction for women and especially for historically devalued women in U.S. celebrity culture. The "Bad Bitch" suggests a black woman from working-class roots who goes beyond the boundaries of gender in a patriarchal domain and plays the game as successfully as the boys by being in charge of her own sexual representation and manipulating it for celebrity and material gain. Yet, like the screen icons of "baad bitches" Cleopatra and Foxy Brown, the careers of some key contemporary rap female stars suggest that they have not necessarily transgressed or radically upset established conceptualizations of black femaleness as much as they are perhaps immersed in the jezebel or bad girl codes long associated with it.

Lil' Kim (Kimberly Jones)—"Queen Bee," "baddest chick," and sex kitten of hardcore rap—is perhaps the most powerful example of this ambivalent persona. Kim has become the premier spectacle of sex queen diva/gangsta rap style, outdoing some of her male peers with an emphasis on "da Benjamins" (money), her sexual prowess, and her lyrical skill. In 2003, Lil' Kim released a new album, *La Bella Mafia*. On the CD, Lil' Kim reasserts herself as the "Queen Bee" in charge, a "gangsta-ass bitch" with big breasts other "bitches" envy and a Louis Vuitton lifestyle. The explicit CD includes proclamations like the song titles "Can't Fuck with Queen Bee," "Beehive," "This Is Who I Am," and the frequently radio-played singles "The Jump Off" and "Magic Stick." "The Jump Off" is a cut replete with Lil' Kim's signature themes—her hot nature and sexual prowess, gangsta rap status, material girl orientation, and claim to "baddest" bitch in rap fame:

Black Barbie dressed in Bulgari . . .
I'm the wicked bitch of the east, you better keep the peace . . .
Or out come the beast . . .
Our presence is felt like a Black Panther movement.

The same year *La Bella Mafia* debuted, new rap superstar 50 Cent's "P.I.M.P."
from his album *Get Rich or Die Tryin'* was still in heavy rotation on MTV,
BET, and hip-hop radio channels with its bleeped proclamation:

Man, bitches come and go, every nigga pimpin' know . . .
Bitch, choose with me, I'll have you stripping in the street . . .
Hoe, make a pimp rich, I ain't paying bitch.

The new gangsta pimp star and Queen Bitch teamed up to perform the
sexually charged "Magic Stick" in which Lil' Kim chants

I got the magic clit
I know if I get licked once, I get licked twice
I am the baddest chick.

While 50 Cent's "P.I.M.P." personified rap music's persistent equation of
women's bodies as merely sexualized commodities for male consumption
and power, Lil' Kim's music showcased her continued elevation of the bitch
as a model of sexual power that provides economic and social status.

Lil' Kim's appropriation of the "baad bitch" persona marks a great distance
between her and another female rapper who also constructed her rap identity as a "supreme queen." With her albums *Ladies First, Nature of a Sista,*
and *Black Reign,* Queen Latifah ushered in a radical black feminine presence in the rap arena. In the early 1990s, she became one of the first highly
visible rap icons, male or female, to offer a crucial interrogation of phallic
constructions of black femininity that relegated them to the low status of
bitches and hos. On the critically acclaimed and still much referenced single
"U.N.I.T.Y." off 1993's *Black Reign,* Queen Latifah encouraged black women
to love and respect themselves. She also called upon black men to love and
respect black women with her challenge to their construct of black women:
"Who you callin' bitch?"

On her 1996 CD *Hardcore,* Lil' Kim presented her signature "Queen Bitch,"
a title she continued to claim on the later *La Bella Mafia.* Collins astutely
observes that Lil' Kim raises a significant question: What do we make of this
female rapper whose mythology is about "pussy . . . the power, pleasure, and
politics of it"?[34] She is also right that the rapper's selling of working-class

black female authenticity depends on her selling sexuality. Yet, Lil' Kim's particular representation of herself must also be viewed as a manifestation of the same patriarchal politics that her persona might deceptively seem to disavow. Lil Kim's ownership of the persona she has clung to is deeply entangled with her mythic (in her own construction) relationship with the late Biggie Smalls, otherwise known as Notorious B.I.G. or, in Kim's most commonly used terms, Big Poppa.

Big Poppa was the most instrumental force in shaping the rap celebrity persona of his protégée and lover Lil' Kim as his hardcore sex diva "bitch." I do not want to negate or judge Kim's own claim to her longtime fondness for dressing sexy and being her own "over the top" self nor suggest that her pleasure in sexiness constitutes an automatic anti-female empowerment aesthetic.[35] However, it appears that rather than create an autonomous, radical representation of her public persona, Lil' Kim has stayed very much within the confines of the "self" styled by her literal and figurative "father" and lover, Biggie.

It is a distinctly phallocentric mythology in the figure of Big Poppa that appears to reside at the core of the Lil Kim "baad bitch" identity. An intrinsic part of that identity remains the idea of a woman who will "trick" for her main man and destroy anyone—other "bitches" or male enemies—who attempt to bring that man down figuratively or literally. As Kim declares on her definitive anthem "Queen Bitch" from the *Hard Core* CD, a "Bad Bitch" does anything for the one "baad Nigga" who commands her devotion:

I am a diamond cluster hustler
Queen bitch, supreme bitch
Kill a nigga for my nigga by any means bitch.

Kim, who took on the moniker of Biggie with her second album, 2000's *Notorious K.I.M.,* has described herself and Smalls as a real-life Bonnie and Clyde. Biggie, according to her, was a "father figure and husband" who taught her everything she knows. His spirit, she maintains, still guides "everything."[36] Despite the violence that is reported to have been a feature of that relationship, for Kim, Biggie remains a godlike phallic figure. There is a sort of kinship here with Pam Grier's Foxy Brown, whose mission of revenge is motivated by her rage over the murder of her man, Dalton. The song "Queen Bitch" hints at the influence of this earlier representation, for Lil' Kim pays homage to the legacy of Grier: "Got buffoons eatin my pussy while I watch cartoons / Seat the loon, this rap Pam Grier's here."

Interestingly, the racist-sexist politics that Grier encountered over her entertainment image in 1970s Hollywood finds an especially striking parallel in the situation of her very different contemporary nemesis, rapper Foxy Brown (Inga Marchand).[37] When she made her debut at the tender age of fifteen, Marchand decided to pay tribute to her movie idol, Pam Grier, by using "Foxy Brown" as her rap entertainment name.[38] Brown says that she chose the name because she loves Pam Grier. In her study on hip hop, *Black Noise,* Rose describes the significance of self-naming by rappers as "a form of reinvention and self-definition."[39] During Marchand's rise to rap diva, Grier became a personal mentor. Grier once addressed the rapper's use of her screen icon name: "Just by using the name, she's saying 'I'm independent and I will try to use my own wits and intelligence to get by, and to get over and learn.'"[40]

The appeal of Grier and her Foxy Brown character to the rapper derives in large measure from the example of black female toughness, but it is also a matter of Grier's visibility as an African American beauty. Rapper Foxy Brown's experience as a dark-skinned young black woman who relies on her physical representation as well as rap skills speaks to the continuing racist ideology informing images of skin color and female beauty in American society. Speaking of her daughter's skin color inferiority complex, Judith Marchand says that while she was growing up, Inga didn't see "anyone in the media who looked like her." Foxy Brown adds that her "number-one insecurity is being a dark female" because it isn't viewed as being cool.[41]

Unfortunately, Foxy Brown's late 1990s reformulation of Pam Grier's "Foxy Brown" did not offer an image of black femininity that transgressed stereotypes of black femininity or the traditional performance of sexuality by black women in popular entertainment. One of the few best-selling female rap artists ever, Foxy Brown became best known for her successful participation in gangsta rap[42] or hardcore rap resulting from her adaptation of the troubling nihilist values that permeate it. She perfected her profane, sexually explicit lyrics and her wild, sexual "tough bitch" image and boldly proclaimed material girl motivations. She has often appeared onstage clad in lingerie and bikini-like costumes, perpetuating the performance of the wild black woman. Similar to Tina Turner's image, as hooks eloquently describes, the rapper appropriates the "wild woman pornographic myth of black female sexuality created by men in a white supremacist patriarchy," exploiting it in order to "achieve economic self-sufficiency."[43]

While Pam Grier's beauty was obviously a resource in achieving her blaxploitation fame, the movie character Foxy Brown and rapper Foxy Brown are women in a male-dominated arena who must use sexual allure as a means to an end. Yet, while for both the metamorphosis into "baad bitch" is initially driven by ties to a lover, their motivations are strikingly different. While

Grier's Foxy Brown was a sister motivated by the murder of her loved one—albeit her man—it did lead to her attempts to dismantle the racist, sexist, and capitalistic underworld syndicate that was exploiting the black ghetto.

Foxy Brown's infiltration of the hardcore rap genre centers on her ability to play the game, as it is for her financial benefit not to disrupt or transform it. Brown seems to view her status as a commercially successful female participator in rap music as the single most important indicator of a radical female rap presence. However, this exemplifies the problematic concept that her participation in the marketing of her public sexualization and appropriation of the bitch label means that she represents a progressive image of liberated black femaleness. In the last three years especially, Brown's well-publicized scrapes with the law have taken center stage, magnifying more her problematic "Foxy Brown," "baad bitch" persona.

In the movie, Grier's Foxy is driven too by rage over the exploitation of the good guy by the bad, powerful white and/or male enemy. While the character's representation encompasses serious problems, as I discuss in chapter 5, she is the antithesis of the extreme capitalistic ethos that privileges money over humanity. In contrast, rapper Foxy Brown's lyrics and public persona demonstrate a distortion of the original Foxy Brown's going-after-what-she-wants tough girl determination. Her music and public presentation of her life in terms of being all about "da Benjamins" reveal the extreme individualistic materialism driving her wild, sexpot "Foxy Brown" image.

Though Grier's Foxy Brown functions in a fantasy world dominated by nihilistic tendencies, there is some suggestion of subverting the stability of hegemonic power. Rapper Foxy Brown has perpetuated the nihilistic tendencies of rap music fantasy, displaying little evidence of the progressive social consciousness that exists elsewhere in rap music. This is not to downplay that the movie's Foxy Brown has to rely on her sexual appeal as a way of gaining access to the drug operation in order to bring it down, a treatment that results in the pornographic treatment of Grier's sexual body. However, while her on-screen persona has been strongly shaped by this dynamic, Pam Grier offscreen does not define or publicly represent herself primarily in terms of the commodification of her sexual body.

In her rap music career, Foxy Brown has tried to affect black female empowerment by using the excessive sexualization of her body onstage and off through erotic poses and ongoing macho bravado about her sexual value and prowess. This provokes questions: Is this exemplary of radical transgression, or the fantasy of it? How much creative freedom or autonomy does Foxy Brown have in crafting a representational space for working-class black femininity within commercial rap music? Her rap career personifies

the tension between the control suggested by her participation in her commodification and the politics of power suggested by the fact that the rules
of this participation are already predetermined. The visibility accorded her
for being one of rap's most high profile "Bad Bitch" divas has thus far been
highly dependent on her positioning herself as ghetto sex goddess: "My sex
drive all night like a trucker"[44] and "Like to be on top or get it from behind
/ Either way I throw pussy like the free throw line."[45]

Brown, like Lil' Kim, projected herself as a "bitch" on top of the rap game
due to her ability to "flow" (rhyme and rap) and be as dirty and profane as
the bad boys of rap. As she proclaims in her song "Saddest Day": "Now I'm
the type of bitch that's one of a kind / Y'all know, the kind of bitch that like
to sip fine wine."[46] Foxy Brown's investment in the equation of her female
power in terms of her ability to make money from selling sex and profanity
remains a troubling, limiting way of constructing female empowerment.

The line dividing Inga Marchand, the product of a middle-class upbringing,
the "ghetto-life"-identified rapper Foxy Brown, and Brown's screen character
originator is very unclear. Brown has expressed an ambivalent interest in
changing the direction of her image. Yet, at the same time, she clings to the
fictionalized creation of herself as the Foxy Brown who is supposedly "keepin'
it real" by continuing the narrow trademarks of black ghetto identity that
many of her male counterparts have glamorized.

Brown's earlier rap music success, as in the case of Grier, has been inevitably tied to the politics of gender and sex. Brown was signed with the male-
led and male-controlled Def Jam record label that has cemented itself as a
rap label with some of the most commercially successful hardcore male rap
musicians today. In spite of her financial success, Chris Lighty of Def Jam
Records acknowledges that decisions regarding Foxy's image and music were
not under Foxy's total control. This is dramatically illustrated by the lack of
control that Brown's own mother says she had over her then fifteen-year-old
daughter's music image and musical direction. A 1999 *Essence* cover story
on Brown discusses contradictions in the matter of who controlled Foxy's
image. According to Foxy, she sought to change or rather tone down her
wild, sexual image but was discouraged by Def Jam executives. In perhaps
her most controversial public picture, Foxy appears on a 1998 December/
January cover of the hip-hop-edged magazine *Vibe* wearing a bikini, clutching her crotch. Brown has said that she asked the magazine and Lighty not
to use the shot, but the picture ended up on the cover.[47]

In 1998, young Foxy Brown started her own label, ironically named Ill Na
Na Entertainment (a term that had become publicly synonymous with her
sexually wild image) in order to assert more control over her own career.[48]

She also released a new album that continued her explicit lyrics yet revealed the contradictions and problems of popular success achieved through her controversial "bad girl" image. Foxy Brown's predominantly problematic or conservative lyrics hint at her potential to offer important social critique within the rap music world:

No more Waitin to Exhale, we takin deep breaths
. . . I be Foxy so peep this
Love thyself with no one above thee
Cause ain't nobody gon' love me like me.[49]

And she appears to recognize the nihilistic quality of her "high price" life in "My Life":

Wanted it all, now it's all mine
Loneliness, sorrow, confusion and pain
Nightmares, headlines, "Rapper found slain"
If it wasn't for my moms I'd drown in this pain.[50]

It remains to be seen how Inga Marchand or her version of Foxy Brown will evolve. The rapper, who became the first female to have an album debut at the top of the U.S. Billboard pop charts back in 2000, has become conspicuously quiet career-wise, while a reported hearing loss and charges of assault and probation violations have kept her in entertainment headlines. The careers of other female rappers in the first decade of the new millennium—Trina, Missy Elliot, Eve, and Kelis—have become more visible. Eve and Missy, for example, continue to achieve success in multiple areas such as collaborations with other pop divas, clothing lines, commercials, and television shows as well as within their roles as two innovative divas in the still male-dominated rap arena.

Both Lil' Kim and Foxy Brown's legal troubles have garnered as much press as their past rap success. In 2005, the hearing loss Foxy Brown suffered became public during media attention surrounding a scrape with the law over her alleged attack on a beauty salon nail technician. In court appearances before her scheduled July 2006 court date, Brown reportedly earned the ire of the judge for behavior deemed disrespectful. During the beginning of her one-year sentence at Riker's Island in October 2007, the twenty-nine-year-old Brown's misbehavior earned her a seventy-six-day stint in isolation, which meant confinement to her cell twenty-three hours a day. Lil' Kim's adherence to her gangsta chick status perhaps contributed to her decision to perjure herself rather than "snitch" about a violent altercation that occurred in a 2001 shootout in New York City between her crew and allegedly a rap posse of rival Foxy Brown. Nevertheless, Lil' Kim's time behind bars seemed to serve and authenticate her tough bitch persona. Her trouble led to a spring 2006 BET reality show, *Countdown to Lockdown,* based on the time leading up to the beginning of her jail sentence in September 2005. Lil' Kim continued to have new music played on urban hip-hop airwaves. She was released from jail in July 2006.

As black feminist Akissi Britton's 2000 letter in *Essence,* "To Kim, with Love," and the 1999 essay "Foxy's Dilemma" in the same magazine personify, the politics that reverberate in the public representation of black femaleness remain a crucial thematic. For a number of black women cultural consumers who appreciate and yearn for alternative manifestations of black female empowerment and more complex identities in both music and film culture, Lil' Kim and Foxy Brown, like Grier's imagery in blaxploitation culture many years ago, provoke an uneasy mix of admiration, tension, and concern. The two rappers get "mad love" from many female rap music lovers because they are viewed as black women trying to assert empowered sexual and celebrity selves within a very male-dominated rap game and Eurocentric entertainment world. Yet, for many black women listeners, fans, and critics, it is difficult to view Foxy and Lil' Kim as icons of true empowerment. In that letter to Lil' Kim, Britton put it this way: while Lil' Kim's music may speak truth to the realities of street life, the lyrics of her music fail to "empower women in these situations to get out."[51]

Foxy's and Lil' Kim's image-making is obviously influenced by the race and class politics that underline notions of beauty and glamour in U.S. culture. While we have seen, for example, pop divas like Britney Spears and Christina Aguilera seemingly trying to follow in Madonna's footsteps by forging celebrity success through a female empowerment forged via sexual and gender transgression, we understand that this is an even more precarious negotiation for black female entertainers. With the rise of the new "black" Cover Girls and beauty icons Halle Berry, Beyoncé, and Queen Latifah, there are still distinctive racial undertones to this emergence, such as the politics of skin color and hair suggested by the blonding fad. There is still a very narrow field of black female representation in Hollywood, where it seems only one or two black female types can be very visible at any one time. Lil' Kim presented a surgically reproduced face and body when she emerged with her 2003 album. We do not know how these rap daughters of Foxy Brown and Cleopatra Jones will continue to evolve or what their screen rebirths will bring. Yet, it is clear that when we observe them in the contemporary hip-hop culture era, we can see their likenesses in the screen divas that came to us out of the blaxploitation cultural moment.

2

Black Power and the New Baad Cinema

> The Black Power Movement was incredible because it was an exuberant, creative burst of imagination. It spread across everything in our culture—from literature to education to politics. Nothing was unaffected. It was like an earthquake.
>
> —Kathleen Cleaver, "Interview with Asha Bandele"

"Everybody knows that all the people don't have liberty, all the people don't have freedom, all the people don't have justice, and all the people don't have power. So that means none of us do. Take this country and change it! Turn it upside down and put the last first and the first last. Not only for black people but for all people."[1]

"Right on, Sista Kathleen! Uh huh, preach girl." My dear friend and colleague April and I were hanging like two excited teen girls who'd just bought the latest hot CD home. Only the sounds we were communing over came from a collection of poems, speeches, and songs that emerged out of the Black Power era. We griped about what we considered glaring omissions and applauded the inclusion of other musts on a CD entitled *Black Power: Music of a Revolution.*

"You gotta understand, girl, this was my generation. I grew up in all this. I listened to this stuff on the street and over the radio." April drifted back to her coming-of-age years during the late 1960s and early '70s. While I had been a very little girl, unaware really of the cultural earthquake that was Black Power, April had been an adolescent, finding herself as black people, she describes, were finding themselves and their way.

"Sista," she passionately reminisced aloud to me, "you gotta believe me when I say Black Power what'n just this catchy political slogan for us. It was this whole energy and it was real. Even to us kids. It was in our hair, words, movies, and sounds . . . everything." She stopped and pressed the pause button on the CD player. "You know, we had this song I remember singing on the school bus: 'We gonna fight the power. Black Power . . . '"

As my friend so eloquently conveyed, the fervor of Black Power energized late-1960s through early-1970s culture. The new political radicalism gave birth to the public expression of alternative definitions of blackness and of the wrongness of America's racial politics through art, song, and most certainly through films that offered larger-than-life black characters winning against the "system."

> Black Power!
> What do you want?
> Black Power!
> What do you want?
> Black Power![2]

Race, Gender, and the Call to Black Power

The cry carried echoes of Malcolm, Marcus Garvey, Nat Turner, Denmark Vesey, and many others. At a Greenwood, Mississippi, rally on June 16, 1966, Willie Ricks and Stokely Carmichael (Kwame Ture), two of the young, charismatic leaders in the Student Non-violent Coordinating Committee (SNCC), helped to popularize "Black Power" among a new generation of black political activists, the black community generally, and the mainstream public. Carmichael explains that in the 1960s, Black Power had been an integral concept in the voter registration drives of SNCC members across the South for some time. In the days prior to the rally, members of both SNCC and CORE (Congress of Racial Equality) had already decided to incorporate the Black Power slogan, marking their open departure from the nonviolent, integrationist-oriented emphases at the core of civil rights struggle strategy. However, because of the media coverage, Black Power gained national attention and became for black people an inspiring call to the fight for liberation.[3]

Black Power thus came to embody the shift in the energy of the black liberation movement to an urbanized sense of black rage expressed in political discourse and cultural representation. Many activists were frustrated with the perceived lack of federal effort in enforcing civil rights legislation—specifically, the 1964 and 1965 Voting Rights Acts—and the increasing disfavor of many black activists with the integration-focused program of the black moderate civil rights program.[4] This was accompanied by a growing denunciation of nonviolence, perceived white liberal influence or control over some civil rights activists and programs, and the recognition that the nonviolent civil rights direct action had not "purged or reconstructed the black ghetto."[5]

In the white and conservative black bourgeois imagination, Black Power was synonymous with racist violence and separatist nationalistic tendencies. The language of revolution offered by militant organizations and activists constructed a war on presumptions of white male supremacy that simultaneously awed and frightened the status quo. They drew on the violence viewed as a necessary component of revolution in radical Third World movements. The Black Panthers, for instance, chanted such slogans as "Off the Pigs" and "Time to Pick up the Gun" in public rallies and blatantly characterized the black revolution using nationalist language that drew on metaphors of masculine violence and war. One Black Panther Party leader declared dramatically, "So the concept is this. Basically the whole black nation has to be put together as a black army and we gon' walk on this nation and we gon' walk on this racist power structure and we gon' say to the whole damn government: stick 'em up mothafucka; this is a hol' up. We come for what's ours."[6] The historical context in which the black militants functioned "magnified their every threat and made it appear that Armageddon was as near as they claimed." The guerilla warfare emphasis of the Black Panthers and other groups, including "underground" contingents, and their efforts to challenge police brutality combined with the uprisings in urban ghettos were viewed as evidence for whites that a violent black revolution was indeed at hand. Thus, J. Edgar Hoover's FBI declared the Black Panthers black racists who were the "number one threat to the internal security of the nation."[7]

Black Power actually encompassed a diverse body of radical black political action, revolutionary discourse, and Black Nationalism. The various organizations that manifested this radicalism included SNCC, CORE, the RNA (Republic of New Africa), RAM (Revolutionary Action Movement), and the Black Panthers Party for Self-Defense, whose doctrine of revolutionary nationalism clashed with black cultural nationalist group Us. These black radical organizations formulated political philosophies that challenged racist and capitalist oppression. Third World–revolution models—the Chinese and Cuban revolutions—and Marxist doctrine had a great influence on them. In their interpretation, Black Power linked the political and the cultural and stressed black pride, self-definition, cultural affirmation, autonomy over its communities, and the destruction of white power oppression. "Black Power" was then a "revolutionary cultural concept that demanded important changes in extant patterns of American cultural hegemony."[8]

In recent years, most black historians, feminists, and cultural critics addressing the era present as an undeniable point its sexist and masculine orientation. Historian Paula Giddings aptly characterizes the 1960s as a "masculine decade," a period of white male revolt against the social and political demands of the feminism of the 1960s. The racial hierarchy and the women who were already a part of the workforce challenged black men.[9] Giddings theorizes that a "desperate need for male affirmation" influenced the interactions of black men and women in black militant movements.[10] In her 1981 book *Ain't I a Woman,* bell hooks describes how white men were articulating anxieties about their masculine roles at the same time black men were publicly declaring that they had "subjugated" black women. The verbal and written expressions of black male activists indicate their tendency to view black liberation as a move toward developing black patriarchy. This frightened white male patriarchs, but they were also, as hooks argues, impressed by the images of black men proudly asserting their powerful, black masculine manhood—an image supported by the historic view of it as primitive and sexually virile.[11] Thus, while the militant Black Power movement certainly did articulate a radical resistance to and interrogation of white supremacy that led to major advancements for black people, it also gave black men a space for affirming patriarchy:

> Militant black men were publicly attacking the white male patriarchs for their racism but they were also establishing a bond of solidarity with them based on their shared acceptance of and commitment to patriarchy. The strongest bonding element between militant black men and white men was shared sexism—they both believed in the inherent inferiority of women and supported male dominance. Another bonding element was the black male's acknowledgement that he, like the white male, accepted violence as the primary way to assert power.[12]

The political discourse of some well-known black male militants, including Carmichael, Eldridge Cleaver, and Huey Newton as well as Black Arts Movement radicals like Amiri Baraka and black female nationalists affirmed black male assertion of their right to patriarchal power over women. This thinking was symbolized through the representation of the virile bodies and forceful masculinity of popular black male icons, both political figures and black athletes like Jim Brown and heavyweight boxer Muhammad Ali.

The configuration of black masculinity versus white masculinity that permeated Black Power culture was a phenomenon shaped by the political and social currents of the time but also an evolution of the historical ideology surrounding the two. Historian Gail Bederman's *Manliness and Civilization* illuminates the historical relationship between race and ideas of virility and manhood in U.S. culture by taking as a starting point the 1910 Jack Johnson–Jim Jeffries fight. The historic fight dramatized the obsession over whether the white or black race could claim to have produced the best model of virile masculinity. Violence erupted after Johnson soundly whipped Jeffries to the chagrin of white American men everywhere.[13] Johnson also added to white male anxiety by his sexual involvement with white women, which he flaunted.[14]

Yet, this historical moment was not a rarity, Bederman reminds, for Americans, particularly middle-class white men long before 1910 and around the turn of the twentieth century, were obsessed about the link between manhood and racial dominance. The idea of manhood has been articulated differently during various time periods because it is a "historical, ideological process" that shapes how individuals situate themselves as men or as women. Ideas of manhood, then, are not fixed but affected by shifting political, economic, and social issues, views about men's and women's roles and identities, and challenges to middle-class male authority by women and laborers.[15]

The Black Power period reflects the evolution of competing racial and sexual ideologies that shape notions about male power. Black male militant activists now employed the dangerous primitive black male image as a mode for projecting a challenging posture of black manhood toward white male supremacy. The expression of Black Power through sexualized masculine imagery became a key signpost of the political cultural era. Black Power became observable through "codifiable images of black masculinity. The black leather jackets, dark sunglasses, big afros, and bigger guns made visual the myths of uncontrollable aggression and rampant sexuality."[16]

Indeed, sexuality became a crucial site in the ideological war between white and black masculinity. Themes of castration and emasculation referenced the literal historical reality of white male terror toward the black male body and black men's exclusion from the rights of patriarchal power. The themes came to stand, too, as metaphors through which Black Power spokespersons condemned the historical white supremacist persecution of black men and projected their new super-macho politicization. Such rhetorical framing elevated the historical oppression of the black man—his castration or denied manhood—as a popular mechanism for dramatizing collective black oppression. This sexualized language magnified the racialized patriarchal struggle between white men and black men as in part a sexual competition between them. Black male virility became another "dis" to white male supremacy as public discourse on the sexual appeal of black masculinity to women, white and black, grew parallel to discourse that configured white masculinity as sexually impotent and effeminized.[17]

Black men now utilized the mythology of black male sexuality and helped perpetuate the pornographic objectification of black women. The phallic construct of black revolution as a masculine domain throughout the political discourse of the 1960s and early 1970s reveals several dominant strains in thinking about black femininity. At one extreme, in both the political and cultural imagination, the misogynistic attitude toward black women construed them as sexual objects and bitchy, potential emasculators who should be willing subordinates to black patriarchal authority, especially since black men were on the frontline of the black revolution. When it came to black women, they too frequently appeared "as the iconic gun-slinging, baby toting, Afro-coifed Amazon warrior."[18]

The other strain, overlapping with the first, was the paternalistic vision of black women that affirmed their beauty and value as African queens, a critical part of the revolution of the mind. Black men were African kings who "protect" their black queens, thereby reifying the traditional association of manhood with the ability to protect as well as rule over women. Though organizations like CORE, SNCC, and the Black Panthers were held together by black men and women working together to achieve black liberation, several of the women who held leadership roles have acknowledged the male chauvinism and sexism that hindered this collective effort.[19] When such identifiable Black Power figures as Eldridge Cleaver, for instance, constructed the liberation movement as a war for black manhood—"We shall have our Manhood or level the earth in our attempt"[20]—it was amplified in a cultural period radicalized also by second-wave feminist activity and rising black feminism.

There was a disturbing devaluation of black women and the assertion of their inherent subordination in the rhetoric of too many Black Power advocates, from artists to social theorists and activists, including the aforementioned Baraka, Robert Staples, cultural nationalist Maulana Ron Karenga, and intellectual prisoner George Jackson.[21] Sexist thinking permeated the extremely misogynistic political writings of militants, most famously Cleaver's prison essay collection *Soul on Ice*. At different points, militants insisted on the rightness of traditional gender roles and suggested the potential emasculating force of black women if displaced from their "natural" sexual roles. Even the politically progressive Carmichael's infamous "joke" that the position of women in the movement was "prone" perfectly illustrated the problem of male chauvinism and conservative gender politics. Indeed, "pussy power" was an actual term that existed to relay that women served the crucial role of servicing or supporting their male comrades through their sexual availability to them.

The macho representation of Black Power owed much to the imagery of the preeminent icon of militant black manhood, Malcolm X, who continued to inspire models of black manhood after his death in 1965. Malcolm's ghetto background, passionate dedication to black freedom, bold condemnation of white supremacy, and affirmation of blackness shaped the visions of young black male activists, including the founders of the Black Panthers, the militant young members of SNCC, black male prisoners, and the masses of frustrated black urban youth. Beloved by black men and women then and now, Malcolm X beautifully personified black rage directed toward white supremacy. He also personified thinking about the link between manhood and the protection of women and children. His ever-evolving black political vision manifested the conservative and at times contradictory tendencies in black male discourses about black liberation, manhood, and gender roles.

Though certainly not exemplary of some of his contemporaries' blatant misogyny, Malcolm was attached to a very patriarchal vision of women and men throughout most of his life. His attitudes toward women were shaped during his early street hustling days, a lifestyle defined by the masculine posture of the hip urban pimp-trickster figure that personified the patriarchal orientation of "street life." In "The Riddle of the Zoot," historian Robin D. G. Kelley writes that Malcolm was a part of a community of black hipsters bound by "gendered ideologies, power relationships, and popular culture." He observes that for black hipsters or hustlers, resistance to "wage labor" often involved an increase in the "oppression and exploitation of women," black women in particular.[22]

Cultural critic Michael Eric Dyson has unpacked such urban versions of black identity that developed after the Great Migration of blacks to northern cities, explaining how they served as masks and modes of resisting dominant definitions of blackness and counteracted the particular powerlessness and demeaning aspects of poor urban life. According to him, "subversive exaggeration" characterized the mack, pimp, hustler, and player, archetypes that evolved out of urban mythologies of blackness.[23] The elevation of sexuality as a site for black males to demonstrate their masculine manhood further hints at its role in counteracting the historic devaluation of black men and their sexuality, which was problematic thinking in the sexual and racial discourse of the time. [24] The cool persona and masculine power associated with these figures were tied to their exaggerated sexuality and sexual power over women, whom they were able to exploit economically. The urban hipster or hustler depended on his ability to "hustle" whites as well as women.[25]

Malcolm's gender views were influenced by a "suspicion" of black women as potential controllers of black men. Sociologist Patricia Hill Collins has argued that he tended to categorize them into groups: Eves, who were "deceptive temptresses who challenged male authority" through manipulating their sexuality for personal gain, and Madonnas, sacrificing mothers and wives, personified in his view by the modesty and femininity of Muslim women in the Holy Land.[26] Malcolm's early personal relationships with women, particularly with his mother, the one who whipped him, and beloved older half-sister Ella, reveal a tendency to fear women he perceived to be overbearing. Malcolm describes Ella, probably the second-most influential woman in his young adult life, as having "broken the spirits of three husbands, more driving and dynamic than all of them combined." She was expelled, Malcolm explains, from the mosque in Boston because of her "domineering ways."[27]

Several other passages in his autobiography highlight Malcolm's early psychology toward women. Reflecting on his education in the streets of Boston and Harlem, Malcolm notes that the prostitutes willingly schooled him about the true nature of their sex. It was these "tough women" who taught him that women needed to be treated firmly. Women, "by their nature, are fragile and weak" and desire men who are strong. Furthermore, he theorizes, "women love to be exploited," and if they are not, they will exploit men.[28] Malcolm reemphasizes such points several times throughout the autobiography. His views are dramatically tinged with classed notions of women. He admired the prostitutes for being "honest" and "realistic" about the nature of men and women and for providing comfort and ego-stroking to the many men who were constantly being beat up by their wives.

According to Malcolm, many women, particularly wives, drove men to prostitutes before even going to work in the morning: "Domineering, complaining, demanding wives who had just about psychologically castrated their husbands were responsible for the early rush. These wives were so disagreeable and had made their men so tense that they were robbed of the satisfaction of being men. To escape this tension and the chance of being ridiculed by his own wife, each of these men had gotten up early and come to a prostitute."[29] Such views even skewed Malcolm's perceptions toward his surprising proposal to Betty Shabazz. Though he pursued her and proposed marriage despite his misgivings about wives and women generally and with virtually no initiation from Shabazz, Malcolm frames their union as if she might have had some kind of power over him. As he relates it, maybe she had known somehow that he would propose, and thus she'd managed to "get me." He grew to love her nevertheless, and she became, in his words, one of only four women he ever trusted.[30]

The Nation of Islam's doctrine about women fit Malcolm's already established feelings toward women. The gender roles were clearly defined: women were elevated to a level of respect by men as their virtuous, submissive helpmates who needed the unquestioned leadership and safety offered by strong black men. Malcolm became the celebrated embodiment of this ideal by both black men and women. Farah Jasmine Griffin insightfully explains that Malcolm offered black women the "promise of protection, an acknowledgement of the significance of white racist assaults on black beauty and an affirmation of black features, particularly hair and color."[31] Though it was predicated on a presumption of male power, for black women historically devalued and excluded from feminine idealization, the idea of protection and valuation of their feminine racial attributes was attractive.[32] The patriarchal nature of Malcolm's masculinity was thus affirmed by black women and by poets and male admirers, for whom he was a "black prince" emblematic of a majestic black manhood.[33]

Malcolm often articulated black oppression through sexualized and gendered language similar to his construct of how men were often castrated by their women. His emphasis on the historical exclusion of black men from the power structure subsumed gender issues and women under the "black man" terminology. He explained to an audience once, "I live in a society based on the political, economic, and social castration of the black man."[34] "Black man" and "black men" referred specifically to black men but also stood for "black people."[35] Collins points out that Malcolm's gendered thinking aligned with the gender ideology permeating African American political thought and activism during the 1950s and 1960s, which insisted on inherent male and female roles that were biologically rooted.

It is easier perhaps to anticipate Malcolm X's potential thinking about race, nationality, and civil rights than about gender. He remained attached to the belief that revolution was work for real men and that the protection of women and children was an inherent quality of true manhood. He never radically backed away from this ideology of proper sex roles. However, in an interview in 1964, when he was sensitized by his travels throughout Africa and by time with formidable women like Shirley Graham Du Bois (widow of W. E. B. Du Bois), Malcolm thoughtfully made a measured observation about how the education and progress of women paralleled the progressive development of the societies he had visited.[36]

The sexist thinking of Malcolm and other black men and women did not exist in a vacuum shaped entirely by the new political agenda, of course, but was a manifestation of the long patriarchal orientation of American society. In addition, the politics of gender that reverberated in Black Power poetics was exacerbated by mainstream negative constructs of black women in the ghetto ethnographies of the period, most famously Daniel Patrick Moynihan's 1965 *The Negro Family: The Case for National Action*. Moynihan's much-cited study touted the black matriarchal family dysfunction theory in which black men were disenfranchised from their proper familial leadership role as their women assumed the role of economic and social head of the family. The report held black women, especially single mothers, responsible for such social ills as crime, poverty, and sexual immorality and suggested that black men could be saved from the black female dysfunctional oppression by being placed in "an utterly masculine world."[37] Black male disempowerment theories were also disseminated in studies by black male sociologists. These studies, Giddings opines, were more sexist than racist. hooks adds that these affirmed the historical notion of black women as "too uppity." Though a storm of challenges from black men and women followed Moynihan's report, some black men employed the black matriarchal thesis to support the idea of black female subordination yet affirm black manhood.[38]

The matriarchal image of the strong black woman tied into the older archetype of the mammy, a stereotype of a black woman who was submissive to white control but too dominating over her own men. The representation of black women as unfeminine in comparison to white femininity and as "dangerous, deviant, castrating mothers divided the Black community at a critical period in the Black liberation struggle."[39] The image of the "black bitch" intensified in the political and cultural environment of the era, particularly when black women in various black radical organizations functioned in leadership roles and dared to address black male sexism. For instance, in her autobiography, former Black Panther Party leader Elaine Brown recounts her struggle with the macho orientation of the party when she assumed leadership in the early 1970s. She recalls addressing the disrespect of the sisters by their male comrades in one instance when one of the latter inquired, "I hear we can't call them [sisters] bitches no more."[40]

By 1970, literature by black women political activists about white supremacy, black sexism, and the particular oppression experienced by black women had emerged more visibly in black public discourse. Individual black women like political activist Angela Davis, organizations such as SNCC's Black Women's Liberation Committee, and major black feminist works such as Toni Cade Bambara's 1970 anthology *The Black Woman* challenged black and white patriarchal notions of black women's roles and privileged fighting race, class, and sexual oppression. Kay Lindsay's "Poem" spoke poignantly to the problematic gender politics underlining black revolution discourse:

> But now that the revolution needs numbers
> Motherhood got a new position
> Five steps behind manhood.[41]

In her essay "Double Jeopardy," also in *The Black Woman,* Frances Beale critiqued the racist capitalist model of black manhood and womanhood as well as black people's complicity in its perpetuation. While her essay supports the leadership of black men in the liberation struggle, Beale challenged the neglect of black women's oppression in the movement's emphasis on the historic castration of black men and the matriarchal stereotype of black women. As she wrote, "It is true that our husbands, fathers, brothers, and sons have been emasculated, lynched and brutalized. . . . However, it is a gross distortion of fact to state that Black women have oppressed Black men." Indeed, Beale went on, the assertion of manhood through the insistence that women stay in their prescribed, passive roles was "counter-revolutionary."[42] Several more essays in the anthology take up similar arguments, including Lindsay's "The Black Woman as a Woman" and Jean Carey Bond and Patricia Perry's "Is the Black Male Castrated?"

Besides major collections such as *The Black Woman,* other radical writings by black women address racism and sexism in the political movement. For example, Mary Ann Weathers offered a pointed indictment of the "myth of matriarchy" and the idea that black women's liberation was anti-male in the 1969 manifesto "An Argument for Black Women's Liberation as a Revolutionary Force." Weathers affirmed that black women should take the lead in fighting for their liberation as women and that this effort tied into the battle for black people's collective struggle for liberation.[43] A plethora of critical literary work by emerging black women writers centered the oppression, triumph, and freedom struggle of black women. Toni Morrison's narrative *Sula* (1973) chronicled the friendship of two young girls coming of age in a society where they realized early they were neither "white nor male," as does a young Maya Angelou in her powerful autobiography, *I Know Why the Caged Bird Sings* (1970). Women playwrights and poets in the Black Arts Movement, most famously Sonia Sanchez and Nikki Giovanni, participated in the pro-black rhetoric of the era but also crafted pieces that signified on the sexist engendering of the movement. In "Woman Poem," Giovanni declared that women could be castrated too and signified, "i wish i knew how it would feel to be free."[44]

Popular culture then and now seized on the matriarchal image of black women and the black masculine persona associated with Malcolm's street hip image, elevating in particular the sexualized, masculine posture definitive of his pre-conversion, Detroit Red days, an indication of the popularity of the urban trickster figure mythology. By the early 1970s, the late Malcolm's masculine image clearly influenced the popularity of the "baad nigger" against "whitey" motif in black cultural productions such as *Sweetback*. Later films like Spike Lee's 1992 *Malcolm X* overly privilege Malcolm's Detroit Red days prior to his spiritual and political conversion in prison.[45] In the early 1970s, the influence of popular black masculine urban identities was no more evident than in the black action vehicles and blaxploitation films that exploded on the scene after the economic success of *Sweetback*.

Race, Gender, and the Rise of Baadasssss Heroes

Globe-sized Afros, platform shoes, bell-bottoms, black leather, super-sized collars, pimped-out hats, animal print furs, superfly Caddies with "diamonds in the back," Uzis, coke rings, bare titties, wigs, funky rhythms, sexy lyrics, Chicago, Harlem . . . folks never run out of words whenever I've mentioned blaxploitation. I might start out answering their question about the subject of my book by saying it's about sexualized film representations of women in 1970s black action films, but it's always when I say, "You know, *Shaft, Super Fly, Foxy Brown* . . ." that their eyes light up with recognition and they begin to giggle and laugh. "For real, girl? You writing about that?"

Controversial history or not, "blaxploitation" has long become the popular label for the formulaic cycle of black-centered action films produced in the early to mid-1970s.[46] The word derives from the collusion of "black" and "exploitation." Blaxploitation shares the typical aspects of exploitation cinema in that it hinges on the exploitation of sex and violence. Plots are "purely accidental" and driven by the film producers' exploitation of spectatorial desire—that is, the desire to view sex and violence. Blaxploitation specifically signifies on the exploitation of black audiences' desire to see black folk and black culture on the big screen and encompasses the marketing strategies of the films, especially the blatant sexual and violent overtones of the ads and posters.[47] Blaxploitation has long been a contested label, raising questions about how it denotes exploitation, who and what is being exploited, who gets to name the genre as such, and whether or not it is an adequate or appropriate label for this body of films.

In *What It Is . . . What It Was!*, the 1998 book homage to the striking posters that helped market the black action films of the '70s, visual artist David Walker attributes the blaxploitation term to Junius Griffin, a press agent and head of the NAACP's Hollywood branch. Griffin used the term "black exploitation films" in an August 1972 *Variety* article. It then came into popular use that same month as Griffin, along with CORE's Roy Innis and other activists, organized the Coalition against Blaxploitation. The term, Walker describes, "took on a life its own."[48] Blaxploitation filmmakers, actors, and actresses tended to resist the labeling of the films as such and responded to the increasing black criticism, questioning "blaxploitation" as an apt term.[49]

Looking back at the film era twenty years later, Gloria Hendry, perhaps the most visible black female actress within the genre after Pam Grier and Tamara Dobson, insists that it should have been more aptly called a "Renaissance." Hendry explains her resistance to the term blaxploitation because "all films are exploitation."[50] Black film critics have employed and continue to utilize the term to suggest the economic and social implications of a group of films that were primarily subject to white Hollywood control. I use "blaxploitation" as way of referring to this unique, popular genre and as a way of signifying on the specific exploitative nature of films that capitalized on black audiences' desire for more empowering, culturally familiar black heroes.

Cheaply produced action flicks with black heroes who buck "whitey" in plots revolving around sex, drugs, and violence provided Hollywood with a profitable market. At the same time, film historian Ed Guerrero describes, this formula served to distort, contain, and marginalize the seriousness and scary specter of Black Power liberation struggle:

> Hollywood was able to combine its traditional moneymaking ingredients of violence and sexploitation, wrap them in the distorted and grotesque signs and imagery of the urban black underworld, and at the same time keep the insurgent black political thought and cultural expressions of the times to a minimum. The resulting product was racially targeted for the huge black audience eager to see a broader representation of its humanity and aspirations validated on the commercial screen. Hollywood was able to play on black people's new-found identification with its increasingly politicized and militant underclass while shifting the industry's black imagery and stereotypes, in the words of the critic Daniel Leab, "from Sambo to Superspade."[51]

Film critic Jesse Algernon Rhines echoes Guerrero, asserting that the films employed a "sex, violence, and 'super-cool' individualism" that was then the "antithesis of what contemporaneous black political organizations, like SNCC, the NAACP, or SCLC" advocated.[52] It is also important to note that though the genre depended on utilizing black actors and actresses, their desire to work as such was exploited, for they were not well paid or necessarily involved in the control of the films. In one of the most commercially successful films, *Shaft,* for instance, star Richard Roundtree was paid only about $13,000; after the film's success, director Gordon Parks fought for Roundtree to be better paid for the sequel.[53]

Sweetback, Shaft, and *Super Fly* established elements of a black action film formula that proved popular and profitable, hence its confiscation by the Hollywood industry. In addition to the impact of Black Power on black popular imagery, the films exploded onto the scene because of the economic plight of Hollywood. Television's rising popularity, the high rate of leasing for Hollywood films, and the failure of studios' big budget films had Hollywood hovering on the edge of economic collapse.

These factors coincided with rising black criticism of the mainstream model of black heroism exemplified by Sidney Poitier's screen persona. Dissatisfaction with an image that was out of tune with the energy of the Black Power age helped birth a new black machismo presented on the big screen by black athletes like Jim Brown and Fred Williamson. The NAACP had long sought to challenge Hollywood's racist imagery, but in the 1960s this effort intensified amid the atmosphere of bold radical political activism and rebellion signaled by social factors, including the urban riots, beginning with Watts in 1965. In films like *The Dirty Dozen* (1967), Guerrero describes, Jim Brown exuded a boldly violent as well as sexual machismo—unlike Poitier—emphasized by his ability to attract women of all races and sleep with them. Yet, he reminds us, this new stereotypical black image signified how racial coding and devaluation evolve and shift in the midst of the contemporary cultural and social environment. The black macho hero was still controlled by white authority.[54]

Sweetback's depiction of the "baad nigger" who revolts against the police and triumphs brought to the screen a black revolutionary macho model who deviated dramatically from the traditional cinema model of black heroism or what Mark A. Reid calls the "black-as-martyr" characterization in Poitier's signature roles.[55] *Sweetback* proved a profitable venture that showcased the potential profit to be gained at targeting a black urban audience through utilizing the appeal of the black hero–winning motif.[56] At first, the film was released only in two major cities but went on to gross $10 million.[57] Its domestic rentals totaled over $4 million. The formula was solidified with *Shaft* and *Super Fly* and finally collapsed after many cheaper imitations and much black criticism.[58]

Sweetback invoked the challenge that Black Power consciousness posed to white male supremacy in the dramatization of Sweetback's revolt and subsequent fight to escape the relentless police. Because of its sexual stud protagonist and the prominence of sex as a narrative strategy, some Black Nationalists and Black Power activists embraced it as revolutionary, while others condemned it as counterrevolutionary.[59] Nevertheless, it was distinguishable from the other two popular black male action films that quickly followed, *Shaft* and *Super Fly.*

Shaft and *Super Fly,* two of the most technically polished black ghetto action films of the era, solidified *Sweetback's* black triumph plot strategy and helped to popularize the less overtly Black Power–politicized action. They exemplified the commercialization of the "new" empowered black hero thematic and the new celebratory sense of black cultural aesthetics or soul culture. *Shaft,* straddling "Hollywood and black independent cinema,"[60] was directed by the multifaceted black director Gordon Parks and released through a major studio. John Shaft, the private eye protagonist, was originally supposed to be played by a white actor, but the success of *Sweetback* changed this as Hollywood recognized a new market and film type. *Super Fly,* directed by Parks's son, Gordon Parks Jr., financed by Sig Shore and some black businessmen, and then distributed by Warner Brothers, offers a glorified black pimp/drug dealer in Priest, a black hero trying to get out of the cocaine-dealing game with some financial security.

Shaft and *Super Fly* embody the key formal and thematic features that came to define the aesthetic style of the developing blaxploitation genre, taking the model of *Sweetback's* black male hero up against white male power into the crime or underworld action drama genre. The representation of the black ghetto and soul culture in *Shaft* and *Super Fly* ushered in an unprecedented visibility of the black urban underclass and black culture, particularly in areas such as music. Music occupied a prominent role in the films with a cadre of significant black music artists producing commercially successful soundtrack albums. Rather than being relegated to background instrumentals that might signal climactic dramatic moments, the soundtracks of the new black action films articulated character representations and personified the social, cultural, and geographical setting.

The critically acclaimed soundtracks of Isaac Hayes's Oscar-winning *Shaft* and Curtis Mayfield's *Super Fly* utilized various historical and contemporary styles of black music, including blues, jazz, gospel, and emerging '70s soul music styles such as funk. Wah-wah and bass guitars, electric piano, strings, drums, congos, bongos, and call and response chorus segments fueled Hayes' and Mayfield's long instrumentals and lyrically driven songs often titled after characters' names. They offered funky beats, sexually charged boasts that portrayed heroes' heterosexual appeal, and melancholic, searing social commentary about the realities of racism, poverty, drug use, and other harsh features of black urban ghetto life. The "Theme from Shaft," with its magnificent instrumental sequence and Hayes's playful question "Who's the Man?" to a female chorus answering "Shaft," is arguably as well known as the film itself. Elsewhere on this lyrically driven soundtrack, Hayes offers such memorable tracks as the gospel-infused ballad "Soulsville," a poignant portrait of black ghetto life, which plays as Shaft goes into Harlem in an early scene.

On Mayfield's *Super Fly* soundtrack, which sold over two million copies, he displays his insightful humanistic values, mellow vocal style, and music production skills on a rich collection of tracks, including the gold singles "Freddie's Dead" and "Theme of Super Fly," which plays in its entirety during a long montage sequence in the film. Mayfield does not merely chronicle black ghetto life and drug culture but theorizes about the psychic, social, and physical causes and costs with songs like "No Thing on Me (Cocaine Song)." The artistic album covers of these notable soundtracks also served as marketing tools that helped draw audiences. Like the film ads and billboards, album covers presented the screen heroes in full "baad nigger" character with sexy images and recreations of scenes from the films.

Bitches, Hos, and the Rise of "Baad Supermamas"

The macho hero in blaxploitation fantasies generally has a number-one lady who has his back by remaining endlessly sexually and socially accessible to him. The hero's "baad nigger" status is symbolized by his control over and appeal to a bevy of sexually hot women. In such cinematic representations, the threat of domineering, bitchy black women and feminism is contained. The fervor of Black Power consciousness and lower-class black ghetto culture and black identities are simplified while the disturbing gender politics are amplified in the exhibition of pimp-powerful black male heroes and white underworld kings who control "bitches and hos." Women function as the major signs of the power competition between white and black men. Whether the hero is a pimp or drug dealer, private eye, cop, or rising revolutionary, his sexual prowess and hold over women help to establish the fantasy of the character's agency. The power of white enemies is also conveyed via the representation of their sexual and economic ownership over all women. In a sense, women are quite literally the "spoils" of war.

This was not solely a feature of black action films, because they in fact followed action cinema's representation of male power through violence and dominance over women that has always characterized popular American tough-guy action cinema—westerns, gangster cinema, spy thrillers, criminal action films, and by extension exploitation cinema. The centrality of male violence as a hallmark of phallic social, economic, and political power is a key feature in the popular hit 'em up, underworld, B-grade and commercial blockbusters of the period. *The Godfather* (1972) may be viewed as the premier embodiment of this representation. The film achieved and continues to pose a spectacular pleasure for white and black male viewers in particular.

In the black action vehicles of the era, women's preeminent characterization as sexualized, phallus-adoring girlfriends and working-class tramps or prostitutes indicates an extreme confiscation of sexist thinking and the elevation of black urban trickster figures as examples of black masculinities romantically defiant of white patriarchal authority. In films like the three signature films where black men had major input or control over the production, the heroes Shaft, Priest, and Sweetback personify the sexual allure ascribed to the player or mack. Their soulful cool relies significantly on the display of their ability to "fuck" any of the women they choose and on women constantly desiring to be "fucked" by them. Likewise, other black popular films (the 1973 blaxploitation pimp feature *The Mack,* for example) and mass popular literature of the day (most notably former pimp Robert "Iceberg Slim" Peck's 1969 popular autobiography, *Pimp: The Story of My Life Slim*) elevated glamorization of the pimp figure and male misogyny.

The prevalent use of the terms "bitch" and "ho" as names that signify the status of woman equates a sense of degraded womanhood inscribed as malicious. "Ho" references "bitches" specifically positioned as prostitutes and oversexed females. Women positioned thus often refer to themselves and each other as "bitch" and "ho" as they compete for men's favors. Many critics decried such constructions and both the real-life and fictional pimp or hustler figures that thrived on the exploitation of women and the community, but, as the mixed but popular reception to *Sweetback* demonstrated, the allure of such masculine figures was quite strong.

The increased filmic visibility of them helped to establish "bitch" and "ho" as part of a normative lexicon that made these acceptable labels for women, ones that conveyed their ideological and social subordination to phallic power. In part, this phenomenon suggested a backlash against the visibility of feminism and black feminist consciousness on the cultural landscape. In the 1970s black ghetto action films, both males and females are sexualized, but the differing pornographic treatment of the female body is evident in the prominence of nude and scantily clad women who drape the background of the narrative action. Furthermore, the racial inscription of these gender politics is a central aspect of this treatment.

As in the real-world street culture described by Malcolm X in his autobiography and in American society generally, white and black women in '70s action cinema occupy a different status. Middle-class, poor, and lower-class black women are often construed as more inherently bitchy than white women, potentially traitorous, and sexually loose. "Bitch" then signified too the idea of black women as potential traitors to black men and their race because of their perceived bitchiness and sexual potency unless subdued by the revolutionary black man. The pornographic objectification and exploitation of the black female body is elevated in these pop culture productions, creating a visual spectacle of black femaleness in terms of freakish sexuality, animalism, and powerlessness. They are frequently the recipients of overtly racist violent treatment. Collins notes the link between controlling images of black women as prostitutes and subordinate "pets" and systems of domination, which helped justify the negative treatment of black women.[61]

The signature white whore in the films is pornographically objectified as well, of course, but with different signification. She is central to black and white men's power relations. The ownership of these very often blonde, "trashy" female character types and the act of "fucking" them operate as a metaphor for "fucking" whitey, that is, black male rebellion against traditional racial patriarchal positioning. She is then a "fist" sticking in the face of "the Man" to signal a black man with atypical agency. The image of the white female whore worshiping the black phallus and under black male "power" becomes a crucial aspect of the racialized, gendered, and sexualized spectacle that the films offer. As such, white female characters often appear as the head of the stable or as number-one prostitute; at the least, a bedroom or sex scene between a black man and white woman is usually included. Though male property too, she operates as the "ultimate booty."[62] This suggests the historic valuing of white female beauty and worth—though certainly not in the sense of the middle-class model of white female purity and perfection. Black women are valued less for their beauty and sexual economic worth in the realm of male-controlled female prostitution.

While *Sweetback* and *The Spook* posit women primarily as sexualized objects, the white female figure becomes symbolic of the historic danger white women posed to black male survival and of black men's subordination to her in the racial status quo. Her visual femininity and whiteness thus serves as a reminder of black men's exclusion from the American cult of true manhood. The avoidance or sexual conquering of her by the pimp or black militant hero is crucial.

The strongest exceptions in the typical constructions of women during the period comes with the brief but notable entry of tough black woman narratives that capitalized on the popularized physical image of the Afro-wearing black power woman personified visually by Angela Davis. Davis, an intellectual and radical political activist, became famous for being a fugitive and political prisoner after the brother of militant black prisoner George Jackson used guns registered in her name to orchestrate a deadly courtroom siege. The major popular entertainment examples of the tough black woman persona came via the black female star film vehicles that appeared in 1973–74. Cleopatra Jones, Coffy, and Foxy Brown were offered up as the personification of "baad bitches"; they were marketed as exceptional black women characters who broke with the traditional marginal and subordinate role of black women. Hence, they were not merely sexualized "bitches" owned by men.

The maternally inscribed "supermama" or more familiar "mama" was a popular slang expression used by men as a term of endearment or expression of admiration of sorts. It accesses all kinds of layered constructions of black femininity, including a heterosexually fine or sexy woman who may be considered an atypically tough feminine figure and/or a potential devourer and destroyer of men or a mythic nurturer of her man and her community. The sexualization of the term becomes evident in the ads for such films as *Coffy*, where a sexily posed Grier is presented as the "Godmother of them all."

The construct of the "bitch" denotes a "difficult woman," according to Elizabeth Wurtzel in her "praise" of such women in the book *Bitch*. Wurtzel focuses primarily on white female icons of this figure but usefully explains that the bitch functions as role model, icon, and idea. It can act as a "mask," a role to be played that allows for the expression of a sort of "female resentment" that often comes out of disturbance, fear, anger, and rage.[63] The moral badness associated with the icon of the bitch suggests a woman who doesn't behave according to proper or traditional feminine mores. She does as she wants and demands rather than asks for what she desires. She has large ambition and uses her sex appeal or sex to her benefit. As a woman who possesses a dangerous persona and/or dangerous curves, violence and sex tend to be associated with her. The bitch then encompasses the femme fatale in that she particularly poses danger to men. She possesses an erotic female potency.

The heroines of blaxploitation fantasies are bold, uppity black women who "don't take no mess" and defy staying in their place. As sassy supermamas, they visibly pose the threat of castration to men. They challenge and destroy powerful white and male enemies. Luckily, unlike the many iconic real-life and fictional bitches that Wurtzel references in *Bitch*, black supermamas are not destroyed in blaxploitation fantasies, since the formula dictates that they must win in the end. Yet, as I explore throughout the chapters to follow, the supermama "wins" in narratives that simultaneously glorify and objectify her and at points punish her for being so "baad."

3

What's Sex and Women Got to Do with It?

Sexual Politics and Revolution in Sweetback *and* The Spook

"Girl, they ain't lying about *Sweetback*. Now if I don't remember nothing else about it, that movie had lines way down the block. And people went to see it two or three times, okay? I think about it now, I was just a child seeing that movie. Can you believe that?" As a lovely, ageless black California artist shared this with me, I listened like a kid voyeuristically experiencing *Sweetback*. I'd seen the movie many times before this conversation, but through her remembrances, I was feeling the magnetic aura of the film in its time.

It seems as if I've always known about *Sweet Sweetback's Baadasssss Song*, the infamous film that inadvertently spawned the blaxploitation genre. Years before actually viewing it, I'd heard all about it and read all kinds of black film histories that addressed the film. I knew that part of its controversial though legendary status stemmed from its graphic sexual scenes, one in which the director's own son played the boy in the encounter with an older prostitute. And still, the movie jumped off the screen and slapped me upside the head when I finally watched it for the very first time several years ago now. I sat stupefied as the warning "Watch Out A Baadasssss Nigger Is Coming Back To Collect Some Dues" faded from the screen. The hype embodied in the well-known declaration that the film "raged" and "screamed" was justified. Whenever I show the film in my classes, it shouts loudly at my diversely mixed students, provoking anger, confusion, and discomfort for many and passionate political enthusiasm and love in others, particularly my black male students. Once we grapple with its form, themes, and problems and continue our viewing and discussion about the black action movie culture of the time, it is always the one film that they are drawn to return to over and over again.

Perhaps because of its unabashed Black Nationalist action center, another boldly political revolt–themed film, *The Spook Who Sat by the Door*, provokes some of the same responses. I had long heard of this film as well, but it wasn't until about 1999 that I finally viewed it for the first time. I watched it with a boyfriend who prided himself on his black radical intellectual consciousness. For him, the film was a sacred manifesto about true Black Power political action and change.

Created and written by Sam Greenlee and produced with other black male collaborators, it offers an unusual, serious dramatization of Black Nationalism and revolution. Though there were also critically significant black dramas like *Lady Sings the Blues, Sounder,* and *Black Girl* in the early 1970s, *The Spook* was released during a period when the crime world–oriented blaxploitation formula was being exhausted in black-marketed, studio-supported action films like *Super Fly. The Spook* reflects a black male political perspective with its extraordinarily strong critique of white supremacist, capitalist oppression and due in part to the control that black men had over the film's vision. Like *Sweetback, The Spook* does not employ the individual criminal/drug action plot or employ and marginalize the black militant image as merely a sensationalist element in the narrative. Rather, it attempts to evoke the black protest struggle emphases on the empowerment of the black community and resistance to the racial status quo.

Despite its technical roughness, I was captivated by its intensity. When the last scene faded, my boyfriend immediately launched into a spirited discourse about the film's revolutionary import and carried on with platitudes about the black male hero's brilliance and the like. He finally calmed down and excitedly awaited my confirmation. Of course I delivered. I agreed on its explosiveness and commented on how interesting it would be to see a remake of it, but I ended with a few deadly serious questions as to whether women would be in the black revolution or not and how. There were women in it, my boyfriend reminded me; didn't you hear the hero tell the brothers how important the sistas would be? I did at that, I answered, but the comment was sort of overwhelmed by the film's representation of black women through two main characters—a traitorous, black bourgeois bitch and a noble black whore with African queen potential. To say the least, the parallels between *The Spook* and its predecessor, *Sweetback,* were quite striking to me, and I felt a great need to talk back to them and insert a black woman's voice. So, after some time being enthralled and infuriated by *Sweetback* and *The Spook,* this analysis serves as my feminist love critique to Melvin, Sam, *Sweetback, The Spook,* and the primarily black male critical vanguard that has unfolded the film in many provocative ways.

What interests me about *Sweetback* and *The Spook* is how they enter into the problematic cultural representation of women and gender politics that permeated black revolutionary discourse. The two films offer bold depictions of women as mechanisms for black phallic empowerment, a depiction that echoes the sexualized masculine perspective that permeated Black Power poetics. *Sweetback* and *The Spook* present women as potential hindrances to black revolution and most certainly to black patriarchy. Their contribution to the black male–led liberation movement rests in their sexual and emotional submission to the demands of the black male revolutionary's noble fight for black liberation. This is not ultimately a point of critique in the film but an affirmation of the hypersexual machismo and traditional gender politics that reverberated throughout the black liberation struggle in the 1960s and early 1970s. Ultimately, in *Sweetback,* female bodies serve as texts for the imaginative depiction of the black man's violent fight for freedom, survival, and his manhood. Melvin Van Peebles's engagement of sex perpetuates a creative mythology revolving around images of black female primitivism and phallic adulation.

Here's the plot: A black sex show worker (Melvin Van Peebles) is spirited away by the police, who need a token black downtown to feign interest in solving a black-on-black crime. In the course of the drive to the station, the two white cops pick up a young black militant, MooMoo, and proceed to beat him while Sweetback is handcuffed to him. Against the background whir of an industrial machine and the sound of the cops beating MooMoo, Sweetback emotionally snaps and proceeds to whip the two cops with the handcuffs dangling from his wrist. Sweetback flees with a battered MooMoo, and so commences the tale of Sweetback's flight and ultimate escape. It's not difficult to understand why *Sweetback* provoked such public controversy. It is a fascinating mix of elements, given its sexual representations, ghettocentric black cultural aesthetics, and resistance to classical Hollywood cinema form. The making of the film is legend itself because of all the strategies Van Peebles used to get the film made on a shoestring budget, like playing Sweetback himself. Part of *Sweetback*'s legacy is its unintentional role of setting up features that would be exploited in the emerging white Hollywood–supported blaxploitation films. It has enjoyed more sustained attention from black film criticism than most others, but there has been a noticeable lack of black feminist reading.

Sweetback investigates the historical social condition of the black lower-class community through the metaphor of dominant notions of black male sexuality—the sexual stud image specifically—while critiquing dominant conventions of classical Hollywood cinema. The police represent institutional

white patriarchal authority that can manipulate, and of course violently assault, the black male body.[1] However, though on one level it signifies on historical constructions of black masculinity and classical Hollywood cinema,
Van Peebles fails to offer radical disruptions of notions about gender power
and, by extension, white and black women.

While how and to what extent the controversial *Sweetback* can be considered politically revolutionary remains a contestable point, it is clear that Van
Peebles captured the energy of the militant expression of black rebellion that
came to be personified by the call for Black Power. *Sweetback*'s employment
of black cultural aesthetics and the approaches the director utilized to get the
film made signifies an artistic adaptation of features valorized in Black Power
discourse, especially self-reliance, black cultural affirmation, and emphasis
on the black lower class as a crucial force in revolution. In a 1971 *Life* article,
Van Peebles declared, as Black Panther Huey Newton did, that *Sweetback* was
the "first black revolutionary film."[2] Though Black Nationalists were divided
in their reaction to *Sweetback*,[3] Van Peebles connected his film with the Black
Power sensibility. "As you'd entertainment wise be blown out your seats," Van
Peebles says, "I hoped at the same time you realized that you could do it for
yourself not just in cinema but in life. 'Power to the People.'"[4]

The male critics of the film since Lerone Bennett Jr.'s provocative read on
Sweetback's manipulation of "emancipation orgasms" have continued to comment at least briefly on gender, though not extensively addressing enough
the absence of dynamic female characterization and the female presence in
key scenes throughout. The lack of black feminist perspectives is perhaps in
part because "a politicized black women's agenda was generally submerged
under a male-focused black nationalist discourse aimed at rediscovering and
articulating the mystique of a liberated 'black manhood.'"[5] Black male critics
continue to address *Sweetback,* exploring the film's appeal to male audiences.
Mark Reid, for example, explains that its appeal to black inner-city youths
can be connected to its politicized street orientation, which Newton, for example, personified. The Black Panther leader expressed "the street ethics of
manhood which equates sexuality with a form of masculine power."[6] Reid
just mentions the film's lack of "dignified portrayal of black women."[7]

In his insightful 2002 book *Soul Babies,* cultural critic Mark Anthony Neal
offers an insightful comment on the sexual and gender implications of *Sweetback.* He observes Reid's discussion of the film's representation of Sweetback's
"workmanlike" sexual encounters, which are not reflections of "emotional
desire." Neal argues accurately that while Reid's comments here suggest how
Sweetback revises historic associations of black male sexuality with animal-

ism and promiscuity, he does not address how the "warlike" sexuality presented in the film "informs sexual violence against black women and others by black men." Neal's next brief but key observation alludes more specifically to my interest in *Sweetback*'s gender and sexual politics when he cites the two instances where a black woman and white women are "constructed as gatekeepers or obstructions to Sweetback's desires for freedom." Neal concludes that while the sexual "'satisfaction' of the black woman challenges the legitimacy of historic claims that black women are insatiable, the sequences do not adequately problematize the use of sex as a tool of control."[8]

In another impressive book, *Black Film as a Signifying Practice,* black film theorist Gladstone Yearwood offers a particularly thorough reading of *Sweetback,* including its formal devices, sexual representations, and political implications. However, his efforts to rescue the film from a lack of complex treatment of its intersecting aesthetic, political, and sexual radicalism result in a tendency to obscure too much its problematic, raced constructs of sex and gender. Yearwood makes a great case for his claim that *Sweetback* is "a commentary on the fundamental structuring function that gender roles and sexual positioning imposes on society" and Hollywood cinema, but it is achieved through very problematic representations, particularly of women.[9]

Van Peebles's text thus participates in the masculine literary, artistic, and political tendency of configuring black female bodies in particular as sexualized and racialized political signs. On one hand, *Sweetback,* as Yearwood and others have suggested, does deny easy dismissal as pornography or complacency with the dominant mode of film representation and filmmaking. Yet, on the other, it offers a conservative gender politic that ultimately reinforces a version of black patriarchy even while it interrogates the historical implications of racial oppression and the dominant obsession with black male sexuality. The particular prominence of sex in Van Peebles's creation and production of *Sweetback* parallels the sexual and gender politics that propel the narrative.

The Sexual (Re)Birth of a Politicized Imagination

I was in a time bind so I was trying this new Experimental crash method. I called it semen-shock. Maybe I could have brought a girl or a couple of girls with me to ball but that would have meant dividing my attention. . . . Yum-yum (pound, pound) yum-yum (pound) oh heavenly (pound). God-damn, just then my muse announced it was ready to escort the idea forward. Yum-

yum (pound), change hands (pound). Yum—I'll be right with you—yum. Amen-yum. My muse copped an attitude, you suppose to be trying to get in touch with me. . . . I'm your reason for being here. Yeah, yum, right (pound), (pound) yum-yum, w/you. Wham, Shazam. . . . My first thought was that the entire thing had been set-up to rationalize my beating my meat and that I was pretty Goddamn old to be out in the sand & sagebrush masturbating. Then I realized that it had worked after all—that the muse had rolled the stone away from the cave. I peered into me and saw I was tired of the Man (this was new, already?) but there was more. I was going to do my Own movie.[10]

So recounts Van Peebles about how the idea of *Sweetback* came to be. His account of *Sweetback*'s birth, of how sexual orgasm through masturbation fueled his creative psyche, sheds light on the prominent sexual politics that shape the film. Van Peebles goes out to the figurative wilderness, the desert, and in lieu of "balling" a couple of girls, he masturbates in order to stimulate his creative psyche. His orgasm results in physical and psychic release as well as creative clarity, that is, the "birth" of a film project that will be reflective of his dissatisfaction with "the Man." Great emphasis is placed on "own" with the capitalization of the word, signifying a project that will be shaped by his vision rather than by dominant Hollywood convention.

This mythic account of *Sweetback*'s birth via orgasm in a symbolic primitive setting has much in common with the Western patriarchal artistic tendency to utilize racialized phallic symbols and metaphors of black femininity and sex to artistically articulate a mix of raced anxieties and desires. Modernist art and literature in the early twentieth century provides a famous point of reference. English writer D. H. Lawrence, for example, perhaps the iconic literary figure of the modernist, masculine construct of sexualized primitivism, wrote literature that tied the physical, creative, and psychic source of modern white men's phallic renewal to the raced female figure. Lawrence's writing in the first years of the chaotic twentieth century reverberates with sexual anxiety linked to issues of gender and white patriarchal authority during a period of the political interrogation of gender roles and British imperialism. Lawrence emphasized recovering a primitive sex consciousness or phallic consciousness, as he referred to it. The "primitive" construct of African women's wombs and genitalia in particular and the language of orgasm serve Lawrence's creative efforts to articulate his vision of the white Englishman's renewal through the primitive sexual instinct.

In his novel *Women in Love* (1922), for instance, the inanimate nude statue of an African woman giving birth and another nude African female statue operate as the dominant symbols of Lawrence's sex consciousness mythology.[11]

Lawrence also tended to associate the retention of a powerful sex instinct in lower-class whites in contrast to middle-class Westerners, whose sex consciousness was being civilized out of them. This sensibility shapes his most infamous works, including *Lady Chatterley's Lover* (1928), a novel in which the middle-class female protagonist, Connie, returns to her true female sexual primitivism and submission to the white phallus. The culminating moment occurs when her working-class lover declares that he thought there wasn't any real sex left besides that which one could have with black women, who came naturally.[12]

Harlem Renaissance writer Claude McKay, an artistic predecessor of Van Peebles who was heavily concerned with the political issues of black people in his time, interrogated dominant, romanticized gendered versions of African primitivism, articulating his creative vision through images of black femaleness. He critiqued Western bourgeois cultural values through a contrasting non-Westernized, black primitive sensibility that was shaped in part by his rural, Jamaican background. Black women occupy a pivotal role in his literary theorizations about the crises of contemporary black masculinity during the early twentieth century. In his controversial 1928 novel *Home to Harlem,*[13] McKay dramatizes black male crises through his romantic portrayal of a working-class "primitive" hero, Jake, an intellectual counterpart, Ray, and their interactions with black women.

Jake's primitive nature is imaged in part through the metaphor of black women, who are represented as being simultaneously mythic sexual nurturers of black men and at the same time the embodiment of danger to black male survival. McKay makes distinctions between lower- class and middle-class black females; lower-class black females are closer to primitivism and thus sexuality, whereas the middle-class black female embodies the confines of middle-class culture. There is concurrently "peace and forgetfulness in the bosom of a brown woman."[14] As Jake tells Ray, "White against white and black against white . . . We's all crazy-dog mad. Ain't no peace with the women's and there ain't no life anywhere without them."[15] Van Peebles's treatment of women and sex in *Sweetback* echoes the problematic politics of gender not only in Black Power political representation but also in the tradition of Western heteropatriarchal, artistic culture that constructs the racialized female body as creative "juice." Van Peebles's description about the moment of his film's conception suggests how sex and female bodies are imagined as vehicles to access and articulates the creative and/or political visions of men.

The controversial early scene in *Sweetback* between an older prostitute and a young boy (Mario Van Peebles) invokes the tale of *Sweetback*'s birth. Only now, masturbation is replaced with the initiation of a boy into his sexual identity and hence his phallic power through sex with the experienced older black woman. Let me pause here and distinguish between the spectator's and film critic's possible interpretation of this scene and the director's construct of its symbolic meanings. The charge that *Sweetback* glorifies the rape of a child with this sequence is certainly understandable, though as several black film critics explain, Van Peebles complicates easy reading of the scene as a rape, as I believe our social codes may demand. He pointedly plays the encounter as a baptism of a boy into manhood and his sexual power, signified in part by a gospel song explicitly associated with black religious baptismal rites, "Wade in the Water."

The subtle facial demeanor of the boy, which moves from dispassionate acquiescence to the woman's sexual demands to a hint of arrogant satisfaction upon recognizing his sexual power, further supports the director's construction of it as a moment of initiation. The nameless boy's baptism as "Sweetback" by the woman who tells him he has a "sweet sweetback" affirms this. The end of the scene, when the movie credits roll against the backdrop of the boy, in between the woman's legs, transforming into the grown Sweetback, further conveys his new sexually masculine role. "Sweetback" operates as a vernacular term for the boy's sexual organ, the symbol of his sexual power; this becomes especially crucial later when it acts as a tool for his survival amid an awakening political consciousness.

In a class viewing of *Sweetback,* I turned the lights on as the end credits rolled. One of my students, a white woman in her fifties, gathered her belongings in furious haste, seething with anger. It was hardly the first such reaction that I'd witnessed. The vast majority of my students have been unfamiliar with *Sweetback.* They do not know what to make of it upon seeing it for the first time and struggle with processing the film. Its technical roughness and resistance to the linear narrative style that dominates contemporary popular movies, as well as the racial orientation and graphic sexual content that defies expectation of erotic titillation, often confuse them. The most curious and disturbing aspect of the film for them is the sex scene with the boy and grown woman. It has provoked strong sentiments from my students and thus highlighted interesting differences in viewing positions.

I've shown the film in classes diversified across academic majors, class, race, gender, and age and have been able to observe some interesting trends in student responses. Many of my nontraditional female students, particularly those who are Caucasian and mothers, have been horrified by *Sweetback* and sometimes outraged. Black male students generally have focused on and endorsed the black revolt ethos of the film while not expressing much surprise or discomfort by the film's sexual politics. White male students, on the other hand, have tended to dismiss the film as a dated and technically rough piece of propaganda or have been intrigued by the filmmaking techniques and by director Melvin Van Peebles. My black female students tend to call *Sweetback* out for its depiction of black women. Both they and young white female students are usually the most vocal in discussing the film's treatment of women in the context of the gender politics infusing the political era of the time.

Sweetback's initial sex scene sets its focus on the historic white supremacist construct of black male hypersexuality and taps into the political revision of black male sexuality as a sign of black masculine power. It thus references the mythic sexualized male heroes of black urban folklore who are in part defined by an unquestioned sexual appeal to women across race and age. My major contention about this scene and the opening shot immediately before it, in which a group of black women stand staring as the boy hungrily eats, is that they quickly establish the black phallocentric perspective that dominates the film. These opening scenes, furthermore, signal the contradictory radicalism and conservatism that permeate the film.

During the sex scene, there is a tension between the sound and the visual, inviting contradiction into interpretation of the visual. This controversial sequence introduces the question of *Sweetback*'s exploitative politics and the dismissal of it as inappropriately pornographic, given the role of the boy. Yet, the song—a signature black religious baptismal song—helps complicate for us the ability to easily categorize it as such. There is a contradiction between what is seen and heard. The deployment of sound gives sociohistorical knowledge, linking the present and past and the community and Sweetback, thus amplifying the black historical communal experience.

Sound, like visual representation, then, signals the film's politics. The narrative does not rely on extensive dialogue and is especially characterized by Sweetback's absence of verbal expression. The community's spoken-word chants, the jarring mix of spiritual songs with secular music, and, tellingly, the cries of women in the sexual encounters with Sweetback all help to articulate the masculinist codes that dominates the text's phallic vision of awakening black revolutionary consciousness.

Sweetback's first version of black male identity occurs via Sweetback being bathed in the black woman's body and her verbally signifying this when she excitedly declares him to have a "sweet sweetback." While I do not mean to negate the problematic implications of a young boy in a sexual encounter initiated by an experienced older woman, it is necessary that we consider the multiple codes that underline the framing of the scene from the directorial perspective. Such a frame is not unique in popular cinema, for in a sense it taps into the long-held patriarchal, cultural construction of sex with an older woman as a romantic, erotic initiation of a boy into manhood, which we have seen played out in a number of popular films.[16]

The opening scene might appear to offer a sort of reversal of the usual controlling male gaze that frequently sexually objectifies women.[17] The as yet unnamed boy sits eating voraciously while a group of black women stand over him, staring at him with intensity. Yet, considering the dominance of the film's black masculine center, the moment reinforces the centrality of the black phallic figure. The women are spectators directing the gaze on him, but we, the spectators, are positioned, as are women in the film, to feel for Sweetback's plight—to accept him as the representative of black lower-class males, who are in turn the preeminent symbols of the black community's oppression. His physical hunger here conveys his social lack. Sweetback's transformation into a sexualized adult male whose sexual power transcends words and whose need to pursue sex aggressively complicates reading the film as a radical reversal of gender politics.

According to Yearwood, the most significant element of Van Peebles's narrative strategy is his movement away from stereotype to "deconstructing and reformulating the familiar representation." The film thus stands as a signification on dominant constructs of sex and gender:

> There is the related focus on how social power is reproduced as the natural order of things in the classical narrative. Although the women seen at the beginning of the film are presented within the space of a whorehouse, they are not represented specifically as prostitutes. Prostitution is the commodification of a sexual act performed in exchange for some form of compensation, usually monetary. The system of relations developed in the act of prostitution is based on the dominant patriarchal paradigm that characterizes most other social relations and the distribution of power in society.[18]

Yearwood further suggests that the positioning of women in traditional sexual relations is reversed because the woman becomes the "sexual aggressor" who demands sex of Sweetback; thus, there is a reversal of the "distribution of power in society."[19]

This particular reading downplays too much the historic import of the association of prostitution with black women. Prostitution is a real social reality, and the presence of a black prostitute in a black film does not necessarily mean mere perpetuation of black female sexual deviance. However,

Van Peebles's treatment of it fails to offer a "critique of the socio-economic conditions that often force women, particularly poor women," into prostitution.[20] He refuses to fully humanize and complicate prostitutes or lower-class women but instead relegates them to a representative unquestioned type of sexual female useful for the survival needs of Sweetback. Thus, *Sweetback* does not offer any radical revision of traditional gender positioning; women's stake in the sexual contract does not even contribute to their material or political survival but rather resides in the portrayal of Sweetback's phallic appeal and their excessive sexual orientation.

Critics have continued to cite the director's rather sterile or mechanical representation of sexual activity that avoids offering us the traditional Hollywood film representation of sexual pleasure. Yet, even this is a bit curious, because while the film shows Peebles as Sweetback in that light, it does not show the women he has sex with in that mechanical manner. Indeed, Sweetback's mechanical manner, which his lack of verbal expression and blank face help to convey, is heightened by the representation of the women being exhilarated by Sweetback's "sweetback." Hence, the black whore's urging of the boy to "fuck" her like a man and his baptism into manhood doesn't upset notions about the hypersexual nature of black women but rather supports the decidedly determined vision of black phallic empowerment. The so-called rejection of male sexual pleasure, then, signified by Sweetback's quietness and emotionless demeanor, does not disrupt the concept of female phallic adulation. The idea of black male sexual potency and female subordination to it functions as a critical part of *Sweetback*'s politics.

Let me point out here too that Sweetback's taken-for-granted appeal to the sexual desire of women without seemingly acting as the aggressor does not mean that he is subordinate to women or that women are in a controlling position—the narrative simply doesn't support this. Again, the text privileges the particular plight of the lower-class black male and the increasingly aggressive use of undisputed sexual power as a tool of survival while it contains lower-class women's presence largely in the role of sexual gateway. Consider the scene in which a handcuffed Sweetback goes to a black woman for help and she demands sex first. Sweetback doesn't appear merely as a helpless male at the mercy of a controlling woman. Recall the woman's statement to Sweetback that he "gave her" to her Old Man as he stands before her, his gaze conveying his demand for her help. This intimates that Sweetback exerts influence on her and can presume to expect her support.

Ultimately, *Sweetback* contends that everybody wants a piece of the black man, white men and women too, the latter signified by their sexual demands.

Though the denial of the erotic pleasure usually intended by the film depiction of sex and women's bodies offers some signification on cinematic and racist representation, Van Peebles's treatment of these establishes the black phallic orientation of the text.

Sex as a Means of Film Production and Aesthetic Strategy

Sweetback's construction of sex and women as fundamental resources to black male survival continues the sexual politics that were so critical to the production and marketing of the film. On several levels, sex was crucial to the filmmaker's street hustler, "Guerilla Cinema" methodology.[21] Van Peebles forthrightly explains that positioning his figurative masculine protagonist as a sex worker and subsequently sexualizing the text offered a way to appeal to his targeted audience. He knew that a politicized film wouldn't draw the black masses that he was looking to attract; as he states, "Brer"—the black community—had to be entertained.[22] The sex dynamic provided a mechanism through which he could present a film with a veiled politicized fervor.

The money necessary to get the film made posed a major issue for the director; he had to negotiate through the financial demands of filmmaking in addition to Hollywood restrictions and moral codes. He in part addressed these by utilizing a multicultural group of actors and crew, playing Sweetback himself, and shooting the film in twenty days.[23] Van Peebles then had his film distributed through a small company, Cinemation Industries, which specifically catered to low-budget exploitation films.

Van Peebles utilized the guise of making a pornographic movie as a way to veil his film and sidestep union obstacles.[24] This helped set the stage for his struggle with the Motion Picture Association of America (MPAA) over the X rating it gave his film. However, the writer-director strategically used this censorship in order to elevate his film's commercial appeal to black audiences and at the same time to signify on the MPAA's presumption of naming and dismissing the film's black political and aesthetic value by categorizing it as pornography. He then marketed *Sweetback* as "rated X by an all-white jury."[25]

The trouble that he encountered from the Hollywood regulating organization is not surprising considering that the conservative perspective dominating the Hollywood system was bound to reject *Sweetback*'s racial and political implications and insistence on operating outside of established filmic language. Notwithstanding the debatable standards for distinguishing a "black independent film,"[26] Van Peebles's strategies for getting a film made that retained its political and aesthetic autonomy certainly personifies a creative ghettocentric, "guerilla" methodology that bespeaks an aesthetic of independence from the confines of dominant Hollywood studio control. Yet, a taken-for-granted sexualized view of women, including his references to them largely in terms of "pussy," permeates even the book discussion about the making of *Sweetback.*

The mythic tale of the film's creation has increased in recent retrospectives about it. This historical framing is itself fraught with the masculine poetics that permeate the film, its making, and popular and critical reception. In 2004, Mario Van Peebles, the son of the director, released *Baadasssss,* a dramatization of his father's making of the film. Mario stars as his father, and the film includes commentary from various speakers, primarily male, such as John Singleton, Ossie Davis, and Bill Cosby, who donated some funds toward the making of the original film.

Mario Van Peebles characterizes his father as the "first in-your-face Black Power director." He presents *Sweetback* as an artistic, political, and spiritual odyssey and plays his father, in his words, as a "baadasssss." It is a term that serves to embody the historical significance of *Sweetback,* his father's radical cinematic vision, and creative strategies in getting the film made. Yet, implicit in "baadasssss" too is its racialized masculine signification. Mario celebrates his father as a "baadasssss" in part as homage to the latter's defiance of dominant Hollywood restrictions and cinematic values and to his affirmation of black cultural aesthetics and black empowerment that was embodied in the popular persona of Black Power masculinity. Bill Cosby reflects on how Melvin Van Peebles got *Sweetback* made despite the obstacles: "He broke rules . . . [and the] budget, talking to white people in a certain way." The son's film also engages his father's phallic and rather pimp-like sexual persona. Van Peebles delves into the personal side of his father, such as his womanizing behavior and their developing father-and-son relationship, of which the film's making served as a major transitional period. Ossie Davis maintains that the son's recent film emphasizes or supports the "reestablishment of the black male and of fathers and sons."

The poetics of black masculinity embodied in the persona of Melvin Van Peebles, in *Sweetback*'s making, and in its subsequent legendary film status can help us understand the myriad politics of gender and race circulating within sexual representations. These politics converge most dramatically in several scenes where women's positions are critical, including the two scenes at the beginning. The sex show sequence at Beetle's club early in the film stands as a pivotal example of *Sweetback*'s problematic representations. The scene centers on a theatrical show in front of a mixed but mostly black audience who watch a performance by a black woman and Sweetback—we learn later—who is dressed in a disguise that encompasses lesbianism and androgyny. He wears several traditional signifiers of gender identity, both feminine and masculine, thus rendering sexual identification ambiguous. The woman lies down and the disguised figure gets on top of her to the applause of the spectators. The black male announcer, whose incongruent fairy-ballerina outfit and masculine gender further serve as signification on dominant presumptions of masculine sexual identity, introduces the next segment. Sweetback takes off his transvestite mask, removing layers of clothes, including bra and genital cup, finally revealing his black male sexual identity.

He "fucks" the black woman, seemingly to her delight and that of the onlookers. All this occurs under the representative dominant gaze of the two white policemen, who stand outside the circle of spectators, "monitoring" the sex show with a mix of grotesque desire and racist censorship while harassing Beetle for a black body to "borrow." The male fairy solicits volunteers to test Sweetback's sexual prowess. A white woman eagerly offers, but the fairy rejects her under the threatening watch of the white police officers.

This scene dramatizes the overall glamorization of black phallic power and the positioning of women in relation to it. The sex show sequence offers signification only on the historical racial politics informing black male, white male, and white female relations and the historic social, economic, and physical castration of black men. When the white woman volunteers to "try" Sweetback, the camera cuts to the white policemen, whose expressions instantly become ominous. Here, the white woman invokes her historical construction as a sexual taboo and danger to black male survival. Her social position over black men allows her to gaze at the black male body and to participate in white patriarchal inscriptions of black sexuality. The fairy host's necessary rejection of her attempt to "try" Sweetback sexually reminds us of the historic danger that she poses for black male survival.

The white police officers' authority to usurp Beetle's control over his nightclub space and the black performers who participate in the commodification of their sexual bodies for money also stress white supremacist authority. The police presence and their power to claim any black man, like Sweetback, in order to take downtown—in this case, as a token black in order to show that they're diligently searching for the murderer of a black man—emphasizes the devaluation of black male life and black males' exclusion from bourgeois patriarchal authority. This of course dramatizes as well the passivity necessary for black male survival, as Beetle reluctantly gives up one of his employees and Sweetback goes quietly along. Hence, the scene in part functions as the director's attack on the imposition of white supremacist patriarchal control over black men.

Where is the black female body ultimately confined in this play on these social and sexual relations? What does the brief but crucial camera close-up of Sweetback's penis when he unveils his male body further signal? What else does the scene establish in terms of Sweetback's options and narrative mechanisms? The camera's pause on the penis represents an unusual instance of actually showing the ever-mythic or all-important yet not generally shown sexual sign of phallic power, the penis. This could be taken as merely a part of the film's signification on traditional cinematic language. However, it is significant that transvestism dissolves into the figure of a virile black male, because it seems to affirm the preeminence of the black sexual stud image around which the filmmaker builds his vision and critique. It stands as a reminder of the black phallocentric perspective that *Sweetback* reinforces rather than upsets. The setup of options facing Sweetback—to "live the castrated existence of a sexual 'freak' performing in nightclub acts" or to realize "the potential for revolt"—does not question Van Peebles's or Sweetback's investment in manipulating sex and women as tools that serve the black male revolt. Van Peebles fails to provide an alternative, anti-sexist vision of black male-female relations or, by extension, of black male presumptions of women's sexual submission. Importantly, while the scene critically seeks to address the historic racial politics informing black male–white male relations using the white female presence, the black woman remains literally positioned under the black male.

The increasingly "warlike quality" of Sweetback's sex demeanor isn't convincingly primarily an aesthetic signification on Hollywood cinema form, but it does help Van Peebles sensationalize the plight and politicization of the black man who is racially and economically oppressed by the status quo. Thus, while the refusal to romanticize Sweetback's responses in his sexual encounters conveys the filmmaker's confrontation of the historic white supremacist treatment of black masculinity in and outside Hollywood, it simultaneously supports the racially and sexually coded subordinate positioning of black women. The narrative emulates the tendency of some of the era's Black Power male advocates to articulate the black collective experience of race oppression by privileging the historic castration of and denial of patriarchal power to black men as the defining tragedy of black oppression.

If this were not the case, it would seem that Van Peebles might have at least revised the conventional positioning of male on top, female on bottom. Instead, the mask of sexual disguise during the sex show transforms into the phallic black man, and the scene culminates in sex within the traditional heterosexual positioning. It foreshadows Sweetback's more aggressive use of sex and raced female bodies as devices of mediation throughout his journey to escape. Shortly after this sex show comes the critical climactic moment when Sweetback stops the police from beating young MooMoo and whips them with the cuffs that symbolize his and black men's general oppression. Yearwood argues that the film differs from the features of pornographic film in that the latter celebrates "unequal relations in society through its exploitation of the body strictly in sexual and economic terms within the system of patriarchy characteristic of society" while *Sweetback* "augurs more shock than titillation," and his argument has some validity.[27] Unfortunately, there is an array of unequal representation and gender exploitation in *Sweetback* that is justified when it serves the "noble" cause of black male revolt against racist oppression.

Sweetback's "Primitive" Survival and the Raced Female Body

If the question of how *Sweetback* envisions women's roles in the awakening black political consciousness and black revolution is raised, as I think it should be, it's fair to argue that this represents the least radical aspect of the film. The politicized social vision of *Sweetback* is limited by its failure to critique and re-imagine black male-female relations in the collective black struggle despite *Sweetback*'s black community themes. Sweetback's continued resistance to white police authority, defiance of their brutality, and journey to collective militant black consciousness is a process signified and punctuated by his escapes via sexualized encounters with women.

As I discuss earlier, the exchange between a silently handcuffed Sweetback and the ex-girlfriend whom he "gave" to another man (her jailed boyfriend) suggests Sweetback's masculine empowerment over her sexual body as much as her "First things first" makes clear the price of her help. Sweetback's interactions increasingly occur within the context of the narrative's movement from the urban, industrial setting to the desert, the site where a second "rebirth" culminates. Sweetback's sojourn in the desert, a return to the primitive, provides the final symbolic rite of passage into full revolutionary consciousness. "Fucking" women becomes Sweetback's premier weapon of choice, for the conquering of females, the text conveys, becomes crucial for black male survival since the women are potential obstacles to Sweetback's increasingly more "noble" aim of keeping alive both himself and the future hope of black empowerment, MooMoo. At one point, Sweetback holds a knife on a black woman as he fools the white men looking for him by masking himself as some random "nigger" having a tryst in the woods. In this schema, rape, the violently induced submission of the black female, is not problematized but justified by the construction of women, both black and white, as potential threats, that is, as tools in white patriarchy's efforts to castrate the black male or the potential allies of black male survival.

The later scene in which a black woman performs a monologue in one of the "I haven't seen Sweetback" sequences could potentially signify on dominant notions of black femininity. It's staged as a performance of the black female bitch or Sapphire archetype that the woman puts on for the white male spectator as part of the community's support of Sweetback. Clad in a blonde wig, the ex-prostitute loudly and sassily tells the silent white man off. She declares that she's clean and off the street and demands the Man get off her back. She threatens him, "Get the fuck off my back, man. . . . When I get pissed off, man, I will throw a natural-born nigger fit on you." After the silent white man walks off, she laughs outrageously, takes off the wig, and says, "Sweetback, man, shit!" The camera then cuts to the same woman singing onstage; she laughs and declares, "I love you," presumably to Sweetback, who's on the run from police.

This performance illuminates the historic import of wearing the mask for black survival but also plays with notions of black female bitchiness in a way that doesn't radically challenge the construction. It reinforces the idea that black women should contribute to black liberation by supporting the more endangered black male through any means. Black women's "Sapphire bitchiness" shouldn't serve to emasculate black men, but it could aid the black man's—and therefore black community's—liberation by being a strategy of protection as it is for Sweetback. Black women must be willing to play various identities in order to support the survival of the potential black male revolutionary.

At the other end of the black female spectrum, there appears briefly a maternal figure—an older black woman shelling peas, surrounded by black ghetto children in a documentary-like scene. As if responding to an anonymous interviewer, the woman says that when the children get older, the county takes them away. The camera cuts quickly from her to Sweetback running from his pursuers, then back to a repetition of the woman's comment. Finally, the woman responds to an inquiry seemingly about Sweetback, saying that she could have had such a boy once. In one sense, this scene emphasizes the invisibility of poor black children like Sweetback and the socioeconomic treatment of them within the system. Yet, it also underlines how female figures serve to help dramatize a distinctly black male–centered plight.

In the second major scene with a white woman, Van Peebles offers a revision of the historic black male–white female positioning that we see imaged in the sex show at Beetle's club. MooMoo and Sweetback face a white motorcycle gang, of which knife expert Prez, also known as Big Sadie, is the tough leader. When he must fight Prez for his and MooMoo's escape, using his choice of weapon, Sweetback stands in quiet assessment. At that instant, the tall, masculine Big Sadie takes off her helmet and tosses her red hair, thus revealing her female identity. Sweetback finally responds with one word: "Fucking." She agrees; they strip off their clothes and take to the center of the excited onlookers. The motorcycle gang sex scene shows Sweetback in a more theatrical appearance as he prepares to do "sexual battle" with Prez. Again situated on top, he at first dons a top hat and white bow tie, then removes the hat and settles himself in between her legs. It is staged as a struggle at first, a competition, with each determined to forcefully "fuck" the other into submission. We then hear her guttural scream of pleasure; her legs flail open, and her cry of "Yeah, Sweetback" seals her acquiescence to black male sexual power.

Later, after MooMoo and Sweetback take refuge in a shack of sorts with the aid of the bikers, Big Sadie protects Sweetback by sending a black biker (John Amos) to rescue him upon learning of a planned double cross by the white male bikers. Big Sadie's initial masculine black leather biker wear, fighting skill, and physique might initially appear to signify on the presumed stability of film images of gender identities. The surreal, theatrical quality of the scene might further mark a critique of the traditional fetishistic treatment of feminine markers of women's identity, like hair. However, such readings don't ultimately register as a rupture of conventional signs of racialized gender identity. First, the popular symbol of true white femininity—flowing hair—reestablishes gender boundaries. Prez first appears as a masculine or phallic female, but she is conquered and "feminized" when Sweetback sexually subdues her. This then accomplishes only a revision of the historic black male–white female relation to exemplify the projection of black male power or the journey toward it.

Sweetback's shift from his earlier "acceptance" of women's sexual expectations and sex for economic survival to his more noble employment of sex to preserve his and MooMoo's lives and the future of black revolution does not stand as a radical movement. Rather than sex with the white female equaling death, it is "necessary" to facilitate their continued freedom. Yet, the historical legacy of racial danger for the black man is ever present; Big Sadie's male biker peers double-cross Sweetback even after he supposedly secures his and

MooMoo's escape by winning the fucking duel. Still, the actual act of sexual triumph over the white woman marks Sweetback's growing empowerment, his breaking beyond the established boundaries of white patriarchal power. Big Sadie thus becomes an ally and sends someone to help Sweetback when she learns of the double cross.

In the last major action sequence, Sweetback flees from two rednecks and some hunting dogs, a moment that obviously hearkens back to the black slave experience. At the end of the scene, the skinned body of one of the dogs floats in the river. Through first having Sweetback survive the treacherous trek across the desert by utilizing primitive means of survival and ultimately making it across the river to freedom in Mexico, the narrative celebrates the vision of black masculine virility as a sign of true manhood. The stunning intensity leading to the narrative's dramatic conclusion builds through Sweetback's running and the simultaneous sound of the community's call and response voices at once mockingly warning and urging Sweetback on against the background music of the gospel song "Wade in the Water." The chorus is mixed with masculine and feminine voices, with the feminine sounding more prominent in the responses:

Lead: They won't waste me.
Response: You can't make it on wings, wheels, or steel, Sweetback.
Lead: We got feet.
Response: You can't get away on wings, wheels, or steel, Sweetback.
Chorus: They bled your brotha. They bled your sista. We got to get it
    together. . . . Don't let them get you. He ain't gon' let you stand tall,
    Sweetback. The Man know everything. He oughta know I'm tired
    of him fucking wit' me. Right on brotha. . . . Run, Sweetback. Run
    mothafucka.

Sweetback's last long trek heralds the birth of a revolutionary black masculinity and subsequently the possible defeat of white supremacy patriarchy. Yet, in achieving this vision, *Sweetback*'s problematic gender politics compromises the meaningfulness of Sweetback's growth from individualist sex stud for hire to politically sensitized survivor and supporter of black collective liberation. The text makes the limited move from interrogating the dominant stereotype of black (male) sexuality and black male powerlessness to a sexualized black patriarchal aesthetic sensitized by revolutionary consciousness. The ending declaration in bold capital letters proclaims the supremacy of the revolutionary black man: "WATCH OUT A BAADASSSSS NIGGER IS COMING BACK TO COLLECT SOME DUES . . ."

Gender Politics and Black Revolutionary Vision
in *The Spook Who Sat by the Door*

Thirty years after its mysterious disappearance from theaters after a successful three-week run, the historically overlooked *The Spook Who Sat by the Door* has garnered new attention and appreciation. In retrospect, it is a rather stunning melodrama driven by the energy of author Sam Greenlee's self-avowed propagandist position. *Sweetback* was made through Van Peebles's guerilla cinema tactics, the result of which is an experimental text that suggests the fervor of Black Power consciousness. *The Spook,* released two years later, similarly reflects the Black Power era. However, while it too was made using "guerilla style" tactics, it is a protest film that depicts the warfare methodology of revolutionary nationalism being put into action. Perhaps its greatest appeal to the few audiences that saw it then and to subsequent viewers is the film's success at capturing the energy of anger and unrest that had erupted in the streets of black urban America in the mid-1960s. *New York Times* film reviewer Vincent Canby put it this way: "The rage it projects is real."[28]

Based on Greenlee's 1969 novel of the same name, the radical film depicts a black male revolutionary hero who utilizes the "master's tools" to launch a working-class revolution against the U.S. government. Released when the blaxploitation formula had become a staple product in Hollywood, *The Spook* is the rare serious, dramatic depiction of black revolution in a year marked by more superfly character–driven black action flicks. The film deviates formally too in its prominent visual cues through the manipulation of lighting and darkness to mimic the thematic motifs of invisibility, covert action, and disguise. In addition, the film is accompanied by Herbie Hancock's percussive soundtrack, which importantly intensifies the film's key action sequences.

The Spook has in common with *Sweetback* the valorization of a black lower-class-driven revolution against racist oppression and the phallicization of this revolt. In the years after its release, *The Spook* became something of an underground bootleg video cult classic; presently, it is receiving more visible popular attention with the occurrence of its thirtieth anniversary. *The Spook* configures black women's relationship to the black male–led revolution in a way similar to that depicted in *Sweetback,* but the critique of the black bourgeoisie appears more overtly via the sympathetically portrayed middle-class black male character and hostile presentation of the bourgeois female character. I'm interested in the intersecting class, gender, and sexual politics in *The Spook* or specifically in how they construct black women in relationship to black revolution as exemplified in the two dominant black female presences, the hero's aspiring bourgeois black girlfriend and his other sexual partner, a romanticized prostitute. Ultimately, the sexualized imagery of these women projects them as potential traitors to black liberation who could be used by "the Man" to maintain white patriarchy unless they willingly yield to black male phallic power, both sexually and politically.

Greenlee's novel offers a story about the first black CIA agent, Dan Freeman, who utilizes his training in guerilla tactics to develop and organize a group of Chicago black street youth who launch a black revolution in major American cities. A self-avowed propagandist, Greenlee served with the United States Information Agency in Iraq before resigning in 1965 to pursue writing full-time.[29] While in Iraq, he wrote his first novel, *Baghdad Blues,* which was not published until after *The Spook.* Greenlee wrote the latter after his discharge in the mid-1960s, finishing it in 1966. *The Spook,* set in highly racialized and politicized Chicago, demonstrates Greenlee's intimate knowledge of Chicago's divisive political history, the influence of the Watts riots in 1965, and the intensifying visibility of the Black Power movement.[30] When he tried to get the *The Spook* published, Greenlee encountered a great deal of resistance because of its anti–U.S. government, black revolution themes. Two British publishers finally published the book in 1969, and it went on to become a bestseller in England before finally being published much later in the United States. Echoing Van Peebles's and Newton's declaration about *Sweetback,* the book cover declares *The Spook* the "first black nationalistic novel."

Greenlee co-wrote the screenplay with Melvin Clay and co-produced the film with Ivan Dixon, who directed it. It was primarily filmed on location in Gary, Indiana, and released—reluctantly—through United Artists. Recently, a remastered thirtieth anniversary DVD edition of the film offers commentary from Greenlee, who calls the making of the film an example of guerilla cinema. Much of the story's crucial setting occurs in Chicago, but Mayor Richard J. Daly would not grant permission for shots of Chicago or their use in the film. Greenlee explains, "The pictures we shot of Chicago, we stole."[31] In order to get financial backing or major studio backing, the initial screening of the film to executives played down the nationalistic dynamics. The screening of the final version of *The Spook* did not register well with studio execs; they were shocked by the depiction of black Armageddon. The controversial black political representation led to the film's abrupt departure from theaters.[32]

Historical black film studies in general have tended to acknowledge *The Spook* but not engage it extensively, submerging it under the general address of blaxploitation cinema. My major interest in the film is not whether its structure greatly reduces its "independent" black aesthetic potential, as Yearwood argues. The film clearly does not, at least, fit the frequently drug-themed, de-politicized, superfly ghetto action film prototype. In addition, it is shaped by the heavy control of the black male creator and film collaborators, who retained the book's black revolutionary, nationalistic vision of radical societal transformation. In this sense, the black (male)-defined political aesthetic certainly represents a not-to-be-taken-for-granted element of "independence" from a mainstream Hollywood perspective.

The relatively little critical treatment of *The Spook* has not tended to address significantly its gender politics but has rather focused on class, the film's political influences, and the mention of its quick withdrawal from theaters. In *African American Nationalist Literature of the 1960s,* Sandra Hollin Flowers offers a helpful analysis of the book version. She argues that its execution of revolutionary nationalist theory suffers because "characterization is sacrificed to political expediency." Flowers focuses on the flawed treatment of class representation without addressing the relevant gender implications. This is curious, considering how the two female characters serve to affirm the black phallic perspective and its vision of the black lower class as the foundation of black liberation and the black middle class as a threat to collective empowerment. The "faithful rendition" in the book and film of revolutionary nationalist theory and the Marxian theory of class suicide revealingly emulates the problematic gendered politics of this representation.[33]

Enemy of a "Black" Revolution: The Gendered "Bourgeoisie"

"Spook," a double entendre, functions as a code word for a CIA agent, but it also signifies the historic racist construct of blackness. Here "spook" denotes the derogatory essentialization of black identity that hinges on the idea that "all blacks look alike." The CIA term "spook" refers to the invisibility necessary for an agent to be effective, whereas its racial meaning refers to the invisibility and at the same time negative hypervisibility accorded to blackness by the dominant status quo. Greenlee revises the implications of this trope in that his protagonist uses the racist "spook" construct as a mode for concealing his radical political intentions. Freeman later teaches the political usefulness of white presumptions of black invisibility to his young black male trainees in Chicago, telling them that "a black man with a mop, tray, or broom in his hand can go damn near anywhere in this country and a smiling black man is invisible." Through his CIA agent training, Freeman learns the tools of the U.S. government's system of power, including war techniques.

It also enables him to construct the middle-class disguise that conceals his political radicalism and plans to forge a revolution directly under the nose of the white power structure.

Freeman then presumably wears the middle-class mask in order to explode the classist and racist structure of American society. The narrative condemns black people who choose to assimilate individually into the established race and class hegemony and its values rather than to support black collective empowerment. Flowers argues, however, that this is a contradictory theme, for Freeman's middle-class lifestyle—for example, his fancy apartment—is not consistently or convincingly portrayed as merely a means for a political end.[34] Nevertheless, the film's anti-middle-class sentiment is dramatized sharply through two central characters, Freeman's old friend Dawson (J. A. Preston) and longtime girlfriend, Joy, played by Janet League. Upon leaving the CIA in order to work toward the social "uplift" of his people, Freeman returns to Chicago, where he becomes reacquainted with Dawson, a prominent cop, who has uniquely come to a place of some prestige within the criminal justice system.

The film invites the spectator to view Dawson sympathetically, a factor conveyed through Freeman's desire to recruit him as a "double agent" for the revolution. This is further dramatized through Dawson's actions on behalf of the people on the night of the riot, which becomes the sequence that sets up Freeman's launch of the revolution. After the death of Shorty, a young petty street dealer, the atmosphere is ripe for a potential riot in the black community. Two white police officers bring dogs to threaten the angry residents, elevating their rage. At the end of *Sweetback,* the act of Sweetback killing and skinning the hunting dog that has been sent to catch him by his redneck pursuers operates as a key symbolic gesture, since the dogs hearken back to the plight of black slaves who ran away and were often pursued by hunting dogs. Hence, *Sweetback* and *The Spook* utilize this historic symbol of black oppression to emphasize their liberation and survival ethos. In the latter film, the people become angrier with the appearance of the dogs, and Dawson, who understands this, demands the white police remove the dogs immediately or he will shoot them.

The problem with Dawson, the narrative insists, lies in his loyalty to the system that he serves. The police here, as in *Sweetback* and other "black" films of the period, represent an arm of U.S. institutional oppression of black people. Hence, Dawson must lose his naive belief that he can make a difference for the masses of black people from within a system rooted in the unequal distribution of race and class power. The struggle between Freeman's radical plan for rupturing the system from outside and Dawson's positioning within it and his rejection of revolutionary nationalism comes to a head in two pivotal scenes.

In the first, Freeman and Dawson convene in a car several mornings after the riot inevitably breaks out. Both men are deeply disturbed about the National Guard's forceful occupation of the community and the socioeconomic condition that they recognize to be the root cause of the riot. Dawson remarks that there were good people out on the street the night before, not "hoodlums"—a comment that counters the mainstream interpretation of a riot as merely proof of black criminality rather than as an expression of black frustration about the reality of their condition. Though conflicted, Dawson insists that law and order must be maintained. Freeman responds that the "ghetto is a jungle" that cages "people like animals," and thus the people cannot be expected not to rise up and fight back. Dawson persists, though, "The streets have to be safe." "Safe for who?" Freeman questions. This exchange magnifies the growing tension between them caused by their ideological distance as the true Freeman begins to emerge from his mask and Dawson senses that the old "radical" Freeman of their college days still exists.

The tension culminates in the last major action scene in the narrative. A furious Dawson holds a gun on Freeman, having discovered that the latter is the "Uncle Tom" whom he, the police, and the CIA have been trying to catch. The moment highlights that Dawson, no matter how noble his ideological confusion, has chosen to remain loyal to "the system." Freeman sums up Dawson's delusion, saying, "You can't be with your people without betraying that badge. And you can't be a cop without betraying your people, you hypocrite." Dawson condemns Freeman for using kids and responds to Freeman's presumption of reading his "blackness": "You think you the only nigga with a sense of outrage?" Freeman declares that he has offered these young men freedom rather than jail or meaningless death. They fight, and Freeman ends up stabbing Dawson. Dawson's death symbolizes the "death" of a counterrevolutionary, middle-class sensibility.

It is the girlfriend Joy, however, who personifies most strongly this perspective and simultaneously the idea that black women can either advance or obstruct the aims of the masculinized black political revolution. In an early scene between the two, we see Joy in a hotel with Freeman as he is about to successfully complete the CIA training program. Joy informs him that she's getting married, to which Freeman replies coolly, "Doctor or lawyer?" Joy answers that he is a doctor and explains that she's not getting any younger. Freeman seductively suggests that they say good-bye "right." She complies, removing her long synthetic wig and joining him on the bed.

Such scenes distinguish Joy as the representative bourgeois black female whose loyalty problematically lies with the dominant model of social mobility. For Joy, marriage to a man with social status is more important than love for a revolutionary-minded black man or the condition of the black masses. Joy and Freeman supposedly share a similar impoverished childhood background. The great contrast between them is that Joy seeks to move beyond lower-class black identity to middle-class status. She desires to never be poor again. This takes precedence over her "love" for Freeman, whose militancy she'd always disliked.

Joy's representation exemplifies then the narrative's condemnation of the perceived disregard for the less affluent black masses by those of the black bourgeoisie who seek integration into a dominant middle-class value system. As the revolution begins in Chicago, Joy reacts with fear and anger that white acceptance of black middle-class individuals is being compromised by the insurgent activity, which, unbeknownst to her, Freeman has organized. In a scene shortly before Dawson and Freeman's fight, Joy argues with Freeman about the "niggas who know nothing but hate and revenge" who are making innocent and decent people suffer. Joy's husband, who never appears in the film, has been a causality of the war, having lost his position at a white hospital.

During the course of their heated discussion, Joy becomes alarmed by Freeman's sympathy for the "hoodlums" as his mask slips momentarily in front of her, and she urges him not to "romanticize" those people. They are not, she tells him, "freedom fighters," as Freeman proposes, but murderers. This pivotal moment anticipates Joy's betrayal of Freeman. In the next scene, she meets with Dawson in a restaurant and tells him that she's worried that Freeman is mixed up with the freedom fighters. She seems aware of the magnitude of sharing this thought with Dawson, a cop, for she asks him if she's doing the right thing. The answer, of course, according to the narrative perspective, is no, a fact dramatized by the climactic scene between Freeman and Dawson.

Joy's characterization is problematic in several ways. The weak, one-dimensional representation of the Joy-Freeman relationship demonstrates the film's use of racial inscription, effecting, at times, almost stocklike characterizations. Joy's ideological distance from the radical, committed Freeman makes it difficult to conceive why the noble Freeman "can't shake her loose," as he tells Dawson at one point. Supposedly they share a similar social background, yet other than some infrequent sexual interludes, there is nothing that lends credibility to Freeman's involvement with Joy, even after she's married. Their relationship perhaps might support Freeman's disguise of middle-class complacency, but her marriage means that she cannot serve as his "public" girlfriend. More important, the narrowly defined Joy characterization confines black female bourgeois identity to the role of "the Man's" tool and of traitor to the "true" black man and black revolution.

One of the interesting aspects of the Joy characterization is the crucial change made from the book to the film depiction of her. The book offers a far more sinister version of Joy's betrayal as a willful, vicious move. She actually goes into the police station to reveal "Uncle Tom's"—Freeman's—identity. The film, however, tones this act of disloyalty down, depicting her betrayal as stemming in part from some misguided worry for Freeman as well as from her selfish desire to see the end of the troublemaking freedom fighters. Both book and film make it clear that her ideological delusion—her commitment to the white status quo—stands as the great flaw that makes her dangerous to the militant black man. I surmise that the film version tones down her "betrayal" so that it does not undercut the theme of black solidarity, which the text espouses is crucial to the effectiveness of the revolution. In addition, it could be that the filmmakers attempted to make it somewhat less hostile toward black women, a sensibility perhaps influenced by black feminism's increased visibility. In addition, though the film is decidedly phallocentric, black female spectators would certainly be expected to be a part of the black viewing audience.

The "Dahomey Queen" Prostitute and Phallic Power

The prostitute (Paula Kelly), whom Freeman dubs the "Dahomey Queen," stands at the other end of the spectrum of black female representation in *The Spook*. The contrast made between Joy and her also manifests the political symbolization of color; the middle-class, "sell-out" Joy is lighter skinned than the noble, lower-class prostitute. Freeman becomes acquainted with her when he picks her up at a bar while on a break from his CIA training. Later in a hotel room after sex, Freeman tells her that she reminds him of someone. She thinks he's putting her on, but he's piqued her curiosity. Freeman tells her that she resembles a picture of a Dahomey queen in a book, but the queen's hair is "natural." The prostitute admonishes him to just act like a "trick" and "quit talking shit about queens." But still, it's clear that Freeman has gotten to her with his alternative view of her potential identity, for she asks him if he really has such a book with a queen who looks like her in it, and Freeman promises to show her.

Obviously, this exchange echoes the era's Afrocentric nationalist consciousness. By basically proposing that the prostitute could be that Dahomey queen save for her artificial hair, the wig, Freeman signals the prominence accorded cultural signs of black affirmation. In suggesting that her "real" black female identity is that of an African queen, he also emulates the rhetoric of an idealized black patriarchal sense of black femaleness and Africanness that permeated constructions of black identity.[35] Freeman represents a sort of salvation for black women like the prostitute because he makes visible her supposedly "true" black or African-rooted woman identity—a construct contrary to the low social status accorded a sexualized black female who earns money by selling her body. Interestingly, she is not given a formal name; rather, she is designated the "Dahomey Queen" by the black hero. Kelly's gritty but dignified portrayal of the prostitute adds to the narrative's elevation of her as a character with the potential of Afrocentric, queenly nobility.

At the same time, the prostitute-Freeman relationship manifests the sexual politics defining the film's phallic representation of black revolutionary heroism. Freeman's intellectuality and masked political passion is stressed throughout; his heterosexual appeal is a key feature of his heroic masculine characterization. Notably, the text does not pose an interrogation of Freeman's sexual behavior; at the point he is supposedly seriously involved with Joy back home, he goes out to the bar as a "trick" looking for sex in between Joy's visits to D.C. This is an acceptable feature of Freeman's "normal" heterosexual male appetite, evidence of his masculinity. The businesslike, cool aura of the sexual interaction between Freeman and the prostitute implies that Freeman should not be emotionally distracted from his noble revolutionary cause by romantic involvement. Yet, his healthy male heterosexual desire for sex on a regular basis should be satisfied. This can be met without a too-distracting emotional investment through the exchange of sex for money with a "whore" and distant "legitimate" woman.

The association between Freeman and the "Dahomey" prostitute personifies the narrative's sexist idea of black male and black female unity, which hinges on the latter's sexual support of the black male, who carries the burden of actually leading and fighting the black revolution. If the black woman is willingly loyal to black male revolutionary power and thus the cause of black liberation, she can be of help, because her sexuality allows her access to men of both races. The prostitute depiction proposes black women as key devices of mediation in the war between black men and white men; hence, the conquest of them, so to speak, is crucial. A couple of scenes after Freeman and the prostitute's initial encounter, a white agent grills her about Freeman in a last attempt by the CIA to find a reason to thwart his so-far successful completion of the training program. The agent hopes to find some sign of sexual deviance in particular, so he inquires whether Freeman is a "homo" or into "weird" sexual acts. The prostitute proclaims him very much a man who just "likes to screw," no kinky stuff. She supports Freeman, thus unknowingly helping him fool the CIA with his mask of assimilation.

Freeman's "relationship" with her affirms the heterosexist black masculinity valorized by the definitive voices of Black Power and revolutionary nationalism. The crucial change in the depiction of the prostitute's sexuality from the book to the film version further supports such an interpretation. In the book, the prostitute is a lesbian who has a woman; she engages in heterosexual sex for pay only, for "men were not her scene." Only Freeman becomes something of an exceptional male figure to her because of his different demeanor toward her.[36] One can reasonably assume that the lesbian orientation of the prostitute was left out or rather ignored in the film because it would not neatly concur with the decidedly idealized heterosexist black perspective that dominates the text. Sexual freedom in terms of heterosexual sex is acceptable; Freeman can engage in intercourse freely without moral stricture, and the prostitute can practice her trade with men. Lesbianism, however, might appear counterrevolutionary.

In the prostitute's last appearance, she arrives in Chicago after the national outbreak of the revolution. She is now being "kept" by the white CIA general, Freeman's former boss and the head of the search to find and destroy "Uncle Tom" and the black insurrection. Her appearance is dramatically changed: she wears full African regalia, including a flowing robe and a short natural under a headdress. The shift symbolizes her evolution into the Afrocentric consciousness that Freeman introduced to her. At the same time, the disguise supports the general's idea of her as merely an exotic sexual primitive whom he (thinks that he) controls. It thus serves as a useful mask, since the general's presumptions about who she is accord her an invisibility that allows her to hear classified information, thus personifying Freeman's earlier statement to his all-male trainees that women can go places and do things that men often can't.

The following meeting between the prostitute and Freeman confirms her still-sexualized yet Afrocentric awakening; she warns Freeman—whom she suspects is Uncle Tom—that the general and his white peers are out to get him by placing a spy inside his organization. The "snake strategy" here signifies on black traitors of the cause who were planted inside black revolutionary organizations like the Panthers to serve the government's efforts to destroy them. When Freeman questions her motives for sticking her neck out for him, she revealingly replies, "I'm black, ain't I?" The prostitute's aid to Freeman sanitizes her in a sense; as she tells the white agent earlier, Freeman doesn't treat her like a whore but rather a queen. All of this elevates the black female use of sex from its individualist, if understandable, means of material survival to its more noble use as an aid to the black male–led war for black liberation—as I suggest happens in *Sweetback*. In addition, as the Dahomey queen mentions to Freeman, through her exclusive liaison with the general, she's making money and now amassing some property. Freeman instructs her to continue her relationship and act as a spy for him. While it is not a woman's place to lead or organize the core of the black revolution liberation movement or engage in the necessary violent actions of war, women *serve* the men who intellectually lead and wield the gun. Thus, the classed women in the *The Spook* are primarily sexualized beings who are attracted to black phallic power.

The marginalized positioning of women reverberates throughout the film, as in, for example, the nightclub scene when Freeman first reunites with Dawson. A bare-midriffed black woman in an Afro and skimpy outfit dances provocatively alone on a small stage. She remains in the background of the camera frame as Dawson, with two attractive black women, and Freeman meet. The four sit down at a table, and the women are immediately cut out of the camera frame, even when Dawson directs a comment or glance to them; at one point we glimpse only their legs. It may perhaps be explained as one of the exemplary technical flaws of the film, but it is a telling one in terms of the gendered sexual politics.

The only other peripheral female presence is Mrs. Johnson, Shorty's mother, who appears to be an obvious signification on an old Negro type, the mammy. Mrs. Johnson lacks any sense of political awareness and if anything, the film implies, facilitates her son's social irresponsibility. Freeman tries to penetrate her ignorance when he attempts to discuss her son's inevitable downfall due to his illegal street activities. He even proposes that Shorty fight his way out of ghetto powerlessness through education, but she remarks, not wholly unjustifiably, that school contributed to Shorty's frustration. Most problematic is her lack of understanding that her son's drug use and dealing helps to hurt both himself and the community; she insists that Shorty isn't in it too much.

Ultimately, the provocative *Sweetback* and *The Spook* do not revise gendered sexual positioning. They primarily try to re-imagine the racial phallocentric order and echo the public self-representation of the Black Power movement by affirming the black phallus as the dominant signifier of Black Power revolution. Both films configure classed black women as primarily sexualized women motivated by counterrevolutionary aims. The whore is situated as being romantically antithetical to the sexualized bourgeois black woman who tricks, in a sense, for middle-class status or for the favor of "the Man." Both imply that she is the kind of black female "bitch" most likely to betray the black man. The two films thus steadfastly assert heterosexuality and female submission to the black male hero. Nevertheless, it is also true that these problematic dynamics do not erase the alluring fact that *Sweetback* and *The Spook* admirably attempted to offer black audiences cinematic entertainment that spoke to the black political fervor and social unrest of the era.

The politicized agenda of *Sweetback* and later *The Spook* unfortunately morphed into a dominance of ghettoized, underworld depictions with the hypersexual machismo that marked the two films' conservative representation of gender. By 1973, black-oriented urban actions films demonstrated the precariousness of projecting black empowerment and political radicalism within the context of mainstream perspectives and of Hollywood's commodification of black films. Black power became apoliticized and largely transformed into a violent and racist phallicization of desire, a desire projected in great part through the spectacle of female bodies. The genre increasingly manifested a host of anxieties related to the receding politicized era's impact on traditional ideas about sexuality, femininity, and masculinity, even as they offered up fantasies about transgressing traditional boundaries of racial and gender power.[37] *Sweetback* and *The Spook* together demonstrate the exhilarating possibilities of imagining black political and social empowerment on the big screen; at the same time, they anticipate the limitation of that fantasy when filtered through conservative models of gender.

4

Race, Gender, and Sexual Power in *Cleopatra Jones*

"You know, I wanted to be just like Cleopatra Jones. She had this cool vibe and she was tough. She didn't get all abused like a lot of women in those movies. I had never seen a black woman like her on-screen before. Especially not in a movie built around her." I can understand why a good friend of mine, as more than one black woman who experienced seeing *Cleopatra Jones* back in the day expressed to me, found it such compelling fantasy. I love looking at Tamara Dobson playing Cleopatra. She exudes this unapologetically majestic, cool, chocolate, regal, and diva-like 'tude. If you turn down the sound when you're watching *Cleopatra Jones,* as I once did, her vivid, visual aura alone compels your gaze.

Cleopatra Jones stands as the quintessential example of the potential of a new sensibility for shaping the black female presence in popular action cinema. By the early 1970s, the Hollywood studio–supported cycle of black urban ghetto action films had evolved into four dominant narrative tendencies: the black pimp and/or ghetto drug hustler "hero" on a mission for material wealth and autonomy from "the Man's" capitalist control (think Goldie in *The Mack* and Super Fly); the black militant egoist run amok after seizing power from white institutional control (think *Birth of a Nation*'s version of demonic black male power, blaxploitation-style, in 1975's *Black Gestapo*); the lone hero straddling the black ghetto and white institutional power and motivated mostly by self-preservation rather than political allegiance(Shaft, for example); or last, the rare, "legitimate" baadasssss hero (like Cleopatra Jones) whose mission is to stop the influx of drugs into the black community.

Cleopatra Jones, released the same year as *The Spook,* fits this latter type but importantly stands as the era's first commercially successful tough black woman action film.[1] The movie revolves around a ghetto-compassionate black heroine and U.S. special agent, Cleopatra Jones (Tamara Dobson), who is on a crusade against white drug enemies. The fight becomes personal after the police, on her enemy Mommy's order, attack Cleopatra's drug rehabilitation haven in Watts for inner-city black youth. Cleopatra's lover and partner, Reuben Masters (ex-football player Bernie Casey), runs the B & S House. Max Julien, who starred in the seriously misogynistic blaxploitation classic *The Mack,* originally created the character with a specific woman in mind to play Cleopatra Jones, though Dobson won the role in a national casting call. Julien cowrote the screenplay with Sheldon Keller, Jack Starrett directed the film, and William Tennant produced it. Julien has explained that he initially took the story idea to Columbia Pictures, but after beginning work on the project, he clashed with the company over its desire to make the film a comedy. He then took it to Warner Brothers, which allowed it to be featured as a dramatic action movie.[2] This detail behind the evolution of *Cleopatra Jones* signals the racialized patriarchal politics then infusing Hollywood studio filmmaking as much as the movie that came from the collaboration between this black writer-actor, his white colleagues, and a major studio reveals the politics of women's representations in black action fantasies.

I'm intrigued by the radicalism and problematic conservatism that underline the film's gendered, racial, and sexual politics. The representations of the black female heroine as well as of black masculinity, white masculinity, white femininity, and lesbianism present a stunning visual spectacle that indicate an ambivalent, sometimes hostile engagement of the political implications of racial, sexual, and female agency. The portrait of heroic black femininity stands as a departure of sorts from the typical black female presence within blaxploitation and Hollywood film in general. And despite the phallocentric framing, *Cleopatra Jones* revises the exclusively sexual, marginalized position that black women are relegated to in the revolt- and underworld-themed blaxploitation films. *Cleopatra Jones* presents a challenge to the traditional hierarchy of race and gender power. At the same time, the character depiction reverberates with historic tropes of black femininity—the black Amazon and black animalism—while projecting a glamorous image of the heroine as a tough soul diva.

Cleopatra Jones differs substantially from the two other major 1970s tough black woman vehicles, *Coffy* and *Foxy Brown,* in its less pornographic treatment of Dobson. In contemporary film studies that address the blaxploitation genre, the primarily black male critics have largely categorized *Cleopatra*

Jones, with Grier's *Coffy* and *Foxy Brown,* as failed representations, to para-phrase Gladstone Yearwood, of "phallic" heroines:

> This "new" black woman seems to break out of her containment. . . . We find a black female heroine who appears to have captured the power from a male-dominated world and is out to seek revenge. Yet, her representation in traditional gender terms equivocates any change in the narrative representa-tion of the black woman. Instead of reformulating the traditional signification of the woman in popular entertainment, the phallic black woman reaffirmed and celebrated the sexual objectification of women. The "black woman as heroine" series of films falls far short of presenting a new problematic of the woman in cinema, for there is a certain regime of traditional male pleasure in these films. Hence, the sexy, guntoting heroine in these narratives is but a variation of the traditional treatment of women in society.[3]

Yearwood echoes pioneering black film historian Donald Bogle's descrip-tion of the films as "high flung male fantasy" that embody a "hybrid of ste-reotypes."[4] Mark Reid similarly remarks that Dobson's and Grier's films are "made to engage male fantasies." Furthermore, he concludes, the "penetrating male heterosexist gaze does more to disarm these heroines than their actions do to empower them."[5] Since these critics identify a phallic orientation of the films that caters to male pleasure, they argue that there is little for black women to relate to, implying that spectatorial pleasure belongs primarily to men.[6]

This quick dismissal of these rare black woman fantasy action heroes poses a problem because it does not account for other dynamics, including the feminist as well as racial and patriarchal implications of the characters. This narrow reading also obscures the significance of this particular historic cultural moment in black female media imagery and collapses the major contrasts that should be made between the treatment of black femininity in *Cleopatra Jones* and Grier's two films.[7] Furthermore, it fails to acknowledge the possible appeal of these female fantasy characters to black women cultural consumers.

When Cleopatra Jones premiered on July 4, 1973, it marked a key moment in black women's imagery within the popular culture of the era. Between 1973 and 1974, the ABC black policewoman drama *Get Christy Love* premiered, though it lasted only a season. Like her film counterpart Cleopatra Jones, Christy (Teresa Graves) was a beautiful, kick-butt, crime-fighting black ac-tion heroine. *Coffy* and *Foxy Brown,* released in 1973 and 1974 respectively, offered another version of the tough black woman action figure.

The James Bond spy thriller to which *Cleopatra Jones* has been compared, *Live and Let Die,* also premiered in 1973. *Live and Let Die* exemplified the popularity of blaxploitation, as the film's plot and long opening sequence with the dancing nude silhouettes and profiles of black women strongly indicate. The film was historical in that black actress Gloria Hendry was cast as the first black Bond girl of romantic interest. Between 1973 and 1974 alone, the regally beautiful Hendry played a tough woman in 1973's *Black Belt Jones* and the girlfriend (or something akin to it) in several other popular vehicles— *Black Caesar, Slaughter's Big Rip-off,* and *Hell Up in Harlem.* Hendry never achieved the leading supermama star status that Dobson did briefly and Grier achieved, but she was perhaps the most regularly cast black female supporting actress alongside the array of new baad superheroes.

The Black Power movement, second-wave feminism, and an increasingly visible black feminist agenda were influential dynamics shaping the social backdrop to *Cleopatra Jones's* debut. In San Francisco in 1973, black women organized for action, and the National Black Feminist Organization (NBFO) was founded in New York City.[8] Film roles such as Cleopatra Jones suggested the cultural impact of not only black political activism but also, significantly, women's rights efforts. As one feminist film scholar explains this influence on exploitation cinema in particular, "A popular version of 'women's lib' was celebrated in sexual role reversals in which strong, assertive women, often brandishing weapons, took their destiny in their own hands."[9]

The few reviews of *Cleopatra Jones* written by black women at the time suggest its import as a film that affirmed the black community and black women in particular. In a September 1973 review of *Cleopatra Jones,* "Brother Caring for Brother," Mary E. Mebane wrote that *Cleopatra Jones,* like another contemporary black film, *Gordon's War,* is "revolutionary" because it shows strength in the black community, "unlike such recent films as 'Superfly' and 'The Mack.'" Further, she proclaims, *Cleopatra Jones* can be commended for dealing with the harsh realities of black inner-city life and for offering a story that depicts black people "loving and helping each other."[10] In her 1974 *Ms.* essay "Keeping the Black Woman in Her Place," black feminist Margaret Sloan critiques the violent black male heroes of *Sweetback* and other blaxploitation films for whom women function in the role of sexualized helpmates. However, she applauds *Cleopatra Jones's* contrasting treatment of black femininity. Sloan assesses the feminist potential of black female empowerment signified by Cleopatra Jones: "She defends against attack and aggression without becoming brutal or violent. She doesn't use men or depend on them for survival. She is her own woman."[11] Unlike many exhibitions of "tough" female characters in exploitations films, *Cleopatra Jones* also cannot easily be characterized within the woman's exploitation revenge film cycle, since stylistically it does not include a lot of the graphic nudity and sexual violence so typical of the genre. In addition, the heroine is a "legitimate" crime fighter motivated by her black-identified personal commitment to save the B & S House from being wrongly shut down rather than by stereotypical "female" passion born out of the loss of a lover or revenge for rape.

Jennifer DeVere Brody's 1999 essay "The Returns of Cleopatra Jones" marks a rare black feminist and queer address of *Cleopatra Jones*. Brody too takes up the narrow black male critical readings of the film. She describes Cleopatra Jones as a "magnificent mahogany diva" who is simultaneously a "handmaiden to the black revolution and hired handgun for the US government."[12] Brody and I share a similar effort in unpacking the myriad visual aesthetic and political implications posed by the unusual presence of a black film heroine of feminist significance. While Brody addresses the implications of the Dobson/Cleopatra Jones photos that accompany much of the aforementioned black male criticism of the film, I provide specific focus on the visual imagery of Dobson within the film. Though I address the white female butch imagery in *Cleopatra Jones* later in this chapter, my discussion does not proceed from the very useful "black queer aesthetic" framing that Brody's does. I primarily focus on the original film characters; in contrast, Brody offers more focus on the 1990s popular "queering" of the Cleopatra icon and intensive review of sexual politics in the 1975 sequel, *Cleopatra Jones and the Casino of Gold*.[13]

Brody's interrogation of male critics' conclusion that the "phallic" perspective precludes any "relevance" of the Cleopatra Jones character to black female viewers is particularly useful, given my attempt to explore the film's progressive and problematic features as well as the appeal of this fantasy heroine to various black women fans. Referencing Kobena Mercer's understanding of the "complexities of identifications," Brody illuminates this possible appeal:

> Given that all action movies are in part fantasy projection, these films might recall the fantasies of power many black women desired. Such low-budget, mass-marketed films directed to a black urban audience need not "reflect" *a* reality. . . . Some critics believe that a focus on "realism" and "positive" . . . images counters the "negative" images of blackface performances . . . that marked "black" performances in Hollywood; but, rather than rehearse the call for such "reality," one might make a plea for "reel-ism"—for reveling in the fantasy of filmic images that does not simply replicate an already known "reality."[14]

Brody's comments and the other cited women's reviews of *Cleopatra Jones* help to highlight how too-narrow readings of the film and of its heroic black female character obscure the complexity of representation and spectatorial desire.

Supermama "Vogue": Imaging Cleopatra

Baby you walk right
You smile and you talk right. . . .
You move like the desert wind
Make me wanna love you again and again.[15]

In the opening scene of *Cleopatra Jones*, Joe Simon's bluesy, raspy vocals announce the striking appearance of Cleopatra through invoking the historic Egyptian queen of the same name. Lyrically and musically, the moaning, wailing homage to Cleopatra heightens the framing of her as a mysterious and important foreigner as she arrives on a plane in a windy Turkish desert. Swathed in a hooded, long fur animal-print cape, she glides forcefully between two lines of male Turkish officers as the music fades. The incongruities of patriarchal authority, feminine glamour, and "blackness" in the primitive patriarchal setting signify the relationship between power and exoticism that we see projected in Cleopatra's image throughout. *Cleopatra Jones*'s male filmmakers structure the aura of glamour and power that defines their heroine by emphasizing Dobson's six-foot two-inch awe-inspiring physical body.

As an unusual black superwoman, Cleopatra inspires a mixture of masculine admiration, sexual desire, and anxiety as the filmmakers purposefully manipulate several contemporary and historical tropes of black femininity. Michelle Wallace identifies one of these as the Amazonian or superwoman archetype in part 2 of her 1977 book *Black Macho and The Myth of the Superwoman*:

From the intricate web of mythology which surrounds the black woman, a fundamental image emerges. It is of a woman of inordinate strength, with an ability for tolerating an unusual amount of misery and heavy, distasteful work. This woman does not have the same fears, weaknesses, and insecurities as other women, but believes herself to be and is, in fact, stronger emotionally than most men. Less of a woman in that she is less "feminine" and helpless, she is really *more* of a woman in that she is the embodiment of Mother Earth, the quintessential mother with infinite sexual, life-giving, and nurturing reserves.[16]

In the marketing of the two Cleopatra films, colorful, cartoonish print ads emphasized Dobson's lithe body. Film posters for the original film and its sequel, *Cleopatra Jones and the Casino of Gold,* declared her "6 ft. 2 in. of dynamite" alongside illustrations of a gun- or knife-wielding Dobson in short fur jacket and Afro or a tight, futuristic cat suit and bright, heavy makeup.

Prior to her blaxploitation fame, Dobson was a model who appeared in a few commercials and ads in *Vogue,* where she was cast as an exotic black female entity in a magazine that specifically showcased white feminine beauty and glamour. Her modeling image and background plays an interesting role in the treatment of glamour in the film. Numerous shots frame Cleopatra in a series of dramatic, erotic poses that evoke runway and print modeling strategies. Cleopatra is simultaneously superwoman hero and aesthetic object of the male gaze within the film. The fashion modeling tendencies that the film employs suggest the heroine's unique presence in a screen space traditionally reserved for the display of male physical action and white female beauty.

Dobson's positioning as a black icon of female glamour in a historically exclusive space exoticizes the screen space. Cleopatra's race and gender, glamorous appearance, atypical feminine physicality, and extraordinary "special" status within white male institutional power make her a stunningly unique presence in the tradition of masculine action criminal fantasy. "Cleopatra" signifies black female power and at the same time a racial exoticism because of its obvious reference to the famous foreign Egyptian queen, an association that is played up in the narrative and on the soundtrack for the film.

J. J. Johnson, a musician who had played with such jazz greats as Count Basie and arranged the *Troubleman* soundtrack, produced the soundtrack for the film. He utilized oriental music with jazz, bass, and strings to invoke an exotic aura. On the album's cover, an Afro-chic Cleopatra strikes a karate pose that highlights her lithe, long body. It is set in the forefront against smaller illustrations of scenes, including a fur-clad Cleopatra holding an Uzi. In her insightful study about the shifting imagery of the Cleopatra icon, *Becoming Cleopatra,* Francesca T. Royster summarizes the dualities underlining the film construction of the Cleopatra Jones persona: "Tamara Dobson is a lost African queen, dripping in furs and silk robes. She is a hybrid of an exotic queen from the past, a homegirl who knows her way around her old neighborhood of Watts and a special agent for the CIA. In the film, we see a double act of appropriation made possible by the ambiguity of the Cleopatra icon."[17]

The camera frequently isolates Dobson, magnifying her racialized, gendered, and sexualized body as a visible sign of exotic difference. In several scenes, long shots of Cleopatra are imaged through the male gaze. In one early scene, for example, two working-class black men watch her stride away down the street, hips swaying provocatively in high-fashion, chic supermama attire. They stare at her backside. One of the men comments that he'd like to have "that," while the other counters with a message that she is not your ordinary sexy woman—the last guy that tried was hurt. As Cleopatra continues her majestic stroll down the street, we see her catch the desiring looks of a bevy of men across race and age. Two very young black boys stare at Cleopatra, their awakening macho sexual awareness obvious. As she speeds off in her racy Corvette, one of the boys proclaims, "Right on, Sweet Sister." In another scene, a young black boy declares, "Man, that is some kind of woman!" Such responses continuously affirm Cleopatra's heterosexual appeal, mediating her distinct positioning as an unusually empowered black woman. Royster maintains that these arrival and departure scenes perform the "queenliness and pageantry of Shakespeare's Cleopatra," though here in the context of action hero.[18] The street and the male gaze in the film function as runway and audience for the spectacular display and consumption of Cleopatra's brilliantly arrayed body.

Cleopatra's high-fashion wardrobe circa the early 1970s emphasizes Dobson's dark skin and towering frame. She appears in rich reds and yellows, tailored pantsuits, slightly revealing, clinging silk shirts, voluptuous fur jackets, turbans, silk headdresses, and hooded capes. These outfits, of course, help create the glamorous persona that is so integral in establishing Cleopatra's fantasy identity as a unique hero because she is beautiful, black, female, and endowed with unusual social empowerment.[19] Annette Kuhn's explication of glamour and women's imagery somewhat illuminates the dual functions of glamour in the film. She explains that in its almost complete exclusive application to women, glamour implies "a sense of deceptive fascination, of groomed beauty, of charm enhanced by means of illusion." She develops her description further: "A glamorous/glamourised image then is one manipulated, falsified perhaps, in order to heighten or even to idealise. A glamorous image of a woman (or an image of a glamorous woman) is peculiarly powerful in that it plays on the desire of the spectator in a particularly pristine way: beauty or sexuality is desirable exactly to the extent that it is idealized and unattainable."[20] As the opening shot and title song signal, the construction of racialized feminine glamour is critical in establishing for us Cleopatra's aura of untouchable beauty. Cleopatra is the object of the male gaze in the film, but while they get to "look" at her, their desire is held at a distance.

Cleopatra's positioning as a glamorous diva on the big screen invites dual readings. On one hand, the constant affirmation of her as a heterosexually desirable woman serves to negotiate her positioning as a tough hero who appears visually more physically powerful than the men around her and who can outfight them and win. As the song "Theme from Cleopatra Jones" personifies, she poses the fantasy of erotic pleasure for men: "You're so sweet and strong. . . . / Touch me like the desert wind." She also presents the threat and thrill of painful eroticism:

> You take my pride and you throw it up against the wall
> You take me in your arms, baby, and bounce me like a rubber ball. . . .
> Dontcha know that it hurts so good.

Yet, on the other hand, her construction as admired, glamorous diva is significant, particularly since black women haven't traditionally been portrayed in such terms in cinema and commercial beauty culture generally. As a heterosexually appealing and glamorous superwoman with phallic power, Cleopatra embodies an image rarely assigned to black women in cultural productions.

The inscription of Dobson's Cleopatra with a racialized glamour mimics the high fashion exotica associated with black femininity in addition to manifesting the impact of the Black Power "Black Is Beautiful" mantra. Interestingly, reflecting on the same 1973–74 period, Barbara Summers begins her study of black model history with the "breakthrough" moment of the 1973 Versailles international fashion runway show where the American designers triumphed through clothes worn by African American models. She observes the symbolic significance of the presence of Josephine Baker, the premier "exotic" black diva of the early twentieth century, who sang at the gala.[21] In 1969, several major beauty magazines—*Cosmopolitan, Glamour,* and *Mademoiselle*—featured black models on their covers for the first time. In 1974, model Beverly Johnson became the first black model to receive the most prestigious commercial beauty assignment of all, the cover of U.S. *Vogue.* Leslie Uggams became the first African American woman to portray Cleopatra on Broadway in 1968's *Her First Roman.* That same year, Diahann Carroll began her television star turn in *Julia.*[22]

Yet, white rhetoric about black models revealed the tendency to view them in *racially* exotic terms. In much the same way, film ads for *Cleopatra Jones* and film review comments on Dobson's physicality reverberate with notions of black exoticism and animalistic imagery.[23] The film narrative plays on the historic stereotypical inscription of black femininity as erotically animalistic through the appearance of the long-limbed Cleopatra in elaborate fur coverings and dramatic makeup, especially around the eyes. Lisa Anderson describes such imagery in her discussion of the jezebel trope of black women: "The animal metaphors resurface; the jezebel is represented as a tiger, a puma, a panther, or other large, sleek cat who slinks up and pounces on her prey. She is a frightening apparition in the white imagination."[24]

Hair politics also figure importantly in Cleopatra's visual effect. Her hair is not prevalently visible. In one rare action sequence in the film, Cleopatra wears an Afro wig when she visits the B & S House in Watts, where black people work together to save neighborhood youth from the ravages of drugs. The Afro serves as another visual marker of the distinctly black feminine beauty aesthetic and soul culture that Cleopatra is supposed to embody. The Afro was a cultural signifier of black affirmation during the Black Power–generated "Black Is Beautiful" consciousness.[25] This filmic display of a black-identified cultural signifier underlines the commodification of soul culture by Hollywood. Hairstyles and head coverings help distinguish Cleopatra as a distinct black feminine figure in the masculinized crime action world, where she is the dominant figure. Historian Robin D. G. Kelley has explained too the history of the Afro as a sign of a "new female exotica" in high fashion circles and among the white and black elite in the late 1950s.[26]

Throughout most of the film, Cleopatra's head is covered with colorful, elaborate, wide-brimmed feathered hats, scarves, and turbans. In several scenes when she fights Mommy's white male hoods, Cleopatra dramatically removes her covering—fur or cape—and whips off her hat, sometimes revealing a tightly tied scarf. Our attention is constantly brought to Cleopatra's "striking" body and face accentuated by the model-heavy makeup and colorful head coverings. Rather than her hair functioning as the quintessential signifier of feminine beauty, it is mostly obscured. Is this, then, to be read as resistance to the white patriarchal positioning of "flowing hair" as a sign of feminine sexual beauty?[27]

It could indeed suggest a departure from the convention of a glamorous (white) woman's hair operating as a visual sign of beauty and feminine softness, since she is supposed to be a black-identified heroine. Yet, it more obviously functions to underscore the racial and gender difference and hence exoticism associated with Cleopatra's imagery. The tight-fitting scarves, hats, and turbans that adorn her dark brown skin and brightly colored outfits heighten her striking African features and physique. The last visual of Cleopatra especially personifies the black high exotica the film's representation of her projects. On the lawn of the B & S House, against the backdrop of the black community, Cleo looks like the consummate "African queen" with her body enveloped in a thick gray fur and her hair adorned in elaborate cornrows and crowned by beads and feathers.

(Un)James Bond-ing Cleopatra

Cleopatra's appearance contrasts sharply with the white male bourgeois con-servative dress that is privileged in such government institutions as the CIA and worn by the police in the film. This establishes some distance from the tough male and white centers of action cinema and especially the iconic James Bond model of "normative" masculinity in spy thriller action cinema. Cleo-patra's special agent status affords her international movement and fluidity to navigate the tight confines of the law enforcement system with a great degree of independence. Her consistent poise, cosmopolitan demeanor, and expert skill align her quite obviously with the James Bond model. A one-woman force, Cleopatra alternately uses martial arts to whip the bad guys or expertly wields one of her high-powered guns, taken out of a secret compartment in her sporty car. She maneuvers her personalized car like a professional driver in the long car chase scene and rides a motorcycle up a steep hill just as expertly. Yet, it is important to the imagery of Cleopatra that she registers as a rare entry in the masculine action cinema tradition. Her hypervisible physical presence denotes her unique identification as a black woman action hero, much as James Bond's more conservative but classy dress conveys his bourgeois white masculinity.

The obvious influence of the famous 007 film series on *Cleopatra Jones* as well as on other blaxploitation films such as *Shaft* has been noted. In addition to the notable Bond-like elements above, Cleopatra Jones shares with Bond a "special agent" status. Rather than going "undercover" on their missions, both have a certain level of fame rather than anonymity. Yet, the contrasts between the two are extreme in that each has a specific racial, class, national, and gender identification. In the essay "Cleopatra Jones 007: Blaxploitation, James Bond, and Reciprocal Co-option," Chris Norton argues that Cleopa-tra Jones offers a critique that encompasses the whiteness that 007 upholds. "Both the Bonds of the 1960s and *Live and Let Die*," Norton writes, "can be seen as efforts to stabilize white hegemony in the face of global nationalist tensions and rising black militancy."[28] Indeed, in *Live and Let Die,* which again premiered during the same period as *Cleopatra Jones,* Bond battles black bad guys. Cleopatra's blackness, Norton points out, establishes a distance between her and Bond, since racism is indicted too in the former film.

While Norton's point about Bond is well taken, the political implications of the revised Bond model offered by *Cleopatra Jones* are more ambiguous. The mere presence of white criminality that is defeated does not provide an adequate refutation of the white hegemony that Bond upholds; Cleopatra's atypical, empowered presence in the white male system can be taken as a limited critique at best. The narrowing of the black liberation struggle to one hero against a drug underworld figure and two minor cops leaves the hegemony intact while offering the entertaining fantasy of white supremacist defeat. Cleopatra Jones, a certainly unique presence in her occupation as "special agent" for the U.S. government, is still an agent for, not against, the government.

Nevertheless, Cleopatra's position as an agent of considerable influence is crucial for the depiction of her as a superwoman heroine. Her "special" status of inclusion in the CIA highlights its pervasively white male hierarchical makeup. Again, though, institutional white male "power" is not a point of critique in the film. In the depiction of Cleopatra as a lone, uniquely empowered black female agent with international jurisdiction, the Black Power ethos of radical transformation of the institutional power does not register in this nonetheless appealing cinematic fantasy of a black female crime fighter who seems to operate without social and geographic confines.[29] Cleopatra's "special agent" crime-fighting status exemplifies the emergence of such law enforcement positions as "compensatory gestures" in film.[30] The black as law enforcement official of some kind in film and television began to occur with growing regularity beginning in the 1970s.

Masculinizing/Emasculating "The Man"

Cleopatra Jones is propelled by a heroine who provokes gender anxiety upon sight and action. On sight, Cleopatra renders other female bodies more traditionally feminine while at the same time she feminizes white and black males. Her long legs become lethal weapons when karate-kicking her male foes and ultimate diva enemy, Mommy. All appear physically helpless despite their guns and machismo. Pam Cook has described such cinematic representations in "narratives of male identity crisis and images of men stripped of phallic power." She argues that they are "a visible response, however phobic, to gay and feminist politics and the perceived empowerment of women." They simultaneously speak to the reality of social transition while "they attempt to recast the roles of victim and oppressor."[31] In the case of Cleopatra Jones, racial coding figures prominently in the configuration of the heroine as a potential threat of castration and emasculation for some black men and white male authority figures.

The castration-emasculation themes play out vividly in Cleo's relationship with the captain of the local police, Lou, a white paternal figurehead and her police ally. Before the two speak directly or meet, we get to see how the all-white male police officers view Cleopatra. In one scene at the police station, they dread her reaction to the raid on the B & S House. The juxtaposition of her super-efficiency with their inadequate crime-fighting skills hints at the notion of white phallic effeminacy. Two of Lou's officers, Purdy and most notably Kirk, are the representative corrupt, racist cops. Both implicate familiar features of blaxploitation—gendered racial caricature and racist speech. Purdy and Kirk's racist machismo make them underestimate Cleopatra. Purdy, a redneck archetype, refers to Cleopatra as a "silly bitch" before his inevitable beating by her. And Kirk, who successfully fools his captain and Cleopatra into thinking that he's one of the good cops, appears condescendingly admiring of Cleopatra.

Lou's attitude and responses toward Cleopatra prove the most interesting indicator of her positioning as alternately a figure of desire, mysteriousness, and female-empowered danger. In the first telephone encounter between them early in the movie, Lou inquires about Cleopatra's welfare after being attacked at the airport by Mommy's men. She answers that her body is okay but expresses anger over the attack on her and the raid on the B & S House. Awestruck, Lou replies that her body is "magnificent." His comment affirms the text's emphasis on Cleopatra's bodily presence with its allusions to an exotic animalism.

In the scene after Cleopatra exposes Purdy's corruption, Lou utters a statement that further reveals the desire mixed with castration anxiety that Cleopatra incites in men. She walks away as Lou and Kirk stare after her in awe. Lou asks, "Kirk, you ever have feelings of inadequacy?" On the surface, of course, the statement alludes to her efficiency, but in a larger sense it hints at the male anxiety that Cleopatra's atypical empowerment or female superiority—physique, ability, and status—motivates. Lou, a middle-aged man of medium height, appears vulnerable or fragile when standing beside Cleopatra, suggesting effeminacy brought to the fore by her. Yet, indicative of the contradictory progressive and conservative elements the film offers, it is worth noting Cleopatra's attitude toward the white male figures of legitimate authority. She interacts with Lou with a cool professionalism, expecting and accepting Lou's respect and cooperation.

The contradictions that Cleopatra's interactions with men present are illuminated by the contrasting depictions of the two primary black male characters. At one end, the uncommon cinematic representation of the black female heroine's lover, Reuben, offers a rather progressive version of a black male–black female romantic relationship. At the other extreme, the comic black male drug dealer–pimp Doodlebug meets a violent end. Frequently in blaxploitation films, black male aspiration to white patriarchal, albeit underworld, power is ridiculed through the subversion of the mythological black pimp or mack who "countered . . . sniveling, deferential, conciliatory, and compliant blacks who lived for white approval."[32]

In many of the studio-produced blaxploitation flicks, this certainly problematic macho-imbued figure mostly becomes an absurdity of comic proportions. The flamboyantly Zip Coon–like, materialistic "pimp" character Doodlebug (Antonio Fargas), with telling name and delusions of phallic power, functions as a spectacle of black male urban posturing that purposefully subverts any real social signification of this figure. The blaxploitation film characters played by Fargas dramatize the cinematic devaluation and exploitation of the black ghetto pimp prototype. With his distinctive physicality—rail-thin frame, prominent African features, and ghetto-jive posturing—Fargas's blaxploitation persona invokes a comedic "eunuch" element, the antithesis of the powerful black masculinity associated with the hustler/pimp and Black Power idea. In his blaxploitation film roles especially, Fargas's ability to portray the ghetto pimp, petty criminal, hustler, and street source–philosopher contributed to his popularity as an icon of black male ghetto identity in 1970s B-grade action film.

Doodlebug's effort to ape mainstream bourgeois culture is a spectacle that spins on his perception of himself as a Big Man achieving the zenith of American materialism and phallic power. Cleopatra mocks Doodlebug's comical imitation of white bourgeois culture upon seeing his white English butler dressed outrageously in mustard yellow. In the one scene between them, Doodlebug is obviously intimidated by Cleopatra; she manhandles his right henchman, who tries to search her, while Doodlebug cowers despite the false macho bravado.

In the war between Mommy—the white female boss from whom Doodlebug fancies himself escaping into independent business—and the "legitimate" black supermama, Cleopatra, Doodlebug lacks "true" power, a fact dramatized by his display of macho bravado and his absurdly exaggerated murder. Indeed, the masculinized war between the two women is in part played out through the treatment of Doodlebug, who has a fatal desire for autonomy in the criminal world. He functions as a mediator of sorts between the two women as they get closer to a face-to-face confrontation. He tells Mommy that she's no match for that "black lady" and declares his independence from her exploitative control. Doodlebug pays for his cocky rebellion against Mommy's paternal control: he is shot to death in the street by her henchmen in a theatrically exaggerated fashion a couple of scenes later.

That Doodlebug's girl is black rather than white—a white girlfriend being the typical sign of the black man's underworld capitalistic, patriarchal elevation—is an unusual aspect of this character. Nevertheless, Tiffany, a petite, young black woman with huge eyes and an air of feminine vulnerability, does appear as the quintessential damsel in distress whom Cleopatra undertakes to help. Mark Reid argues that Cleopatra Jones's empowerment comes from her fights with women—the "antithesis of truly feminist struggle."[33] Though in one sense the visual juxtaposition of Tiffany and Cleopatra emphasizes the latter's uncharacteristic phallic feminine persona and Tiffany's traditional femininity, it is still representative of a black woman willing to fight for another held under patriarchal control. In addition, there is affectionate black female camaraderie between Cleopatra and Mrs. Johnson (Esther Rolle), mother of the karate-chopping Johnson brothers.

The brothers present another example of black male representation that downplays, albeit less grotesquely, the image of black masculine power. They work in concert with Cleopatra in her battle with Mommy, but the film plays Mrs. Johnson as a bit of the matriarchal mama; Cleopatra goes to her first in order to request the aid of the "boys." Full-grown men and martial arts experts, the Johnson brothers are simultaneously played as loyal friends to Cleopatra yet childishly macho. The only other minor black male characters— Snake, a petty dealer, and the victimized, recovering addict, Beekers—are both physically petite black men, like Doodlebug, who appear distinctively weak in the presence of Cleo; she browbeats Snake in one scene and clears the falsely charged Beekers. These juxtapositions serve to emphasize Cleo's superwoman-ness.

Cleopatra and Reuben's relationship presents a more progressive look at black male–black female relations. Reuben is played as a strong black man who tenderly cares for the recovering kids at the B & S House without being made an extreme caricature of either the angry black militant or the feminized black male. The depiction underscores the rarity of such black male imagery within the genre and American popular action cinema. When the police raid the B & S House on a false drug tip, Reuben confronts the police bravely. With quiet force, he challenges the gun-holding racist cops, who look sufficiently inept and inadequate alongside his strong physical presence and proud demeanor despite their guns. After the police decide to shut down the house, Reuben determines that he will literally fight to keep it open for the kids who need it. He tells Cleopatra, "I'll tell you one thing, Mama, if they want this house, they got to bring something to get something."

At the end of the movie, Cleopatra and Tiffany seem about to meet their end at the hands of Mommy and her soldiers, but Reuben comes to her aid with the Johnson brothers; they fight alongside each other. Indeed, rather than undercutting Cleopatra's power, as one male critic says her receiving physical aid from men does,[34] it is a moment of black male–black female solidarity and equity. By this point, remember, Cleopatra's extraordinary self-sufficiency is already well established. It should be pointed out too that women help Sweetback and Shaft. The Johnson brothers and Reuben work in concert with Cleopatra; their interaction is mutually respectful and affectionate. It is also worth noting that Reuben especially has an equal stake in the preservation of the drug rehabilitation house.

The reversion of traditional bourgeois gender roles without using the strategy of merely imbuing the male with traditional feminine qualities and the female with male ones is especially appealing. Cleopatra goes outside the domestic sphere—metaphorically the B& S House—to fight the drug trade, while Reuben fights from home base. Yet, Reuben is not presented as the emasculated or effeminate black male due to his ladylove's untraditional gender role. Instead, they share a social as well as romantic bond. Reuben is not threatened by or antagonistic to Cleopatra's status. There is one subtle sexual scene that, unlike the dominant filming of sexual scenes in the genre, does not occur from the perspective of the black male's control and pleasure. The most "graphic" aspect is the long, sensual kiss between the two before the scene fades to black. Cleopatra's body is not situated as being in service to her lover's sexual pleasure or control. At the end of the movie, Reuben remains in charge of the B & S House and lovingly bids Cleopatra good-bye as she goes off to fight drug crime out in the world.

The White Lesbian "Bitch" and Patriarchal Dilemma

In *Cleopatra Jones,* the black female protagonist takes on a white female nemesis in a world where white and patriarchal power is compromised by the females' atypical empowerment. The film hints at the very real ideological divide between the white middle-class feminist movement and the black feminist platform. In waging battle against racial oppression in solidarity with black men, many black women seemed at best ambivalent or outright resistant to the gender-exclusive fight against patriarchy being forged in the early 1970s. Female solidarity—racially, especially—did not live up to the articulated, public representation of "true feminism" then being espoused. The first appearance of Mommy, in the film's second scene, stresses the spectacle of racial and gender difference at the core of the narrative perspective; race serves as the crucial marker of the super-female divide between them and their "baad bitch" fight as Mommy rants about Cleopatra: "That bitch! That goddamn black bitch!"

While Cleo's supermama image hints at male ambivalence about notions of black and female power amid an era of feminist and arising black feminist consciousness, Mommy poses an overtly vicious backlash to white feminist and sexual politics. Why does Mommy come out so significantly worse than Cleopatra, other than because of her designation as the protagonist's major criminal enemy? The representation of her in this collaboration of sorts between a black man and white men offers the specter of a distinctly dangerous white female power that has historical implications.

In the American master-slave hierarchical system, white women held power over both black females and black men yet were under the domination of the white male—a structure imitated to a degree in the film. The film text is propelled by the spectacular fantasy reversal of this traditional racial and gender hierarchy around which the raced female power struggle occurs. While Cleopatra's energies are directed toward getting rid of criminal drug guys, Mommy operates outside the boundaries of bourgeois morality and patriarchal control while exerting power over the latter. She thus provokes castration anxiety. Her underworld power as the "big boss," a traditionally male role, affords her tyrannical control over men. She owns her white male soldiers and some of the policemen, who sometimes refer to her as "Mother." Mommy is presented as a pathological, violent "bitch," a role emphasized whenever she physically and verbally terrorizes her white male soldiers. The lesbian identification assigned to Mommy is problematically used to make visible her inscribed gendered pathology. Mommy violates traditional white maternal and heterosexual feminine imagery, which in part plays on popular stereotypical 1970s B-grade horror and action film imagery. Judith Halberstam offers a description of the butch or masculine woman in popular Hollywood cinema that explains the depiction of Mommy: "The masculine woman prowls the film set as an emblem of social upheaval and as a marker of sexual disorder. She wears the wrong clothes, expresses aberrant desires, and is very often associated with clear markers of a distinctly phallic power. She may carry a gun, smoke a cigar, wear leather, ride a motorbike; she may swagger, strut, boast, flirt with younger and more obviously feminine women."[35]

Mommy's violent treatment of males, especially white men, is framed in a way that implies that phallic power is misplaced onto her through filtering our view of her through the eyes of her oppressed white soldiers. Camera shots privilege their scarcely veiled looks of disgust and disdaining amusement, a factor that helps to intensify the scary spectacle of white female power.

If the role of Mommy suggests any subversion of the driving patriarchal treatment it receives, it lies in the theatrical performance by Shelley Winters. Her exhibition of Mommy provides a striking contrast to Dobson's austere Cleopatra. Winters plays Mommy in a comically exaggerated fashion, reminding us that her character is a patriarchal fantasy of white female, lesbian-identified power. While she's doubly the object of the spectators' gaze within and outside the screen, Winters gleefully plays the "white bitch" role in a fashion so over the top that it mocks the parody of white female or feminist power. Without the mediation offered through her outrageous theatricality, the Mommy representation might completely reinforce patriarchal anxiety about the potential consequences of feminism's impact.

While Mommy possesses the markers of underworld king status, exploitation fantasy–style—money, power, and women—her desire for the last denotes her deviancy. The homophobic treatment of the Mommy character underscores the film's anti-feminist undertones. The contradictory juxtaposition of the "mommy" endearment and her violent masculinity emphasizes the perversity attached to Mommy's lesbian gangster image. The title "Mommy," an idealized name for the mother figure, and Mommy's maternal bodily appearance provide a sharp contradiction. She brutalizes her male soldiers, pummeling them with a powerful right, but sexually mothers her young female servants and figurative daughters. Of course, the "daughters" are young white, ultra-feminine, pretty blondes and brunettes. Immediately after a tirade, one of her "daughters" enters to soothe Mommy, who coos at her as if at an infant. Then Mommy caresses the girl's backside. Mommy's sexual disregard of men, her man-hating nature, and her lesbian orientation offer a spectacle of white female power bound in grotesque portraiture. Through the film's racialized patriarchal perspective, she is the feminist horror realized in an emasculating, white lesbian freak.[36] Contrasted together, Mommy's whiteness, lesbianism, and phallic power highlight Cleopatra Jones's heterosexual appeal, blackness, and phallic power. The latter's bourgeois sophistication emphasizes Mommy's low-class moral corruption; Cleopatra's feminine masculinity underscores Mommy's "butch" lesbianism. The film posits them as warring "baad bitches," creating an exotic spectacle of racial femininities that resolves the tensions their female power provokes. In keeping with the genre requirement of black triumph at the end of the film, Cleopatra neutralizes Mommy in a mismatched physical fight.

Exoticism and Lesbianism in
Cleopatra Jones and the Casino of Gold

The 1975 sequel *Cleopatra Jones and the Casino of Gold* presents a more bla-tant stereotypical treatment of racialized femininities. The spectacle of black female exoticism and deviant lesbianism is heightened, constructing a far more "cartoonish" version of phallic femininities. The sequel, also a Warner Brothers production, was written and produced by William Tennant and directed by Chuck Bail.[37] *The Casino of Gold* personifies the American fasci-nation with Hong Kong martial arts cinema and the long historical Western association of the exotic with Eastern bodies and locales. The Bond inference is less overt and more symbolic in the backdrop of the casino—a familiar Bond film trope—and the reference to gold in the title and casino location, though "gold" does not actually figure in the plot.

The film has Cleopatra alone in Hong Kong to rescue the Johnson brothers, who have been taken hostage by a white drug lord, the Dragon Lady or Ms. Big, as she is called. The eroticization of Cleopatra Jones intensifies through her more exotic appearance and the contrast between her and an Asian female counterpart. The two team up to topple the phallic Ms. Big (Stella Stevens), through whom the film takes further the association between white female phallic power and lesbian perversion. The exotic feminization associated with the Asian female body and the Hong Kong locale proves a backdrop against which Cleopatra appears ever more visually "other."

Again, the fashion modeling aesthetic plays a significant role, though Cleo-patra's appearance appears more stereotypically animalistic than in the first film. Her costumes range from glitzy masculine evening wear, veiled hats, sequined coats, and black pants to a tight chocolate cat suit. Her hair is hid-den under elaborate head coverings. In the *New York Times* review of the film, Vincent Canby condemned it as a "trashy black exploitation movie" that in his opinion denied the "large, beautiful, overwhelming presence" of Dobson. Instead, he goes on, the film hides her "real sexuality" through the karate-chopping narcotics agent role and "costumes that seem to have been designed for a female impersonator."[38] In one of the first scenes, Cleopatra walks the streets of Hong Kong in a masculine pants outfit and brilliant red hat, drawing stares from the petite pedestrians.

Actress Ni Tien (Tanny) plays Mi Ling, an Americanized Asian operative who comes to Cleopatra's aid despite her initial resistance, ultimately becom-ing Cleopatra's sidekick. Mi Ling is a skilled martial artist and dart expert, a tough woman herself. Cleopatra looms over Mi Ling, with her ultra-feminine appearance and petite frame. Mi Ling's look stays within the confines of the exotic femininity associated with Asian femaleness in the Western imagination. In further contrast to Cleopatra, Mi Ling's flowing, shoulder-length hair swings bouncily, shining and black throughout the action sequences.

In one scene, Mi Ling showers and then dons a short white robe tied with a red sash. Two men break into her room and tie her hands behind her back, but Mi Ling manages to fight them, all the while swinging her hair prettily. Her purse serves as another signifier of her femininity. In the last long martial arts fight scene, Mi Ling climbs up walls and completes daring flips and karate kicks with her red purse intact on her shoulder. In the juxtaposition of Mi Ling and Cleopatra, the latter becomes a more masculine supermama, which their verbal interplay about being the Lone Ranger and Tonto emphasizes.

The contrast between Cleopatra and the glamorous but brutal Dragon Lady or Ms. Big, played by a blonde, green-eyed Stevens, underscores other stereotypical associations. Ms. Big is played as a much less comical portrait of sexualized white female deviancy than Mommy. Her appearance presents an idealized traditional vision of white American female glamour and beauty, but her status as the preeminent gangster of the Eastern drug trade in a foreign environment implies the degradation of this imagery. Ms. Big poses several contradictory ideas of white femininity through the inscription of her power as pathological rather than just criminal.

Her blonde beauty instantly images a heterosexual "to-be-looked-at-ness"[39] as the viewer is invited to focus on her white blondeness. In one scene, Ms. Big walks slowly down the long stairs of her casino, dressed in a sexy, sophisticated green evening dress that heightens her fair skin, blonde hair, and green eyes. Her cold eyes, however, hint at an internal evil that her appearance seemingly contradicts. The exterior of idealized white American feminine beauty elevates the aura of her sinister nature. The rather grotesque competing versions of phallic femininities presented via Cleopatra, Mi Ling, and Ms. Big suggest the filmmakers' preoccupation with the possibility of phallocentric power unseated by women. *The Casino of Gold* explores the consequences of a world in which white male power is nonexistent and native men are castrated, that is, subordinate to women.

Ms. Big's sadistic brutality toward her male servants and girls exemplifies the implied social dysfunction wrought when white patriarchal power is transposed onto a white woman. The representation intimates too that the "exotic" Eastern environment intensifies her sexual pathology. One scene in particular brings together this signification. In shadowed light, we see nude bodies behind a thin curtain. Ms. Big lies on a bed with two girls, kissing one while the other massages her body. She dons a sheer, long black negligee when one of her male servants interrupts with information on Cleopatra. She treats him like a eunuch, ordering him to get her dressed, then standing naked in front of him before she puts it on, as if he is not there. In another scene, she brutally kills one of her young Asian girls; the close-up of the girl's tortured body further emphasizes the white female horror that Ms. Big personifies.

The racist sexual politics that define the film's contrasting female imagery culminate in the fantastical physical battle between Cleopatra and Ms. Big. As the casino walls begin to crash down around them, Cleopatra transforms her glittering evening dress outfit, taking off a long skirt wrap to reveal a chocolate cat suit. The skin-tight suit, glittering cap, and heavy eye shadow sharpen her already striking features and elongate her lithe body. Dobson is said to have done her own makeup for the film. Brody remarks that perhaps the heavy makeup and numerous costumes and roles signify the "minstrel origins of American film."[40] However, in the "baad bitch" fight finale, the harsh makeup, cartoonish costuming, and animalistic fight choreography result in a disturbing spectacle of black femininity that does not register as radical signification. Ms. Big appears with her hair covered for the first time with a black scarf—perhaps symbolizing the racial implications of the fight. She wears a loose-fitting black karate-pants outfit. Cleopatra, looking like a futuristic being out of a *Star Trek* episode or a mad panther, leaps across stairs and debris, her face contorted into grotesque grimaces. It becomes clear that Ms. Big is severely outmatched, fighting as she does in a stereotypical feminine manner, lunging clumsily, running and falling, and showing an ineptitude not in keeping with her formidable depiction throughout. The fight concludes, of course, with her bloody murder at the hands of Cleopatra.

The original film unsurprisingly proves the less hostile treatment of black female agency. Yet, both *Cleopatra Jones* and *Cleopatra Jones and the Casino of Gold* offer rather vicious treatments of lesbianism and white female power along with a distinct concern over the potential of white male feminization that goes beyond adherence to the requirement of the genre to offer a white enemy. The reliance on distinct archetypes of masculinities, lesbianism, and femininities illustrates a conservative response to the radical politics of the early 1970s. And yet, despite these troubling features, *Cleopatra Jones* is a pioneering black woman action narrative that avoids some typical features employed in tough woman representations in B-grade action films. The black heroine does not face any serious threat of rape or other violent degradation—signature features of female-centered exploitation flicks. It also avoids an overly pornographic treatment of Dobson.

The only other near competitor to Pam Grier's reigning supermama status, Tamara Dobson fell out of film-lead favor after the demise of the genre, when Hollywood no longer saw the economic benefit of even attempting to invest in films starring black women. During the writing of this book, it was difficult even to discover Dobson's whereabouts, an apt metaphor for her film career post-Cleopatra and for the neglect of her in black and feminist film criticism. In October 2006, the beautiful, luminous Tamara Dobson resurfaced on the public radar. At age fifty-nine, she died from complications of pneumonia and multiple sclerosis. Cleopatra Jones's creator, Max Julien, commented on Dobson's combination of beauty, skill, and screen presence and concluded quite rightly that Dobson had not been given her due in Hollywood. He blamed the blaxploitation label as the reason she had not been taken as "seriously" as she deserved. However, his additional comment more accurately alludes to the politics that did not allow her better opportunities in Hollywood: "If she had been a white girl doing the exact same thing, everyone would be talking about her today."[41]

I wrote in a tribute that her passing should provoke a genuine moment of reflection, consideration, and respect because the invisibility, neglect, and too-cursory glimpse of her role in black and American popular film history personified by the barely noticeable footnote of her passing provides a sad commentary on too many lost big-screen sisters. So shouts out for the most majestic kick-butt diva of all time.

5

Sexing the Supermama

Racial and Gender Power in Coffy *and* Foxy Brown

Women of the seventies had to be a lot of things. If there
wasn't a man around to do the things that had to be done,
she had to do them. I brought that into the films.

—Pam Grier in *BaadAsssss Cinema: A Bold Look
at 70s Blaxploitation Films*

Growing up, without fail, all the men who I ever heard talk about
Pam Grier did so reverently: "She so baad." They meant "baad" as in "fine"—
sexy and beautiful. It was that beauty and her on-screen persona of a sassy,
surviving black woman that earned the affection of my mother and aunts. I
have no recollection of my actually viewing *Foxy Brown* or *Coffy* in childhood,
but I was very aware of whom Grier was, and I'd certainly seen her on-screen.
Maybe I was half asleep in the backseat as my parents watched her films at the
drive-in, or maybe I glimpsed her while I was curled up on Mama's lap sleep-
ing while she watched *Foxy Brown* on a late-night movie showing or video.
I do know that I understood that the character of Foxy Brown was an icon
and that Grier had the adoration of folk like my uncles and aunts and me for
being an unquestioningly beautiful black woman who was a movie star.

My nostalgic sense of Grier's movie celebrity status clashed rather sharply
with the narratives that unfolded before me when I watched her two iconic
films as a young adult over a decade ago. Foxy Brown will forever define Pam
Grier's screen persona and will continue to stand as a baad supermama in
the popular cultural imagination, but *Coffy* and *Foxy Brown* are spectacles
with disturbing political implications.

In *Coffy,* Grier plays a nurse on a mission to avenge the drug addiction
of her baby sister, Lubelle. Coffy survives attempted rape and murder, finds

out her black politician boyfriend is in league with the drug dealers, kills the traitorous lover, and topples the drug lords. In *Foxy Brown,* Grier plays a woman involved with a noble black undercover agent, Dalton Ford, who is killed by Katherine and her lover, Steve, the white leaders of a drug and prostitution syndicate. Foxy's brother, Linc, a petty drug player, unwittingly sets Dalton's murder in motion and then gets murdered by Steve as well.

Coffy and *Foxy Brown* present the fantasy of a ghetto-smart black heroine who takes aggressive action against racist and sexist oppressors, yet her revenge is more about personal loss than liberation. She lacks legitimate resources of power. Her grit, sass, and skill at manipulating prescribed notions of sexualized racial femininities are weapons she utilizes, but it is "pussy power" that proves her ultimate resource. Patricia Hill Collins reads Grier, as I do, as having established a model of the "black bitch" with her 1970s roles.[1] In several movies, including *Coffy* and *Sheba Baby,* the protagonist is deemed a "bitch" in the negative sense of the word and usually by male figures. She uses the term herself to dis a bad white woman in *Foxy Brown.* However, she becomes a "baad bitch" when she takes on and defeats her enemies.[2] The contradictions underlining this particular vision of a tough black soul diva demonstrate the problems and limits of representing black female heroism through a racist, phallocentric perspective. *Coffy* and *Foxy Brown*'s offering of the "Godmother of them all," of a powerful black female potency, unfolds pornographic fantasies driven by an obsession with racial patriarchy.

In these two iconic films, the threat of female empowerment—of black and especially white women—is explicitly linked to a hierarchy of male power defined by the racial status quo. *Foxy Brown* and *Coffy* offer a series of sadistic acts of racial violence against the female protagonist as well as against black male characters. Castration and rape themes intertwine with the spectacle of masculinity, femininity, and lesbianism. These narratives also—like *Sweetback* and *The Spook*—manifest an obsession with male supremacy configured in terms of racial, sexual, and economic dominance, though as supermama films they might appear to be primarily concerned with woman's power.

In contrast to *Cleopatra Jones,* black female agency in *Coffy* and *Foxy Brown* is more heavily undercut by the configuration of the black heroine in what visual cultural theorist Mark Reid calls a "violent sensuality." The racialized misogyny that defines the spectacle of race, sexual, and gender power reinforces traditional hierarchies.[3] The filmic images of Grier throughout her early 1970s B-grade film roles personify historical, popular notions of black femininity that merged in the "new" image of the baad black, sexy supermama born out of the popular culture confiscation of Black Power and feminism.

The fantastical ghetto underworld provides a canvas for the eroticization of black femaleness through which competing masculine, racial, and gender hegemonies are acted out. The serious political aims that motivated the Black Power movement are rendered rather innocuous in films where racial oppression is conveyed through corrupt whites who represent economic and social power that black men pursue and/or are undone by, and against whom the black protagonist seeks revenge. The lingering masculinist image of the Black Power hero in revolt against white patriarchy that stirred the cultural imagination, though crucial background for the racialized plots and representations, is willfully refuted by the narratives of such films as *Coffy* and *Foxy Brown*.

Inventing the Ghetto Sex Goddess

The commercial success of *Cleopatra Jones* led to American International Picture's quick introduction of a tough black woman action heroine of its own. Founded in 1954 by James H. Nicholson and Samuel Z. Arkoff, AIP went on to build its reputation in the production of profitable cheap horror films, even launching the biker film genre. Larry Gordon, AIP's head of production, desired a "black woman revenge story."[4] Jack Hill, one of the major figures in the evolution of the 1970s exploitation genre, was commissioned to create a black female action character and film. Hill wrote and directed *Coffy* as a starring vehicle for Pam Grier, a young black actress who had been in some of his mentor-collaborator Roger Corman's B-grade films. The success of *Coffy* led to what was supposed to be its sequel but instead became *Foxy Brown*, which sealed Grier's reputation as the reigning queen of blaxploitation.[5]

Credited with depicting "strong women," probably because of his many sassy-mouthed, gun-wielding female characters, Hill helped to popularize the heavily racialized and sexualized 1970s exploitation genre. In his exploitation melodramas, Hill astutely utilized the contemporary political consciousness, situating the struggles of blacks, women, and third world revolutionaries as backdrop to his display of erotic phallic fantasy in films like *Big Doll House* (1970) and *The Big Bird Cage* (1971) (Grier appears in both). "If only I could get laid by a real man once in awhile, I think I could stand it here," bemoans one of the white women contained in the tropical island prison in *The Big Bird Cage*. Grier became AIP's and Hill's black cinema muse, helping to establish Grier's sex goddess screen imagery. His pornographic treatment of her and the gleeful trash quality of the films posits Grier as a black ghettocentric version of the white female Hollywood sex symbol model. But along the way, Grier began to offer some resistance to AIP's investment in this image of her.

In an interview with Nathaniel Thompson, Hill (unintentionally?) illuminates the difficulties facing Grier in the battle of control over her screen image in the early 1970s. Reflecting back, Hill shares that he thinks Grier wanted to be more like Tamara Dobson (Cleopatra Jones) and be "glamorous, wearing nice clothes," instead of being "down and funky the way I had her character played." That's what the audience preferred, Hill continues, and that's why her other 1970s films didn't do well, "because the writers didn't write scripts for her and didn't have a sense of her personality."[6] His comments reveal his allegiance to the ghetto sex goddess construct of Grier, while his interpretation of her fading 1970s career neglects several influencing factors.

In *What It Is . . . What It Was!*, Hill offers a rather contradictory perspective on his racialized treatment of Grier and the films *Coffy* and *Foxy Brown*. He notes that what he did in *Coffy* "was a little bit racist from the Black point of view," which, he shares, he did "deliberately" to try to take a look from the other side.[7] However, according to his observations about black spectators whom he watched viewing the film, *Coffy* received enthusiastic responses. The audience got into it, Hill states, "So is it racism? I plead guilty if it is. So what? It's a good yarn." *Foxy Brown* was supposedly somewhat of a "desperation project" foisted upon him by AIP. Hill says that he threw everything into the script in large part to "spite the company." The company had little "respect" for the black audience and didn't comprehend black movies. They were interested in action only rather than substance. He put in ideas that he thought the company would reject, like the presentation of the white man's castrated penis to his lover at the end of the movie. But AIP loved it, to his dismay, leaving a film with little "humanity" and a scene that he's "been ashamed of . . . ever since."[8] While Hill offers insight into the problematic politics of studio thinking about black-oriented subject matter, he also reveals his own contradictory investment in the particular racist and sexist representation of social identities in blaxploitation films. Though a text marked by a more melancholic complexity than the overtly caricatured *Foxy Brown*, *Coffy* includes the lynching of a black man and concludes with the bloody castration of another. *Foxy Brown* continues Hill's manipulation of the racial and sexual tropes that structure *Coffy* despite his interest in retaining some humanity, as suggested by his fight with the company over cutting some of the less action-oriented dramatic scenes.

Dorothy Dandridge's sex goddess imagery and its implications, discussed by cultural critic Marguerite H. Rippy, share some parallels with Grier's sexual persona in the blaxploitation era. Rippy calls the sex goddess role one "produced by the female body, but elicited by a particular model of heterosexual male desire."[9] The exhibition of women's sexual bodies so central to *Coffy, Foxy Brown,* and other such 1970s exploitation films were enabled by the general relaxation of traditional Hollywood restrictions regarding violence, sexual content, and profane language. However, in the case of Grier, this exhibition is deeply tied to Hill's and AIP's insistence on depicting black female resistance and empowerment primarily through the pornographic treatment of their star, a tendency that the prostitute guise motif in both films dramatizes. The films perpetuate the historical white supremacist construct of black women as "sluts" and "prostitutes" who are "objects of open sexual lust."[10] Camera shots throughout, including those of the male gazes directed at Grier within the films, reveal the objectification of her "black" sexualized body.

In a much more overt way than in *Cleopatra Jones,* the treatment of Grier points to Laura Mulvey's theory of the "to-be-looked-at-ness" that the female presence has historically presented in patriarchal cinema. Here, though, Grier's raced black and gendered female body is subject to the voyeuristic, controlling gaze of the filmmakers and the masculine gaze within the film.[11] Her baad woman characters are inscribed with a hypervisible black female sexuality, a trait strongly linked to her power to act. While they lack legitimate phallic power or male supremacy, Grier's Coffy and Foxy Brown possess an excess of black female sexual power.

The camera exoticizes the heroine with the overfocus on Grier's breasts. Like the butt, which scholar Sander Gilman and others have discussed, the bared breast too plays a role in historical notions of black female sexual excess and deviance. Gilman remarks that the breasts have long functioned as a "sexual sign of physical maturity."[12] In the racist-sexist perspective of nineteenth-century European observers, the unabashedly bared breasts of some African women signaled their sexual accessibility.[13] In her book *Nature's Body,* historian Londa Schiebinger notes that European naturalists frequently "exaggerated the length of African women's breasts." In the male European mind, she continues, the breasts of women of African descent took on "truly mythic portions."[14] While the European ideal breast was firm and spherical, the breasts of women of African descent were portrayed as overly large, pendulous, and often sagging and were taken to be signs of their licentiousness. In turn, this type of breast, identified with primitives, also became a sign denoting lower class. Side-angle shots and close-ups of Grier's breasts constantly emphasize their voluptuousness and convey the contrast between her and the other smaller breasted, primarily white prostitutes.

In the representation of Grier, the stereotypical iconography mixes the primitive African image popular in nineteenth-century European literature and the U.S. mythology of sexually wild black female slaves now evolved into the twentieth-century "sexpot" or "hot mama" image of black femininity. Accordingly, the *Coffy* advertisement—posters and newspaper ads—suggestively declared, "Now meet the Godmother of them all . . . Coffy . . . and she'll *cream you!*" The marketing for *Coffy* and *Foxy Brown* featured large body illustrations of Grier, her breasts overflowing out of tiny bikini tops or tight dresses, her lower half clad in form-fitting pants, against the backdrop of her in a variety of violent, erotic poses.

The soundtracks to the films played up the racialized eroticism that defined the representation of black femaleness in *Coffy* and *Foxy Brown* as well. While the *Foxy Brown* album cover offered a close-up shot of Grier's face framed by a large Afro, *Coffy's* soundtrack cover is a colorful cartoon with Grier overflowing out of a hot pink, midriff-baring bra top and low-cut, tight bell-bottoms. The illustration is set against an equally bright background of renditions of the film's scenes, including an eye-catching drawing of Coffy fairly bulging out of her top as Mystique, her prostitute alter ego. The two albums' many sexually explicit song titles, like most blaxploitation soundtracks, provide social commentary but also prominently emphasize the sexualized characterization of the main character. Roy Ayers produced the *Coffy* soundtrack, which offered such tracks as "Coffy Is the Color," "Exotic Dance," and "Making Love." Willie Hutch, the producer of the *Mack* soundtrack, produced the soundtrack for *Foxy Brown*, offering an even more phallocentric and sexually graphic body of songs, including "Give Me Some of That" and "You Sure Know How to Love Your Man."

Scenes in both films illuminate the fetishistic treatment of Grier's sexual body via her breasts. In one telling scene from *Coffy*, for example, the spectacle of sexualized femininity is framed quite overtly through the eyes of male spectators,[15] as jealousy over the attention that the new prostitute "Mystique" receives motivates a battle among the prostitutes. Hill exploits the idea of female sexual competition between "visibly" different racial groups of women. A series of fast, short shots capture the prostitutes' breasts popping out from their dresses to the amused stares of the male onlookers. Coffy's main prostitute nemesis gets slashed by the razors cleverly hidden in Coffy's wig. Coffy whips the other women over her shoulder, then body-slams them and snatches the dresses from their bodies to the pleasure of Vitroni, the Italian head of the drug cartel, who declares, "I've got to have her. She's like a wild animal."

The opening shots of Grier during the credit roll at the beginning of *Foxy Brown* likewise exemplify the erotic treatment of her body and subsequently the aggressive voyeurism that underscores the film. Against a shifting colored backdrop, Grier dances around provocatively, posing in a variety of sexy outfits. In one particularly long sequence, the camera moves in to present a close-up of Grier in skimpy black bra and panties, next zooming to the center of her breasts, cutting her face off. She then poses in different stances wearing the various sexy outfits worn throughout the movie, including a tight red jumpsuit and her tough woman gear—big Afro and black leather pantsuit.

After the credit roll, Foxy's brother, Linc (Antonio Fargas), calls his sister for help. The camera cuts to Foxy, lying in bed. As she rises, clad in an or-ange negligee, the camera closes in, moving slowly from the bottom to the top of her body as she puts on a bra. It lingers on her breasts, which, again, overflow out of the bra. The eroticism linked to her being an atypical sexy and feminine tough figure is underlined when she sticks a small gun in one of the bra cups. The juxtaposition of her sexual femininity and the phallic or masculine symbol, the gun, highlights the sexual framing of Grier's body. Her difference from the muscular tough guy cinema image is thus emphasized; we are reminded that this is a tough feminine woman with dangerous curves who has heterosexual appeal.

Jacinda Read makes the relevant observation that rather than being mas-culinized, the avenging woman is very often eroticized.[16] Such a common camera shot as the one described above serves too as a reminder of how dif-ferently male and female bodies are treated in popular Hollywood cinema. It continues to be more common for females to be captured on-screen through close-up partially nude or nude shots. I am not saying here that feminine sexiness automatically means that the film thus can pose no potential radical or feminist edge. In her examination of rape-revenge films, Read reminds us that sexiness should not always be interpreted as merely "antithetical" to feminism.[17] However, Hill's depiction of Grier goes beyond "sexiness," for the narrative hinges on a distinct oversexualization of the heroine.

Jezebel, Sapphire, and the Supermama Hero

Since the racial and sexual difference or Otherness inscribed in Grier is so central in *Coffy* and *Foxy Brown,* the strategies that make this difference visible are crucial. The characters' names, for example, serve as one of these mechanisms. "Coffy," "Foxy Brown," and the prostitute names point to the racialized and sexual coding defining the representation of the protagonists. For example, "Coffy," metaphorically invoking black coffee, underlines the protagonist's race and the eroticization associated with it. The repeating hook of one of the songs from the soundtrack, "Coffy Is the Color," indicates the connection: "Coffy is the color of your skin." Another song, "Coffy Baby," more blatantly signals the racial sexualization of the character: "Coffy, baby, sweet as a chocolate bar . . . / You're one of nature's kin."[18] Coffy's prostitute name, Mystique, heightens the inference of sexual mystery and danger associated with the ethnicity of the character.

"Foxy Brown," coined by the sales department of AIP, according to Hill, signifies the "brown sugar" construct of Grier/Foxy and communicates a racially inscribed heterosexual appeal.[19] "Foxy" has roots in the popular urban vernacular words of the period. It was a popular adjective that might be applied by men to refer to a physically attractive or "fine" woman. "Foxy" also plays on the literal dictionary connotation and social concept of "fox," implying sly or cunning, hence suggesting her position as the heroine who will outfox her enemies. Together the two terms help to create the erotic allure of the character personified in Grier's racial sexual imagery. AIP capitalized on the sexual-racial connotation of the name in advertisements for the movie. For example, one trailer declared: "She's brown sugar and spice and if you don't watch it, she'll put you on ice."

The danger linked with the sexual imagery of the black protagonist suggests popular myths of the dangerous woman who provokes castration anxiety. The femme fatale, the dangerous sexual woman, aligns with the white supremacist myth of the excessively sexual black female bitch. In *Femmes Fatales,* Mary Ann Doane explains that the femme fatale image indicates multiple fears connected to primal drives. She writes that this figure is "situated as evil and is frequently punished or killed. Her textual eradication involves a desperate reassertion of control on the part of the threatened male subject."[20] Doane's description, though, does not account for the implications of race so central to the characterization of Grier's dangerous women. Black female representation in *Coffy* and *Foxy Brown* hinges on the racialized spectacle of the femme fatale imagery.

Here, the fatal inscription encompasses tropes that have historically been specifically associated with black femininity. The black jezebel stands as a threat to the supremacy of traditional social institutions and patriarchal hierarchies. Her primal emotive and sexual energy even poses a threat to her own self. Her image embodies, Lisa Anderson describes, "the black widow spider that kills the male when she has finished mating with him, or the *vagina dentata.*"[21]

In Grier's three major 1973–74 films, she plays graphically sexualized protagonists who utilize sex or "pussy power" through taking on the more sexualized identity of the whore in order to get close to her enemies and destroy them. Thus, Foxy and Coffy's creator manipulates what Collins has called the "controlling images" of black womanhood that support the notion of deviant sexuality associated with it.[22] The scientifically embedded association of black femaleness with prostitution is implicit in this notion of black female sexual deviance.[23] The jezebel, Collins details, emerged in slavery and functioned to position black women in "the category of sexually aggressive women" to justify "the widespread sexual assaults by white men typically reported by Black slave women."[24]

Gilman unpacks the historical roots of this phenomenon in the historical European construction of black women as the prevailing "icon of black sexuality."[25] The tropes of deviant, abnormal sexuality that nineteenth-century European naturalists and explorers projected onto the African female body became embodied in the now well-known construction of Saartje Baartman (Sarah Bartmann), the "Hottentot Venus," as the quintessential nineteenth-century sign of black female sexuality. In *Coffy* and *Foxy Brown*, Grier's body functions as a narrow image of ghettoized black female sexuality.

One of the defining traits of the jezebel's sexual aggression is its designation as both amoral and dangerous. In the wake of her wrath, she undermines the power of both black and white male and female enemies who are drawn by her sexual allure and crushed.[26] The jezebel intersects with the Sapphire image—the bitchy and deceptive black female. This dual imagery reverberates in the presentation of a black woman virago who temporarily disturbs the supposedly fixed boundaries of the gender and racial hierarchy through her most potent weapon—her sexual body. Feminist film analyst Jane Gaines calls attention to how the sexualized black female figure signifies a particular threatening presence: "If, as feminists have argued, women's sexuality evokes an unconscious terror in men, then black women's sexuality represents a special threat to white patriarchy; the possibility of its eruption stands for the aspirations of the Black race as a whole."[27]

In a 1997 interview, Grier remembers the early 1970s as "a time of sexual revolution." She asserts that her roles showed the changing racial and sexual politics: "We redefined sexuality for America. Suddenly it was acceptable to desire a black lady."[28] Grier expresses a more critical view in a 1975 interview; here, she critiques her "black sex goddess" image in films that AIP favored. AIP, she continues, thought *Coffy* too strong and serious. They cut it up, "taking out the most important parts," so that all you see is "bang, bang, bang, shoot 'em up tits and ass, bang, bang, bang, shoot 'em up tits and ass." AIP's policy, Grier continues, was to "give the niggers shit."[29]

Racial-Sexual Politics and the Prostitute "Masquerade"

In the "baad bitch" representation forged through the appropriation of the Sapphire-jezebel mythology in the Grier films, we are made aware that the heroine slides into playing the whore as a way of gaining access to her enemies. The conscious wearing of the particular mask of the whore in order to thwart white and male dominance might be read as a radical element, given its motivation.[30] However, such a possibility is undercut by the treatment of Grier, whom the film blatantly positions as a pornographic object even outside the prostitute role performance.

The disguise distinguishes Grier from other racialized female bodies, especially white women, and is the primary mechanism for an action plot shaped by the visibility of gender and racial hierarchies. The recurring use of the prostitute disguise as the mode of depicting black female empowerment raises questions that have been asked before in explorations of sexualized black female performers in the twentieth century. Can a filmic version of black female agency be adequately achieved if the prostitute trope is the dominant mechanism of projecting it? How much could Grier, in the role of a tough black woman figure controlled by the white male director and movie studio, subvert the conventional stereotypes of black femaleness as accessible, sexually promiscuous, and deviant? Do her performances of sexualized protagonists and within those as prostitutes perpetuate or disturb the traditional racial and gender hierarchy of power?

Though *Coffy* was created as a result of Warner Brothers' success with *Cleopatra Jones,* the approaches to the two film portrayals of black female empowerment could not differ more. Coffy is completely marginalized by white patriarchal institutional power; she is a working-class black woman, a nurse, who uses sex to infiltrate her enemies' power structure. Coffy has tried to save her beloved little sister from the demons of urban ghetto life—poverty, prostitution, drugs, and violence. This failed aspiration motivates her mission of revenge when her sister is derailed by drug addiction. In the second film, Hill gives no pretense that Foxy has any "real" occupation or job other than that of avenging angel. Both films problematically position "real" black femaleness in the one-dimensional portrayal of lower-class black females in the figures of the prostitute or hot mama.

Hill's fascination with such stereotypes and reliance on the prostitute plot device intimate the historical association of prostitution and sexual promiscuity with black women.[31] Furthermore, he perpetuates the construct of ghettocentric black femaleness that appeared in mainstream ghetto ethnographies intent on theorizing so-called black ghetto pathology. *Foxy Brown* and *Coffy* offer a pornographic vision of the black female body through a racist, patriarchal narrative structure. Calvin C. Hernton's observation about the racist white male idea of black females as "sluts" and "prostitutes" in his bestselling 1965 book *Sex and Racism in America* offers a relevant point here. He writes, "In the mind of the racist, the northern ghettos are viewed as jungles of smoldering black flesh against which the prejudiced white man can act out his lewd concept of the sex act."[32] The persistent construction of lower-class black femininity in the singular figure of the commodified sexual black woman reinforces the narrow filmic representation of lower-class black female identities within the 1970s blaxploitation/exploitation genres and within American popular culture in general.

The opening scene in *Coffy* sets up the whore motif and subsequently the prominent sexualization of Grier. Two black men, a club manager and an indebted drug dealer, discuss the off-camera Coffy. The manager argues that he already has all kind of "tail," even white tail. "She's real special," insists the other. They go out to the car and peer through the window at Coffy, reclining in a thigh-exposing dress. The two men drive off to an apartment with her. Coffy masterfully manipulates the club manager's lust and kills both men with a shotgun. As we see how the protagonist uses sexuality as a resource to achieve revenge, the film's phallocentric perspective is made clear. Coffy must continually navigate patriarchal power while in severe peril. The film is replete with phallic symbolism, most important the shotgun that Coffy uses. Furthermore, Coffy alternately feigns phallic adulation or is framed through her sexual adoration of her crooked boyfriend. When the club manager asks her, "Is one big enough for you, honey?," she replies, "Do I look like the kind of girl that one man is big enough for?"

After she learns that Vitroni, the drug kingpin, likes "foreign exotic" girls and freaky sex, Coffy disguises herself as the Jamaican prostitute Mystique. This role further projects the continued exoticization of black femaleness that characterizes the text's construction of Grier. As Mystique, Coffy has to first infiltrate the drug operation of black pimp King George, one of Vitroni's dealers. She actually has sex with him to get to Vitroni. Thus, Coffy gains access to the male targets of her revenge mission by dispassionately using sex and her heterosexual appeal. The order in which she attacks her targets parallels the level of their power, ending with the underworld white patriarch, Vitroni. Unbeknownst to Coffy, Vitroni is in partnership with her black lover, Howard, a city councilman and aspiring congressman, and a Latino man, the police commissioner. Vitroni, a white Italian, is strikingly small and soft, which, juxtaposed with the other men, visually implies a potentially degenerate white masculinity due to the threat of feminization and blackness and symbolized by his sadistic sexual appetite for exotic girls.

Interestingly, Coffy gains the information she needs about King George by playing tough guy and intimidating a drug-addicted white prostitute named Priscilla. Priscilla, a sickly, pale-looking woman in a white nightgown, turns male tricks in the place she shares with her lover, a black female butch. At first glance, the scene heightens the impression of the protagonist's toughness by utilizing a popular masculine tough-guy approach in film. Yet, the subtext indicates the racial and sexual politics. Coffy aggressively demands to know where King George, Priscilla's former pimp who maimed her, keeps his drug stash. At one point, she grabs a cowering Priscilla and threatens to cut her. Just then, Priscilla's black female lover arrives home and pauses, framed in the doorway. Her stereotypical overly masculine, butch appearance—tall, large muscular body and black leather biker uniform—immediately establishes a striking racialized, gendered contrast among the three women. Coffy's masculine stance instantly softens next to the more masculine appearance of the black female butch.

The lover flies into a jealous rage and goes after Coffy. Hill offers two linked spectacles here. First, the black-white lesbian relationship parodies the black male and white female relationship image prevalent within the genre, where a trashy white female is the prized sexual property in the black pimp figure's stable. It appears to ridicule the idea of this possession as a sign of black male racial and economic, patriarchal power. It also implies the degeneracy of a lower-class, commodified white female such as the prostitute, Priscilla. Second, the stereotypical black butch dually conjures up the figure of a lesbian identity inscribed with deviance and abnormal masculinity, rendered more so by the visualization of race. Together these images ridicule both black female and lesbian empowerment by recasting them as absurd attempts to emulate masculine and racial authority. In essence, this is another instance that race and gender representation resolves anxieties about the specter of black masculine and female empowerment.

Foxy Brown presents a more contradictory set of implications surrounding the protagonist's prostitute alter ego. Foxy puts on the excessive decor of sexualized femininity: makeup; bright-colored, skimpy, tight-fitting clothes; and the demeanor of the black sex kitten for hire, Misty Cotton. She presents herself as a seasoned professional whore when she addresses Katherine for the first time in a revealing yellow outfit while the white woman appreciatively assesses the capitalistic value of her sexual body. "Now Miss Katherine,"

Foxy declares, "let's cut all the bull. . . . I've come here for one reason only, this is where the money's at. . . . You tell me who you want done and I'll do the hell out of him if the price is right." In the next scene, wearing a tight, plunging red jumpsuit, Foxy catches the desiring gaze of the white henchmen, including Steve, Katherine's man. Right after, Katherine notices Steve staring at Foxy's breasts as she disrobes and changes into a baby blue dress for her first "assignment."

Hair and clothes play a critical role in creating the spectacle of female racial difference. In both *Coffy* and *Foxy,* when the protagonist takes on her prostitute disguise, she dresses in plunging sexy clothes that accentuate her feminine curves and skin color, and she wears a long black wig. Hair has been symbolically important in the historical racial politics shaping notions of black and white female beauty. The flowing hair exemplified by white women was one of the standards for white evaluations of female beauty.[33] Hairstyles signal the difference inscribed in the heroine. As Coffy and Foxy pretend submission to their enemies, the politicized cultural implications of hair must be downplayed.[34] Before Foxy goes on her mission of revenge, her outfits reflect a softer femininity. She wears subtly sexy pants and shirts. When she begins her revenge mission, the clothes shift dramatically as well.[35]

As a Black Power era–influenced heroine, Foxy wears a black leather pants outfit and sports a large Afro, hence conveying her transformation into a kick-ass black soul diva taking on the tough guy persona. In contrast, the flowing black wig that she wears when she dons the prostitute disguise distances her from the tough guy role and instead affirms her as a hot mama, a commodified sexual object. In the prostitute persona, the hair not only stands as a symbol of the "wildness" and "natural world sense associated with Eve in the Garden of Eden" but is also "synthetic and man-made, artificially constructed as is the sexualized image it is meant to invoke."[36]

Despite the ways the prostitute disguise perpetuates traditional racial and sexual notions, there is a shadowy hint of subversion. When Foxy appropriates the Misty Cotton disguise in order to infiltrate Steve and Katherine's drug and prostitution syndicate, she immediately begins to undermine the smooth maintenance of their underworld operation. Sent to a party at a hotel to entertain the white, middle-aged Judge Fenton, Foxy plays the wild black seductress to gain Fenton's sexual interest. Fenton is excited by the fantasy of illicit sexual danger in which he is at the sexual mercy of black female subordinates. Along with another black female prostitute, the light-skinned, fragile Claudia, Foxy manipulates Fenton into a vulnerable position, literally with his pants down, and begins to mock his sexual potency. "The charge, your honor," Foxy ridicules him, "is assault with a very undeadly weapon." She continues, "Talk about your blunt instruments."

The hotel scene bears witness to the text's preoccupation with imagining the horrific consequences of destabilized white patriarchal power. At first, Fenton is certain of his control over the women, who are merely erotic black female freaks to him. But his sense of control is shaken by their sexual humiliation of him, a turn that indicates the castration anxiety that permeates the text. In perhaps the most radical—but brief—moment in the film, the gaze is directed through the women and turned on the voyeuristic white paternal figure. Foxy and Claudia turn Fenton's presumption of class, racial, and gender power into a spectacle controlled by them. Having seduced him with their feigned phallic adoration, the women toss the terrified Fenton out into a hallway of the hotel with his (unseen) penis exposed and demand that he send in a "real man." His "manhood" is exhibited to the horrified, indignant gaze of several "proper" white ladies, who begin to beat him mercilessly. In the next scene, Katherine and Steve learn that their Judge Fenton has thrown the book at two of their henchmen as Foxy helps Claudia escape from them.

It would seem, then, that here at least Foxy's purposeful assumption of the prostitute guise works to her benefit, as well as to another oppressed black woman's. Doane's analysis of femininity as masquerade, a concept introduced by Joan Riviere, may relate here very well. Rather than a "reaction-formation" against woman's tranvestism, Doane writes of womanliness as a mask which can be "worn or removed."[37] She points to a key implication of this that may relate to Foxy's appropriation of the prostitute guise. "The very fact that we can speak of a woman 'using' her sex or 'using' her body for particular gains is highly significant—it is not that a man cannot use his body in this way, " Doane emphasizes, "but that he doesn't have to."[38] In the blaxploitation film cycle and mainstream action cinema, the male hero is a sexual figure but does not generally take on a sexual disguise as his primary way of gaining access to and power over his enemies. In contrast, Foxy can strike at her white enemies only by using her body and performing their notions of black female sexuality.

This element of the masquerade underscores its limited subversive potential. *Foxy Brown* imagines black femininity in terms of established notions of black female sexuality, linking the demonstration of the black woman's agency to sex. The other serious limitation of the whore disguise is that the protagonist does not retain control over the use of her sexual body. Hill cleverly offers the prerequisite revenge moments, where the protagonist appears to come out on top of her enemies. However, the racial and patriarchal relations defining the distribution of power present threat and danger for the protagonist, highlighting the limits of her control. Hence, Coffy is beaten and negotiates countless rape attempts. In *Foxy Brown*, the heroine appears more resilient and triumphant at the end than Coffy, but she is raped, beaten, and degraded along the path to "winning."

The Racial Phallus

"Mmmmph, mmmph, mmmph, dirty dogs . . . know they what'n right." The last time I watched *Coffy*, I was curled up on the couch, tucked in the warm arc of my mother's arm. I was home for the holidays and indulging in some late-night movie watching. To my surprised delight, I'd discovered that my stepfather had spotted *Coffy* and *Foxy Brown* on sale somewhere and brought them home to surprise my mother. He remembered her saying how much she liked Pam years ago, and they knew I was writing something about the films. So we ate popcorn and watched our girl Pam and talked back at the screen, Mama flipping from nostalgic pleasure to shocked discomfort as scenes unfolded that she hadn't seen in probably thirty years. "Now, they just dirty. I never liked the way they did her. All that mess ain't even necessary. . . . I don't know why they gotta do all that cussing either . . ." My mother shook her head, frowning as we watched Vitroni ordering Coffy to beg for his white body.

I know Mama's "they" didn't just mean the characters in the film abusing Coffy but also the "they" off-camera who were treating Pam Grier that way on-screen. The extreme racial eroticization of Grier culminates in misogynistic spectacles. The fantastical display of racial violence in *Coffy* and *Foxy Brown* supported AIP's penchant for horror, which has in common with pornography its foundation in sadism and voyeurism.[39] While the films bring to the fore shifting notions of racial, sexual, and gender identities, they exploit racial and sexual "horror" to produce the sensationalistic action on which the narratives turn. Similarly, as Anna Everett discusses in her study of race in several contemporary films, Jack Hill devised "narrative situations that rely on race to authorize their speaking the unspeakable, performing the prohibited, defiling the sacred, and generally transgressing most sanctioned codes of social conduct."[40]

The film marketing advertised heroic characters who get even against white and male enemies and at the same time promised to satisfy male desire because these characters are presented in overtly heterosexual terms. Yet, the heroine, like the black male characters, is punished for failing to remain in her conventional racial, sexual, and gendered place. Hence, the imagined threat posed by black female agency is contained because at the same time the director offers a heroine who assumes some agency, he also depicts the costs of her aggression against established racial and gender authority.

There are several key instances in *Coffy* where the heroine turns the tables on her male enemies and subjects them to angry violence. Vitroni's sexual interest in Mystique rises when she becomes his embodiment of the hot, wild black woman during the prostitute brawl. In one of the most disturbing scenes that follow, Vitroni enacts his fantasy of black female and white male relations. He orders Coffy to get on the floor where a "no-good nigger bitch" belongs. Coffy, playing along, falls to the floor and crawls, then begs, "Let me have your precious white body just once." He spits on her and calls her a black trash nigger. Suddenly, Coffy pulls out a gun and prepares to kill him. Then there is the countermove: Vitroni's men charge in and unarm her. They slap her around and then hold her hostage in a shed, thus reaffirming Vitroni's white supremacist patriarchal power.

Vitroni controls capital and thus everyone, including men of color, like King George and Howard, and women. That Vitroni can't even entertain the idea that Coffy acted on her own highlights the politics underlining this racial patriarchy. He demands to know what *man* sent her to kill him. Her answer leads to a plot twist that offers a disturbing depiction of black female–black male relations in the racial patriarchal status quo. Coffy seizes the opportunity to set up King George and says that he sent her to kill Vitroni. As a result, King George is roped by the neck and dragged from a car by Vitroni's white henchmen. His lynching takes place under the passive gaze of another black man, Studs, the henchmen's driver, who sits horrified between the two gleeful white men as they drag King George's body in a scene contradictorily tinged with the comedic effect of low-horror film.

The henchmen laugh, "This is the way we lynch niggers," and admonish Studs to be a good "boy." The mythology of the black woman as a castrator of men, black men in particular, hovers over such scenes. Though on the surface it is a plot twist that affords Coffy another opportunity to get at one of the dominating male drug dealers—the bad guys—it is significant that she is the one who facilitates the black man getting lynched. King George is guilty of exploiting women and the community, but he's merely a secondary patriarchal figure in the film's spectacle of racialized masculine power.

I've observed students watching these scenes in class. The more absurd or cheesy aspects of the film offer a means of viewing them with some distance.

At the same time, while students have often smirked in amusement at the now politically incorrect racial language and laughed at the fake dummy that stands in for King George's body as he is being dragged to death, they also shift uncomfortably at what they know is the underlying historical reality of racial terrors like lynching.

The relationship between Coffy and the other major black male character—her lover, Howard—further highlights the politics underscoring the positioning of black femininity against black masculinity. After Coffy's failed attempt to murder Vitroni, Howard is summoned as a possible suspect. Upon seeing the captured Coffy, Howard must declare his allegiance to Vitroni and their capitalist political goals over his love relationship with Coffy. Howard tells Vitroni that he has no genuine sense of loyalty to black collective political and economic interests and no involvement in attempting to kill Vitroni, as it would impede his own progress to attaining power and money.[41] In a final betrayal to black political collective unity and black women specifically, Howard completes the relegation of Coffy to expendable hot black pussy by asserting that she is merely "some broad that I fuck" whom they can take out and kill.

Even before this point, the relationship between Coffy and Howard merely reinforces the film's phallicization and racist sexual mythology. Like King George, Howard is portrayed primarily in relation to his corruption and insatiable sexual desire, playing on stereotypical notions of the oversexed black male; the sexual pleasure that Coffy affords Howard is the defining feature of their connection. This point is exhibited during an earlier penis-centered dialogue that has Coffy praising the potency of the aging Howard's "goody" and performing fellatio. Coffy's childhood sweetheart, good cop Carter, is the only other prominent black male character. Vitroni's henchmen brutalize the sensitive Carter and leave him physically and mentally damaged for his refusal to go along with his corrupt white police peers.

Similar to *Coffy*, *Foxy Brown* manifests Hill's narrative strategy of exploiting the features of the traditional racial and gender hierarchy against a frightening portrait of the new identities posed by 1970s radical politics. Black male figures ultimately lack true capitalist and patriarchal autonomy, for they do not win in the battle with white men. Foxy's lover, Dalton, whose murder by Katherine and Steve motivates her revenge mission, plays the noble black man who tried to work within the criminal justice system to bring down the syndicate. This gets scant attention in the overall narrative, for it is his role as black phallic motivation for Foxy that is most visible. While he loses his battle with the white outlaws, his few scenes serve to emphasize the racist sexism structuring the film.

We figuratively see Dalton's "penis" first when, in their initial scene together early in the film, Foxy visits him in the hospital. Dalton has survived a murder attempt by Steve and Katherine and undergoes plastic surgery in order to assume a new identity. The music shifts to slow, romantic lyrics as Foxy comes in and goes to the bed, where Dalton lies with his face hidden in bandages. She immediately bends her head and begins to perform fellatio. Dalton wakes, moaning. The camera moves to his upper body to show his reaction under the bandages. Dalton expresses doubt about whether he can stand the pleasure: "A little taste of honey isn't enough." Foxy tells him that he's going to get it after he's unwrapped. She expresses concern over his new face, and he reassures her that "the part" that counts is still just the same, to which Foxy replies, "I noticed." After commenting that it's been a long time, he suggests they just pull the curtain closed. He invites her to "come on up here"; they begin to have sex until a large black, bossy nurse interrupts them.

Here, Hill affects a minstrel scene that draws on the white supremacist obsession with the genitalia of black men and black femininity.[42] Sexualized notions of the latter become visible by the juxtaposition of the jezebel and mammy images. That the nurse is a large, dark-skinned woman with an overbearing maternal demeanor, meant obviously to invoke black matriarchal imagery, sharpens the contrast between her and the heterosexually feminine, lighter-skinned, "beautiful" Grier. The contrasting asexualization and sexualization defining the women's differing personas and Dalton's vulnerability in their presence becomes sharper when the nurse scolds Dalton like a naughty little boy: "We'll have none of that nonsense." She rolls her eyes in exaggerated fashion upon pulling the sheet and seeing his erect penis (not visible to the audience). "Clean the body, clean the mind," she says, scrubbing him ferociously as an amused Foxy looks on, "then a body Jesus'll find."

The connection between black male disempowerment and black female agency converges dramatically too in the depiction of Linc, Foxy's brother. Antonio Fargas, an icon of blaxploitation fantasy, plays the "castrated" black man who dreams of achieving social power. Constantly in need of his sister, a maternal figure, to rescue him, Linc keeps trying to gain an economic foothold in the criminal underworld as a numbers runner and drug dealer but constantly ends up on the wrong side of the mob. In one early scene, Linc speaks of the difficulties facing black men who attempt to rise amid the limits posed by a racist society. His speech rearticulates Walter Younger's expression of modern urban black lower-class male frustration in Lorraine Hansberry's *A Raisin in the Sun*: "Foxy, look, I'm a black man and I don't know how to sing and I don't know how to dance and I don't know how to preach to no congregation. I'm too small to be a football hero and I'm too ugly to be elected mayor. But I watch TV and I see all them people in all them fine homes they live in and all them nice cars they drive and I get all full of ambition. Now you tell me what I supposed to do with all this ambition I got?" Foxy's mothering of Linc and her scrappy persona highlight his phallic weakness. Clearly, as the sister who rescues her brother and demands he get his life together, their relationship emulates the pattern of early mainstream cinematic representations of the black Sambo figure being maligned by the matriarchal Sapphire. Linc accuses Foxy of standing in the way of his economic empowerment through the drug trade. He betrays another black man, Dalton, to try to achieve it.

After Linc facilitates Dalton's murder, Foxy transforms fully into avenging "baad bitch," signified by her black leather pants outfit. She bursts into Linc's apartment and shoots at her cowering brother until he tells her who had Dalton killed. Later, Linc is murdered too, like Dalton, the latter for his resistance and Linc for his aspirations. In a familiar Hill and blaxploitation plot twist, Linc has a lower-class white girlfriend who prefers see-through negligees. His murder scene tellingly begins with him "balling" the girlfriend, then being interrupted by Steve and one of his henchmen. They shoot Linc first and then slash the throat of the bare-breasted girl. The murders reinforce the film's racial and gender politics and, by extension, the containment of threatening images of black male empowerment through their violent erasure from the text.

The film's purposeful vision of black male disempowerment is heightened in the case of Claudia, the black prostitute and damsel in distress whom Foxy helps. In the scene before the Judge Fenton setup at the hotel, Claudia encounters her husband, who has brought their little boy to say good-bye to his mother. We learn that the domestic relationship has been destroyed by the master/slave structure of Claudia's entrapment in Katherine's stable. The husband, Willard, a big, angry black man, demands that Claudia come away with him and their son. Since Steve and Katherine "own" her, Claudia disobeys her husband, fearing for both of their lives. "What kind of world would it be if anybody could keep a woman away from her own man and child?" Willard demands to know, arguing that Claudia is his "rightful wife." But when Willard insists on taking "possession" of his wife and resists Steve's attempts to remove him from the property, he is brutally beaten by the white men. The beating, occurring as Katherine, Claudia, and Foxy look on, underscores the politics of the racial and gender hegemony displayed. We are reminded that black men are subordinate to white men and women.

"Put in Her Place": The Rape of Foxy Brown

The rape scene presents one of the most troubling moments in *Foxy Brown*. Whether Hill really attempted to signify on AIP or not with the *Foxy Brown* script, his manipulation of racial tropes to eroticize white supremacist violence against the black female body follows the patterns of his exploitation cinema work and the aesthetic tendencies of female revenge flicks and blaxploitation. The tough, sexy, avenging black woman personified in *Coffy* and *Foxy Brown* emerged during a period that the B-grade rape and revenge films appeared amid the second-wave feminism of the 1970s. Here, rape is envisioned as an act deserving of the most violent punishment. This kind of "female" exploitation cinema, the result of feminism's impact on popular culture, offered the "angry woman image" Carol J. Clover explains. Such an image, she describes, projected a woman "so angry that she can be imagined as a credible perpetrator of the kind of violence on which in the low-mythic universe, the status of full protagonist rests."[43]

In *Coffy* and *Foxy Brown*, rape takes on other significant connotations as a metaphor of racial power relations. The threat of rape is ever present in both films and occurs in *Foxy Brown*. This plot twist has several important implications as it figuratively reenacts the historic function of rape in slavery. Katherine orders Foxy to the "ranch," a metaphoric slave-breaking plantation where troublesome girls are sent. Foxy's punishment stems from her pretense of submission to white control and for daring to disturb Katherine and Steve's operation. In keeping with Hill's exploitation of white supremacist notions of black femininity, Katherine implies that Foxy's turn at the ranch with the redneck overseers will be a sexual pleasure for her rather than punishment. "You know what the boys would do with her," says Steve. "She'll probably love it," Katherine purrs.

The rape scene begins with the camera in blurred focus cutting to Foxy; the lens clears as she wakes, bruised and dirty. Her shirt is torn open, exposing her breasts; they appear fantastically large, bulging out of a tiny bra. Though obviously weak, Foxy tries to escape and makes it outside. Taking the slave narrative even further, one of the burly white men ropes Foxy around the neck as banjo music plays. He drags her across the ground and then ties her to the bedpost. Now, the narrative formula requires that she ultimately "win," since it is supposed to center on a black woman who beats her enemies, but not without a lot of degradation.

The rednecks taunt her, "You a lucky nigger." Foxy curses at them, provoking more abuse. They immediately put her back in her place by beating, drugging, and raping her again. Again, Grier's breasts are situated as prominent signs of a sexual Otherness that justifies misogyny. One of the men refers to her as a "big-jugged jigaboo." He rips off her bra and removes his shirt, coming nearer to Foxy as the shot fades out. The camera next fades in, offering a full-length body shot of Foxy tied up on the bed. It zooms in on her visibly more bruised breasts, now even less veiled by her ragged shirt, which falls away completely to reveal one bare breast.

In her book *Women, Race, and Class*, Angela Davis explains that in slavery, rape was an "uncamouflaged expression of the slaveholder's economic mastery and the overseer's control over Black women as workers" that also served to discourage black male supremacy.[44] "Slave owners encouraged the use of rape to put Black women in their place," Davis argues, effectively serving as well to "remind them of their essential and inalterable femaleness." She also notes the use of rape as a weapon against resistance and as a weapon of "domination" and "repression, whose covert goal was to extinguish slave women's will to resist."[45]

Foxy works a razor off the bedside table, gets free, and enacts her revenge. In keeping with the narrative strategy of punishing the heroine and then satisfying the requirement that she ultimately win against her white perpetrators, she manages to blow up the drugs and the rednecks. The blatant replay of slave-era social relations between black women and white men in grossly exaggerated language and action risks erasing the serious implications of the director's manipulation of this historic, terroristic treatment of black women. The politics implicit in such a scene may be further undercut by *Foxy Brown*'s categorization as cheap or low-grade cinema. It is worth raising questions about the motivations behind and reliance on such "action" and Grier's complicity and/or lack of control in the positioning of her body as such racial spectacle. The fantastical scene resolution—the immediate erasure of the rednecks—denies any physical or emotional signs of Foxy's ordeal. The narrative returns to Foxy's mission of avenging her man's murder without missing a beat, disavowing the historical reality that the rape scene manipulates.

The Politics of Castration

Like rape, the theme of castration hovers over racial and gender relations in both *Coffy* and *Foxy Brown*. The occurrence of castration in the latter marks the culmination of the intersecting play of politics. The castration horror reasserts the narratives' concern with imagining the consequences of white patriarchal authority being challenged by women's liberation and the masculine-imbued Black Power movement. The actual realization of castration also signifies on the masculinist poetics of political discourse that prominently featured the historical castration of black men by white men and utilized the metaphor of castration to verbalize the revolution against white supremacist patriarchy. Interestingly, the first film ends with the castration of a black man, while the second concludes with that of a white man.

At the end of *Coffy*, Grier's character escapes Vitroni's henchmen by once again confiscating the jezebel role. Coffy kills Vitroni and the Latino commissioner and goes in search of Howard, who has gone to his beach house for a sexual rendezvous. Coffy quietly enters with a shotgun in hand. Howard comes down the stairs in a robe; he sees Coffy sitting in a chair, pointing the shotgun at him. Coolly, he begins to appeal to her presumably feminine sexual weakness for him, telling her that she is his woman and that together they can achieve great power. Coffy appears vulnerable to his appeal; the camera focuses on the perceptible lowering of the shotgun.

Suddenly, a female voice interrupts. A very young blonde appears in a white negligee, framed in a bright light that emphasizes her pale blondeness. She stops at the top of the stairs, looking down on them in shocked horror. At the moment of her appearance, Coffy awakes from her half-yielding state and shoots. Howard's face turns grotesque as he crumbles, clutching his groin. The blonde shrieks as a dazed Coffy drops the gun, turns, and exits the house as the light darkens. The last image is a shot of Coffy in shadow walking along the beach. This last action scene visualizes the historical sociopolitical relations among the three. Since the narrative is supposed to offer the fantasy of black female power triumphing, we are intended no doubt to read Howard's castration by Coffy as retribution for his racial sexual betrayal of the black woman, signaled by his "fucking" a white woman and figuratively for "fucking over" Coffy.

The intertwining politics of the castration thematic cannot be fully understood outside its historical and contemporary racial and gender implications. There is a sharp contrast in the violent deaths of men in the film. The two major black figures are castrated and lynched. Coffy's role in their deaths externalizes Hill's use of the historical racial context of looking and sexual privileges, castration, and lynching and of tropes of black female bitchiness. Both Howard and King George aspire to the capitalistic patriarchal power represented by Vitroni. The white female body signals this aspiration, with the imagery of the black male sexual brute and black rapist myth hovering over the representation of the men. Tellingly, King George's lynching occurs in the scene after Meg, his blonde, number-one prostitute, begs him not to go and instead to stay with her so she can "service" him.

Howard's castration at the moment the white female appears luminously on the stairs above Coffy suggests that his downfall is due not to his corruption or betrayal of black political interests or even of his sacrifice of Coffy's life. Rather, Howard pays, as King George does, for his daring to aspire to white patriarchal power—a yearning visually signaled by his sexual confiscation of the white female body.[46] The film thus exploits a series of historically significant racial relationships to effect its sensationalistic action and at the same time to reaffirm threatened racial and gender ideas of power. The black woman's traditional place in racial patriarchy—on the bottom—parallels the position of the white woman, the black man, and the black woman in the final castration scene.

In *Foxy Brown,* the threat of castration hangs over the narrative before its realization in the depiction of Foxy and Katherine as "baad" women. Both are presented as threatening the supremacy of white patriarchy. Katherine is an emblem of white male authority misplaced, according to the film's depiction, onto a woman. Similar to Mommy in *Cleopatra Jones,* Katherine is thus conveyed as a threat to the supremacy of white patriarchy. More than Steve, Linc fears Katherine, who he tells Foxy is "the protection, the fixer."

While Katherine's sexual desire is "normal" (heterosexual), her status as a *female* paternal power head is mocked through her phallic adulation of Steve. Her hypersexual adoration of Steve reminds us that for all her phallic power, Katherine lacks a penis. The visual impression of her tall and thin body appearing almost boyish next to the curvy prostitutes and voluptuous Foxy suggests that she possesses a limited heterosexual appeal—a consequence of her emasculating patriarchal status. The camera offers short but key shots of Steve's desiring looks toward other women and his disinterest in Katherine.

She alternates between being the "baad bitch" whom everyone fears and the needy seductress, swooning over her lover. Katherine is as racially and sexually exploitative of other women, if not more so, than men as well as emasculating to white men. Tellingly, Foxy Brown refers to her as "Miss Pimp" and to Steve as her "faggot boyfriend." Katherine suggests the emasculating possibilities of white female empowerment like her film peers, Mommy and Ms. Big. Her adulation of the disdaining Steve is mocked by the camera's framing. In demonizing white female authority, the representation promotes the reassertion of traditional sexual roles.

In the last scene of the movie, the war between the two women concludes with Foxy's "victory" over Katherine symbolized by the literal castration of Steve. Such a scenario could merely be interpreted as the manifestation of black female triumph via white male castration. However, the peculiar dynamics involved here—Foxy's own phallic motivation and the black male's role in the castration—suggest otherwise. Foxy's motivation for going after Steve and Katherine—the loss of her man—actually perpetuates the dominant phallocentric focus operating in the text. When Foxy goes to the representative black male militant group for aid in bringing down Katherine and Steve's organization, her speech begins like a manifesto against white supremacist, capitalist exploitation and for black collective action as she speaks, surrounded by posters of black radicals on the walls. The end of her speech, however, repositions her with the other apolitical, individualistic blaxploitation male heroes, such as Shaft, yet at the same time distinguishes her traditionally female-oriented motive: "And most of all, I want justice for a good man. This man had love in his heart. And he died because he went out in his neighborhood to try to do what he thought was right." Thus, though the castration in part signifies on white supremacist–economic oppression and exploitation of black people, it does not adequately register as a signification on either the racialized sexual abuse that our sassy supermama endures or as a manifestation of awakening radical political consciousness. Instead, the narrative intimates that Foxy's revenge is not more for brothers like her own brother, Linc, or, in her words to the black militant group, in the name of justice "for all the other people whose lives are bought and sold so that a few big shots can climb up on their backs and laugh at the law and laugh at human decency" but for her lover, Dalton.

When Foxy brings Katherine Steve's penis and informs her that he's still alive, a shocked, distraught Katherine wishes herself dead. The loss of the physical manifestation of his sexual masculine power, his penis, signals a debilitating loss for her, as her own phallic identity now seems to be shattered with Steve's manhood. Foxy's last lines underscore this loss: "Death is too easy for you, bitch; I want you to suffer" *like I've been made to suffer.* Katherine crumbles before Foxy's cold glare.

Steve's castration, though a seductive strategy in a black hero–white enemy blaxploitation fantasy, is less a matter of black female triumph and more a manifestation of white male castration anxiety safely enacted in filmic fantasy. Consider the orchestration of the castration. The black male militants actually perform it as Foxy Brown approves it and looks on. The castration of the dominant white male by the black male militants enacts the mainstream perceived aim of Black Power politics—the subordination of white men and the destruction of white male economic, political, and social supremacy.

SEXING THE SUPERMAMA · 131

We must remember the fear that the Black Power macho image provoked in mainstream America's imagination by 1970 as well as how sexualized racial metaphors have been used in cultural productions to articulate the perceived dangers posed by black masculinity. In addition, public imagery of Black Power presented by black men affirmed an assertive black masculinity in violent revolution against white patriarchy. It was the macho Black Power revolutionists with their ideology of armed self-defense, guerrilla warfare, and societal transformation that came to signify in the popular white imagination perhaps the scariest threat to white supremacist patriarchal power.[47] The fantastical, grotesque portrayal of black power heroism that came to dominate the Hollywood studio–supported blaxploitation films resolves the feared destabilization of traditional boundaries of racial patriarchal power. Ultimately, the white patriarchal orientation that drives the supermama narratives engage the shifting racial, sexual, and gender politics without unsettling the conventional mythology of white phallic authority.

The politics that shaped *Coffy* and *Foxy Brown* were reflected in Grier's off-screen struggle with her white male film handlers. "My movies," Grier tells Jamaica Kincaid in a 1975 *Ms.* interview, "were the first they had done with a strong woman character, not to mention black." Grier notes her open criticism of their black film formula, the "cheesy way" they worked, and the money the company made through her films. While they wanted to keep doing more of the same type of films like *Coffy*, Grier was angry because she felt the goal should have been to make a better product the next time around.[48] In 1975, the last of Grier's roles associated with the blaxploitation genre appeared. These, however, reflected the move to elevate her screen persona through more middle-class or professional heroines. In *Sheba Baby*, Grier plays Sheba Payne, a private eye who returns home to help her father fight off the mob's efforts to take over his business. In the second, *Friday Foster*, Grier is a photographer who uncovers and thwarts a white supremacist plot to assassinate black leaders. Yet, though these films mark a departure from the overt pornographic objectification inscribing her previous roles, the texts still revolve around a distinct sexualization of the protagonist. Fortunately, Grier proved just as resilient as the shadow of her blaxploitation queen imagery.

Despite the difficulty in negotiating Hollywood politics, Grier exhibited a defiant attitude worthy of Foxy. By 1974, she formed a production company, Brown Sun Productions, after a pet named given to her by her grandmother. Her motive, she revealed in the 1975 *Ms.* interview, was to take control of and change the image of Pam Grier in films.[49] However, her opportunities for starring roles dwindled when Hollywood's love affair with the Foxy Brown–Shaft movie models died. Grier later went on to do other unmemorable movies and guest-starred on such 1990s sitcoms as *Martin,* never fully breaking the mold of her popular film image. Ironically, her late major career breakthrough, *Jackie Brown,* borrows from her Foxy Brown fame. In 2004, Pam Grier emerged again, this time on television, with the premiere of the critically acclaimed Showtime series *The L Word.* Still, as a recent cognac ad featuring Grier in Foxy Brown Afro chic attests, she will forever remind us of our mad love for blaxploitation fantasy despite the politics, because in my mama's words, "at least she got they behind."

Superbaad for the
Twenty-First-Century Screen

Through spring and summer 2006, several occurrences dramatized the unique ways in which the social identities and bodies of black women can become spectacle in the public sphere and cultural imagination. Georgia Democratic representative Cynthia McKinney's response toward a Capitol Hill security officer who failed to recognize her gave way to her hair and appearance becoming far more newsworthy than her politics. It became such a hot topic indeed that even some black radio and news shows devoted air space to debating how she should wear her hair and evaluating whether or not her cornrowed hairstyle or straight hairdo made her look more attractive and appropriate for Capitol Hill.

During the same period, the Duke University scandal exploded. In late spring, a young black woman charged several members of the prestigious Duke men's lacrosse team of sexual assault. The case triggered a public frenzy as the social and physical identity of the young woman, a black single mother and student working as a stripper, became a spectacle in which class, race, sex, and gender dramatically converged. Historical and contemporary inscriptions of sexualized women, working-class black women in particular, were whipped to the fore as scholars, legal experts, spectators, and racially divided students and professors debated the authenticity of the woman's claims. The question of authenticity was intimately tied to the social legitimacy and moral caliber of the young woman herself versus that of the socially privileged young men. The public conversation disturbingly centered on the fact that she was a black woman working in a sexualized position designed to illicit the heterosexual gaze of men. This became even more clear as the case began to fall apart amid charges that the prosecutor had mishandled it.

At the same time as the Duke case continued to unfold, Janet Jackson's body became news again. This time it was not a source of scandal but rather celebration. With the infamous Super Bowl nipple flash seemingly all but forgotten, the media couldn't get enough of Jackson's newly svelte body. The late summer cover of iconic hip-hop magazine *Vibe* dramatized the distance between then and now but still centered the attention on Jackson's breasts. Janet, adorned by long tresses and a shell necklace, appears topless in a slinky bikini bottom. Her right arm shields her nipples from view, just covering the rest of her breasts, which peek out from under the arm. So Jackson was no longer at forty a "middle-aged" pop star shamefully offending the public with too much female nudity but rather the latest sex symbol and poster girl for how good forty could look. Jackson, her silent retreat from the media spotlight now over, half-jokingly declared that she wouldn't stop flaunting her body until she was at least eighty. Headline after headline proclaimed her miraculous weight loss. She was suddenly everywhere, usually in a midriff-baring ensemble that accentuated her full breasts and toned abs. Every interview with the pop diva focused on the big questions first: How many pounds had she really dropped, and how had she had done it? Jackson, prepping for the release of her upcoming fall album, smiled demurely and declared again and again that she didn't like to work out, but it was a necessity.

I thought a lot about these women in the late spring and summer of 2006 and tried to process the implications of their public presence. At the same time, I escaped to a lot of movies and was one of the many who flocked to check out several blockbuster action films. They were mostly sequels, two a part of the dynasty that is Marvel Comics. One of these, the third installment of the X-Men series, hit the screen in June. As I was a longtime fan of the comic book and television cartoon versions, there was no question that I'd be on the scene to bear witness to the third and supposedly final film in the series, *X-Men: The Last Stand*. I did so with a little trepidation. The first and second films had offered a disappointingly wimpy and minimal representation of the X-Men character I adored most, the African woman Ororo, known as Storm. This strikingly beautiful, dark, dignified, and wise fantasy sista is so powerful that she not only can sail effortlessly in the air but can whip up a mighty hurricane or blizzard in seconds.

The Storm that debuted in the first film in 2001 and later in the second did not do the character justice. Instead, the filmmakers settled for making this quietly commanding woman a pretty visual, first by casting the talented and beautiful but mistyped Halle Berry in an ill-conceived blonde wig and second by not even bothering to create either action or an underlining story that honored the significance and complexity of the character. I had heard

Berry say in an interview that her role was enlarged for the last film in the trilogy. Indeed it was, primarily because most of the other X-Men disappear early. The blonde wig was more attractive, but Storm still did not translate effectively from comic book page to screen.

After watching the long-awaited *Superman Returns* in June 2006, which hardly offers glimpses of black folk registering on Superman's radar or crossing the street in Metropolis, I excitedly took myself to see the much-hyped sequel *Pirates of the Caribbean: Dead Man's Chest*. Of course, it's a film replete with exhilarating visuals, stuff oozing out of the ghostly faces of the undead, and the hip-switching sway of Johnny Depp as funny, effeminate pirate Jack Sparrow. Yet, even with the spectacle of so many creepy bodies, there was also a physical place and a presence that personified primitive darkness, and it wasn't Jack's heart-empty enemy Davy Jones or Jones's many-legged, Swamp-Thing-like creature. Jack and friends venture into a "heart of darkness," if you will, complete with black night-of-the-living-dead figures swaying in the swamps and a dreadlocked soothsayer mistress of it, Tia Dalma (Naomie Harris). I immediately thought to myself, "Somebody's read his Joseph Conrad or caught it on display in the latest remake of *King Kong.*" What became clear to me as I watched these films is that as surreal and spectacular as the arena of action cinema remains, it is like popular movies by and large, a landscape that has trouble envisioning black femaleness.

Our cinematic imaginings are powerful. With movies, filmmakers attempt to represent reality—not that it *is*—or remake it, theorizing about how it could be and challenging what it is and shouldn't be. They create fantasies that surpass and exist beyond and in spite of physical, social, and political realities and boundaries. Action cinema especially has long been a genre that imagines heroes who surpass, challenge, push, break, or ignore social and physical boundaries. As a pivotal force, it is, as cultural critic Stuart Hall has eloquently described of popular culture, a profoundly mythic arena, "a theater of popular desires, a theater of popular fantasies." Here, we "discover and play with the identifications of ourselves, where we are imagined, where we are represented not only to the audiences out there who do not get the message, but to ourselves for the first time."[1] Sweetback and his predecessors manifest both this hope and the historical problem of stereotypical black cinema representation. Born as they were, out of the interplay of the black audience's demand for empowered black heroes in an identifiable cultural framework and Hollywood's recognition of the economic potential in commodifying this desire, they faded out of vogue with the end of Hollywood's economic need and the death of the political energy that fueled their birth.

The art and business of filmmaking remains, of course, a costly and political enterprise and a notoriously exclusive club. However, Internet-based cinema, the DVD movie explosion, cable television movie networks, and a slew of filmmaking software and camera equipment are making it a bit more accessible for a more diverse body of people to dare to act out their imagination on film and gain an audience. But new technology and access is not enough; there must also be alternative visions of the spectacle that is the body on screen.

I asked a group of young African American adult women, action film fans, what their ideal black woman action star would look like and be in the twenty-first century. The women, most of them students in their twenties attending the Art Institute of Atlanta, answered individually. Yet their responses were not very dissimilar and demonstrated their acute awareness of the lack of black women leads in major action movie releases as well as of the narrow representations of black femaleness imaged in popular film throughout the twentieth century. They did not articulate their disturbance with the screen imagery of black women with terms like "politics" or "racialized" or "patriarchal"; instead, they translated those terms eloquently in their assessment that the big screen failed to imagine black women characters "outside the box." Sadai, one of these bright, hopeful movie lovers, summed up the heart of this sentiment in lines from her original poem:

Urban. She knows the city
Dark brown skin. Curly carefree hair.
Thick hips. With full lips that speak her mind.
Natural appeal, the earthy kind, a poet
standing up for what some women lack
She doesn't need guns, knives, or a sexy suit
to get by. Mentally she's tough, her mind her
superpower. No fancy cars, capes, or wings . . .
just chucks on concrete . . . her mission is the
street. To the rescue of her forgotten black
race. . . . She puts empowerment in negativity's
place. No extensions, but extensive love. Not for
wealth, for a richer community and love for self
made to be heard not only seen.
more than a pretty face on a silver screen.
A real woman. A black woman like me.[2]

Notes

Introduction

1. Rhines, *Black Film/White Money*, 43.
2. Bogle, *Toms, Coons*, 251–52.
3. Yearwood, *Black Film*, 44.
4. Gaines, "White Privilege," 337.
5. hooks, *Critical Thinking*.
6. Willis, *High Contrast*, 1.
7. Ibid., 4.
8. Everett, "Other Pleasures," 281.
9. Reid, *Redefining Black Film*, 4.
10. Tasker, *Spectacular Bodies*, 8.
11. Ibid., 6.
12. Pough, *Check It While I Wreck It*, 20–21.
13. Hazel Carby quoted in L. Williams, *Playing the Race Card*, 4.
14. L. Williams, *Playing the Race Card*, 4.
15. Ibid., 6. Williams argues that the "old" melodrama of Toms, anti-Toms, and racial victims and villains as presented in *Uncle Tom's Cabin* and *Birth of a Nation*, for example, are made "new" in moral shifts and new media.
16. Ibid., 17.
17. Ibid., 19.
18. Ibid., 21.

Chapter 1: The Pleasure of Looking

1. Sloan, "Keeping the Black Woman," 31.
2. Kincaid, "Pam Grier," 52.

3. Grier quoted in Hobson, "Foxy as Ever," 5.

4. Guerrero, *Framing Blackness,* 98.

5. Sloan, "Keeping the Black Woman," 31.

6. Guerrero, *Framing Blackness,* 98.

7. Ibid., 99.

8. Mayne, "Paradoxes of Spectatorship," 158.

9. Ibid., 159.

10. Linda Williams references Judith Mayne here. See Williams, "Introduction," 14.

11. Diawara, "Spectatorship," 213, 215, 216, 219.

12. hooks, "Oppositional Gaze," 289, 291.

13. Ibid., 293, 294, 295.

14. Ibid., 299, 300.

15. Stewart, "Negroes Laughing at Themselves?," 665.

16. Ibid., 653, 661, 659.

17. Ibid., 665, 673.

18. Ibid., 661, 665.

19. Ibid., 665.

20. Tarantino appears in Isaac Julien's 2002 documentary *BaadAsssss Cinema.*

21. Mann appears in *Baadasss* (2004), directed by Mario Van Peebles.

22. In 2003, I went to see *Resurrection,* the powerful documentary about late rapper Tupac Shakur, at the most popular and rather exclusive shopping center in Columbus, Ohio, the Easton Town Center. My black male companion and I stood in line with groups of young, primarily black men, some of whom reached the entrance only to be turned away. We wondered about the reason—were they too young? They didn't appear to be. Was the little-enforced rule of no admittance without an adult if under a certain age being suddenly enforced? No, as we moved up, we discovered that the policy had been changed solely for the Tupac film; the required age had been raised and "children" younger than that age had to be accompanied by adults. In addition, there was no admittance for certain viewers without "proper" identification. The high school–aged young men in baggy pants and Tupac T-shirts in front of us looked around somewhat helplessly but resigned. One turned to my companion and me, imploring us with his eyes. We reached the ticket taker, and I told him that we were a party of four. The two young men thanked me, their eyes conveying more of their gratitude than they could express. We went in, but my pleasure had been dramatically curtailed by the disturbing implications of the difficulties that youthful black moviegoers faced in merely gaining entry to a public social space.

23. Pough, *Check It While I Wreck It,* 18.

24. hooks appears in *BaadAsssss Cinema.*

25. In *Black Noise,* Tricia Rose offers a helpful analysis of rap music and hip hop, calling them "cultural, political, and commercial forms" that are for a number of young people "primary cultural, sonic, and linguistic windows on the world." She

also explains that "hip hop . . . attempts to negotiate the experiences of marginalization, brutally truncated opportunity, and oppression within the cultural imperatives of African American and Caribbean history, identity, and community" (21).

26. For further history on hip hop, see Nelson George, *Hip Hop America,* and Alex Ogg with David Upshal, *The Hip Hop Years: A History of Rap.*

27. Rose, "Hip Hop Summit."

28. Some helpful discussions about the historical roots of the sexist/racist iconography of the black female are provided in Sander Gilman's *Difference and Pathology* and Londa Schiebinger's *Nature's Body.* Also see hooks, *Black Looks,* and Carby, *Reconstructing Womanhood.*

29. hooks, *Black Looks,* 65.

30. Collins, *Black Sexual Politics,* 123–24.

31. Ibid., 126.

32. Souljah, *Coldest Winter Ever,* 4.

33. See Morgan, *When Chickenheads Come Home to Roost.*

34. Here, Collins references a *Vibe* magazine article about Lil' Kim. Collins, *Black Sexual Politics,* 127.

35. Jones, "Lil' Kim."

36. Ibid.

37. This reading of rapper Foxy Brown presents a version of a discussion begun in Dunn, "Foxy Brown on My Mind."

38. Reggae artist Jennifer Hylton has also performed under the name Foxy Brown.

39. Rose, *Black Noise,* 36.

40. Pam Grier quoted in Martinez, Martinez, and Chavez, *What It Is,* 53.

41. See Burford and Farley, "Foxy's Dilemma," 76.

42. Gangsta rap or hardcore rap is a category of rap music noted for its graphic representation of anti-bourgeois black urban ghetto identity, profanity, and sexual obscenity. For further discussion, see Kitwana, *The Rap on Gangsta Rap.*

43. hooks, *Black Looks,* 69.

44. F. Brown, "I'll Be," *Ill Na Na.*

45. F. Brown, "Saddest Day," *Broken Silence.*

46. Ibid.

47. Burford and Farley, "Foxy's Dilemma," 136.

48. Ibid., 137.

49. F. Brown, "Ill Na Na," *Ill Na Na.*

50. F. Brown, "My Life," *Chyna Doll.*

51. Britton, "To Kim," 115.

Chapter 2: Black Power and the New Baad Cinema

1. Kathleen Cleaver appearing on *Black Power: Music of a Revolution.*

2. Carmichael, *Ready for Revolution,* 507.

3. See William Van DeBurg's discussion about the rally night in Greenwood, Mississippi, in *New Day*, 31–32.

4. Ibid., 41–42.

5. Ibid., 43.

6. Quote appears in the documentary *Black Panthers*.

7. Van Deburg, *New Day*, 159.

8. Ibid., 27.

9. Giddings, *When and Where I Enter*, 314.

10. Ibid., 316.

11. hooks, *Ain't I a Woman*, 96.

12. Ibid., 98–99.

13. Bederman, *Manliness and Civilization*, 2.

14. Ibid., 3.

15. Ibid., 4.

16. Golden, "My Brother," 20.

17. hooks charges that the public discourse of black men about sexuality "pointed the finger at white males and accused them of being pussies who were unable to get it up and keep it up." Some of the "hip" literature of the late 1960s and early 1970s by black men and white males such as Beat poet Jack Kerouac demonstrates this. See hooks, *We Real Cool*, 13, 77–78.

18. Kelley, *Freedom Dreams*, 136.

19. See, for example, Giddings's discussion of Angela Davis and Kathleen Cleaver in *When and Where I Enter*, 316–17. Also see Tracye A. Matthews's essay about the Black Panther Party, "No One Ever Asks What a Man's Role in the Revolution Is." She argues that the "gender ideology of the BPP, both as formally stated and as exemplified by organizational practice, was as critical to its daily functioning as was the Party's analysis of race and class dynamics" rather than "secondary" (231).

20. E. Cleaver, *Soul on Ice*, 66.

21. See hooks's comments on the sexist thinking personified in the rhetoric of such black men as Black Arts Movement artist Amiri Baraka in *Ain't I a Woman*, 95–96 and 106–7. See also Manning Marable's "Groundings with My Sisters" in which he critiques the patriarchal implications of the writing, work, and activities of black intellectuals, including Staples, Cleaver, Baraka, and Karenga, as well as some black women. Marable, *How Capitalism Underdeveloped Black America*, 98–99.

22. Kelley, "Riddle of the Zoot," 169.

23. Dyson, *I May Not Get There*, 106.

24. See, for example, Hernton, *Sex and Racism in America*.

25. Kelley, "Riddle of the Zoot," 170.

26. Collins, "Learning to Think for Ourselves," 59, 74, 76.

27. See Malcolm X, *Autobiography*, 7, 319.

28. Ibid., 93, 95.

29. Ibid., 92.

30. Ibid., 232.

31. Griffin, "'Ironies of the Saint,'" 215.

32. Ibid., 216, 222.

33. See Ossie Davis's eulogy of Malcolm X in *Eyes on the Prize: The Time Has Come (1964–1966) / Two Societies (1965–1968)*.

34. Ibid.

35. See Collins, "Learning to Think for Ourselves," 76.

36. In this interview with Bernice Bass, Malcolm supports the idea of mass education for men and women, saying that where women were discouraged from getting an education, their "incentive" is killed and then they in turn kill their children's incentive. The consequence of this is that *the man* will fail to "develop to his fullest potential" and the society is less progressive. See Malcolm X, *Last Speeches*, 98.

37. As quoted in Kelley, *Freedom Dreams*, 142.

38. hooks, *Ain't I a Woman*, 103.

39. Collins, *Black Feminist Thought*, 77.

40. E. Brown, *Taste of Power*, 363.

41. Lindsay, "Poem," 17.

42. Beale, "Double Jeopardy," 148.

43. Weathers, "Argument for Black Women's Liberation," 158–61.

44. Giovanni, "Woman Poem," 13.

45. See Baraka's critique of Spike Lee's *Malcolm X;* he argues that the film exemplifies "absolutizing the middle portion of Malcolm's life," positing his depiction of Malcolm's young life as a "memory in Detroit Red's life." Baraka, "Malcolm as Ideology," 18–19.

46. Guerrero identifies 1970–73 as the blaxploitation high period, which produced about ninety films, forty-seven of which, he offers, exemplify the blaxploitation formula. See Guerrero, *Framing Blackness*, 95.

47. Koven, *Blaxploitation Films*, 7, 8.

48. David Walker quoted in Martinez, Martinez, and Chavez, *What It Is*, 54.

49. See *BaadAsssss Cinema*.

50. Gloria Hendry quoted in Martinez, Martinez, and Chavez, *What It Is*, 108.

51. Guerrero, *Framing Blackness*, 94–95.

52. Rhines, *Black Film/White Money*, 45–46.

53. See Guerrero, *Framing Blackness*, 92.

54. Ibid., 79.

55. Reid, *Redefining Black Film*, 78.

56. Ibid., 79. According to Reid, during the period 1969–71, film consumers under thirty represented the largest bloc of the American moviegoing audience.

57. Rhines, *Black Film/White Money*, 44.

58. Ibid., 71.

59. See Guerrero's detailed account of the mixed reactions to *Sweetback* in *Framing Blackness*, 86–91.

60. See Yearwood, *Black Film*, 90.
61. Collins, *Black Feminist Thought*, 144.
62. Kelley, "Riddle of the Zoot," 170.
63. Wurtzel, *Bitch*, 4.

Chapter 3: What's Sex and Women Got to Do with It?

1. See Eldridge Cleaver's discussion of police brutality against blacks, "Domestic Law and International Order," in *Soul on Ice*. Cleaver calls the police the "armed guardians of the social order" who "protect the way of life for those in power" (134, 129).
2. Guerrero, *Framing Blackness*, 88.
3. In "From a Black Perspective," the Kuumba Workshop argues that *Sweetback* failed as revolutionary black art and in educating black people. As quoted in Reid, *Redefining Black Film*, 81–82.
4. Van Peebles, introductory comments to the VHS version of *Sweet Sweetback's Baadasssss Song*.
5. Bennett quoted in Guerrero, *Framing Blackness*, 90. See also Guerrero, *Framing Blackness*, 87–91. Guerrero refers to Lerone Bennett's condemnation of *Sweetback* as a film that romanticizes black poverty and whose main character "fucks his way to liberation" (Bennett quoted in Guerrero, 90). Bennett's critique is emblematic of that early criticism that rejected *Sweetback* as revolutionary. In contrast, Black Panther leader Huey Newton called the film the first truly revolutionary black film.
6. Reid, *Redefining Black Film*, 80.
7. Ibid., 82.
8. Neal, *Soul Babies*, 25.
9. Yearwood, *Black Film*, 192.
10. Van Peebles, *Making of "Sweet Sweetback's Baadasssss Song,"* 8–9.
11. Lawrence wrote *Women in Love* between 1916 and 1917, but the controversial novel was not published until 1920.
12. Lawrence, *Lady Chatterley's Lover*, 209.
13. W. E. B. Du Bois offered a scathing critique of McKay's novel for its valorization of the black lower class rather than middle-class culture.
14. McKay, *Banjo*, 283.
15. McKay, *Home to Harlem*, 34.
16. It is worth mentioning Gladstone Yearwood's valid point about the differing critical reaction to the "manhood initiation" in *Sweetback* and in the critically acclaimed Gordon Parks film *The Learning Tree*. In the latter, an adult female, Big Mabel, seduces the "dazed" young protagonist Newton Winger after she helps the boy, who has been lost in a storm. However, as Yearwood points out, the initiation in *The Learning Tree* has received very little of the critical commentary that has been directed toward the initiation scene in *Sweetback*. See Yearwood, *Black Film*, 191.

17. See Laura Mulvey's influential discussion of the patriarchal structure of classical Hollywood cinema in which, she argues, men are the active holders of the gaze and women the sexual objects of that gaze. Mulvey, "Visual Pleasure," 33.

18. Yearwood, *Black Film*, 192.

19. Ibid., 199.

20. Neal, *Soul Babies*, 27.

21. Van Peebles, *Making of "Sweet Sweetback's Baadasssss Song,"* 10.

22. Ibid., 14–15. Van Peebles explains that this strategy was meant to offset the boredom of "Brer." In his words, "One of the problems we must face squarely is that to attract the mass we have to produce work that not only instructs but entertains" (15).

23. See Murray, *To Find an Image*, 73. See also Guerrero, *Framing Blackness*, 86. Peebles also used $100,000 of his own money and $50,000 from Bill Cosby.

24. As Van Peebles explains in *Making of "Sweet Sweetback's Baadasssss Song,"* "The unions don't trouble themselves over smut films, that is, pornographic films . . . [so I] told everyone I was making a beaver film (Beaver is Californese for vagina)," 20.

25. See Murray's discussion of Van Peebles's fight with the MPAA in *To Find an Image*, 73–74.

26. Reid states that he doesn't consider *Sweetback* a "black independent film." See Reid, *Redefining Black Film*, 82.

27. Yearwood, *Black Film*, 215.

28. Canby, review of *The Spook Who Sat by the Door*.

29. *The Spook Who Sat by the Door* publicity material.

30. Acham, "Subverting," 118.

31. *The Spook Who Sat By the Door*, DVD, directed by Ivan Dixon, thirtieth anniversary edition (1973; Monarch Home Video, 2004).

32. Bates, "Interview with Sam Greenlee." During this interview commemorating the thirtieth anniversary of the film, Greenlee reveals that he endured U.S. government harassment for years following the making of *The Spook*.

33. Flowers, *African American Nationalist Literature*, 137.

34. Ibid., 140.

35. See Van DeBurg's comments about natural hair as an aesthetic and political signifier in *New Day*, 198.

36. Greenlee, *Spook*, 38–39.

37. In *BaadAsssss Cinema*, Guerrero remarks that "until about '72 and '73 there was a very militant energy that starts to get displaced into fashion, the display. The Afro was out, the floppy hats were in." This reflected the commodification of the Black Power fervor by Hollywood and the emerging shift, in Guerrero's words, from the "we civil rights generation" to the "me consumer generation."

Chapter 4: Race, Gender, and Sexual Power in *Cleopatra Jones*

1. According to Guerrero, *Cleopatra Jones* made $3.25 million and produced a successful soundtrack by J. J. Johnson that sold over a half million copies. Guerrero, *Framing Blackness*, 98.

2. "Actress Tamara Dobson."

3. Yearwood, *Black Film*, 44.

4. Bogle, *Toms, Coons*, 251.

5. Reid, *Redefining Black Film*, 87, 88.

6. See Bogle, *Toms, Coons*; and Yearwood, *Black Film*.

7. Jennifer DeVere Brody usefully addresses the film photos that accompany black male critics' reference to the film, including Reid's and Guerrero's. The selected visuals, Brody's analysis suggests, confirm the too-narrow dismissal of them as phallic figures. See Brody, "Returns of Cleopatra Jones," 96–97.

8. The Combahee River Collective began in 1974. The Boston chapter of the NBFO stressed the significance of women's liberation to "black and other Third World women" and communicated to the black liberation movement that liberation must extend beyond just one portion (men) of the race. It also stressed the "eradication" of homophobia and attention to lesbians in black feminism development. The Collective's manifesto "A Black Feminist Statement" declared that "the major systems of oppression are linked hence integrated analysis and practice is needed" (232–33).

9. Cook, "Border Crossings," xvi.

10. Mebane, "Brother Caring for Brother," 104–5. Cook echoes Mebane's point; she explains that some of these narratives addressed serious social problems such as "rape and unwanted pregnancy, performing a delicate balancing act between the demands of exploitation and politics." Cook, "Border Crossings," xvi.

11. Sloan, "Keeping the Black Woman," 30–31.

12. Brody, "Returns of Cleopatra Jones," 93.

13. Brody proposes that "black queer and/or lesbian readers might see in/as Cleo a representation of their own identities and desires." She argues that in order to consider Cleopatra as a black queer character, one must "see" her in a different perspective. Brody investigates this recovery of Cleopatra Jones in 1990s popular culture and offers these guiding questions: What can it mean that feminist and feminist lesbians have "revived" *Cleopatra Jones*? What do such readers take to be "familiar" about Cleo's character? And finally, how can they see her as a black queer figure? Brody, "Returns of Cleopatra Jones," 102–3.

14. Ibid., 101.

15. Johnson, "Theme from Cleopatra Jones," *Cleopatra Jones*.

16. Wallace, *Black Macho and The Myth of the Superwoman*, 107.

17. Royster, *Becoming Cleopatra*, 146.

18. Ibid., 147.

19. See Annette Kuhn's discussion of performance and gender identity, "Sexual

Disguise and Cinema," in *Power of the Image*. Kuhn notes the operation of clothes as "outward mark of difference" yet argues that as an identification signifier, clothes can also act as a disguise or "embody performance." This indicates that it is not a "fixed signifier of a fixed gender identity" (53). What I am suggesting, though, in *Cleopatra Jones* is that clothes are strategies used in the phallocentric framing of the film to "fix" the racial and gender identity of Cleopatra as a distinctly black and feminized masculine hero.

20. Ibid., 12.

21. Summers, *Black and Beautiful*, 3–5. Summers cites major reviews of the show, which applauded the "showmanship of the black models from America" (Bill Cunningham quoted in Summers, 4).

22. See Royster's excellent discussion in *Becoming Cleopatra*, 135–39.

23. In a review of the sequel, Vincent Canby, for example, refers to "Miss Dobson" as "one of nature's androgynous wonders." Canby, review of *Cleopatra Jones and the Casino of Gold*.

24. See Anderson, *Mammies No More*, 88.

25. See Kobena Mercer's discussion of the 1960s "Black Is Beautiful" relationship to the Afro's (and dreadlocks') function as a signifier of "self-valorization" or "aesthetic idealization" that had been formerly denied. Mercer, *Welcome to the Jungle*, 109.

26. Kelley, *Yo' Mama's Disfunktional!*, 27.

27. In *African American Women and Sexuality in the Cinema*, Norma Manatu reminds us of white men's idealization of the white female form—her virtue, white skin color, and "flowing hair" were marks of her feminine beauty (18).

28. Norton, "Cleopatra Jones 007," 3.

29. For discussion of the Black Panthers' revolutionary aims, see former Black Panther Elaine Brown's autobiography, *A Taste of Power*, and William L. Van DeBurg's *New Day in Babylon*, 138, 153–60. Van DeBurg outlines the Black Power agenda and the Black Nationalist emphases on black self-determination and social, political, and economic autonomy as exemplified by CORE under the direction of Roy Innis when Black Power infused the organization and the Black Panthers.

30. Film scholar Sharon Willis discusses the implications of African Americans as law enforcement representatives "in a system consistently under fire for the inequalities it perpetuates." Willis, *High Contrast*, 5–6.

31. Cook, "Border Crossings," xix.

32. Dyson, *I May Not Get There*, 106.

33. Reid, *Redefining Black Film*, 88.

34. Ibid.

35. Halberstam, *Female Masculinity*, 186.

36. Ibid., 177.

37. I believe that Brody's discussion about the differing sociopolitical period by 1975 is useful here. She argues that by 1975, when the sequel was released, the ideologies of Black Power and white feminism were being reshaped by the heightened

prominence of black feminism. By this late period of the blaxploitation era, she continues, instead of Cleopatra being more a "race woman" who works "against" white feminism, "cultural productions had to be more disavowing of feminism" due to its success. Brody, "Returns of Cleopatra Jones," 115.

38. Canby, review of *Cleopatra Jones and the Casino of Gold.*
39. See Mulvey, "Visual Pleasure."
40. Brody, "Returns of Cleopatra Jones," 106.
41. Julien is quoted in "Actress Tamara Dobson."

Chapter 5: Sexing the Supermama

1. Collins, *Black Sexual Politics,* 125.
2. Ibid., 124.
3. Reid, *Redefining Black Film,* 86–88.
4. By the early 1970s, the company was combining elements of its B-grade horror and comedic action genres in producing its own black-marketed vehicles to profit from the growing popularity of the blaxploitation film. See Jack Hill's commentary in Martinez, Martinez, and Chavez, *What It Is,* 141.
5. According to director Jack Hill, the sales department at AIP canceled plans for a sequel entitled *Burn, Coffy, Burn* at the last minute because it felt sequels weren't doing well. See Thompson, interview with Jack Hill, 6.
6. Ibid.
7. Hill quoted in Martinez, Martinez, and Chavez, *What It Is,* 136.
8. Ibid., 138, 139, 141.
9. Marguerite H. Rippy argues that the sex goddess image is "a partnership between actress and culture in which economic reward results from satisfying a cultural desire for images of sexual victimization." See Rippy, "Commodity, Tragedy, Desire," 181.
10. Hernton, *Sex and Racism in America,* 90.
11. Mulvey, "Visual Pleasure," 33.
12. Gilman, *Difference and Pathology,* 113.
13. Ibid., 114.
14. Schiebinger, *Nature's Body,* 163.
15. See, for example, Mulvey's discussion of the feminine treated as spectacle in "Visual Pleasure."
16. Read, *New Avengers,* 35.
17. Ibid., 52.
18. See Ayers's soundtrack to *Coffy.*
19. Hill quoted in Martinez, Martinez, and Chavez, *What It Is,* 139; Pieterse, *White on Black,* 178.
20. Doane, *Femmes Fatales,* 2.
21. Anderson, *Mammies No More,* 88.
22. Collins, *Black Feminist Thought,* 81.

23. See Gilman, *Difference and Pathology*, 85–89; and Schiebinger, *Nature's Body*, 160–65.

24. Collins, *Black Feminist Thought*, 81.

25. Gilman, *Difference and Pathology*, 83.

26. Anderson writes that the jezebel is "also envisioned as a destroyer of black men and manhood, which she accomplishes by pulling black men down from their 'proper' role as patriarch within the family." See Anderson, *Mammies No More*, 88.

27. Gaines, "White Privilege," 352.

28. Grier quoted in Hobson, "Foxy as Ever."

29. Grier quoted in Kincaid, "Pam Grier," 53.

30. bell hooks offers a relevant discussion of Tina Turner's wild, "hot" sexual woman imagery, projected in Ike's "pornographic fantasy of the wild sexual savage," as an example of the difficulties of black female appropriation of the racist iconography of black female sexuality. hooks, *Black Looks*, 61–67.

31. For a helpful discussion, see Gilman's analysis of the merger between the figure of the black woman and prostitution in the late nineteenth century in *Difference and Pathology*, 99.

32. Hernton, *Sex and Racism in America*, 90.

33. See Manatu, *African American Women*, 18–19.

34. hooks, *Black Looks*, 71.

35. In her book *Tough Girls*, Sherrie Inness points out that masculine clothing, such as a black leather biker's jacket, signifies toughness and "serves as a visual reminder that a woman has distanced herself from femininity" (25).

36. hooks, *Black Looks*, 70.

37. Doane, *Femmes Fatales*, 25.

38. Ibid., 26.

39. L. Williams, "Introduction," 16.

40. Everett, "Other Pleasures," 280.

41. It is worth noting here hooks' comment that representations of black males in white cultural productions "socialize" black males to view themselves as "always lacking, as always subordinated to more powerful white males whose approval they need to survive." See hooks, *Reel to Real*, 84.

42. See, for example, Franz Fanon's analysis of white obsession with black male genitalia and sexuality in *Black Skin, White Masks*.

43. Clover, "High and Low," 76–77. Mainstream feminist criticism regarding this cycle of films has largely ignored *Coffy* and *Foxy Brown* and by extension the politics of race in representations of rape revenge. Jacinda Read critiques Carol J. Clover's psychoanalytic model of the rape and revenge genre, arguing that Clover's work does not effectively address the impact of historical change on the cycle of rape and revenge films. Yet, in her intriguing work, she too fails to examine adequately the issue of race, discussing rape only within the confines of white female rape, briefly touching on the myth of the black male rapist, and omitting critical attention to the

black female rape victim historically and the few avenging black women film representations. See Read, *New Avengers,* 28–29.

44. Davis, *Women, Race, and Class,* 7.

45. Ibid., 23–24.

46. See Fanon's exploration of the mythology of black male genitalia and the function of lynching as "sexual revenge by the white man" in *Black Skin, White Masks,* 159.

47. For an insightful discussion of mainstream reactions to Black Nationalism and Black Power imagery in the 1960s and early 1970s, see Van DeBurg's *New Day,* 145–70; and also Kevin Powell, *Who's Gonna Take the Weight,* 97.

48. Kincaid, "Pam Grier," 53.

49. Ibid.

Afterword

1. Hall, "What Is This 'Black' in Black Popular Culture?," 132.

2. S. Williams, "Original Poem."

Works Cited

Acham, Christine. "Subverting the System: The Politics and Production of *The Spook Who Sat by the Door.*" *Screening Noir* 1 (2005): 113–25.

"Actress Tamara Dobson, Who Famously Played Cleopatra Jones, Dead at 59." *blackamericaweb.com*, October 5, 2006 <http://www.blackamericaweb.com/site.aspx/bawnews/dobson106>.

Anderson, Lisa. *Mammies No More: The Changing Image of Black Women on Stage and Screen.* Lanham: Rowman and Littlefield, 1997.

Angelou, Maya. *I Know Why the Caged Bird Sings.* New York: Random House, 1970.

Ayers, Roy. *Coffy.* Soundtrack. Motown, 1973.

Baadasssss. Directed by Mario Van Peebles. Sony Pictures, 2004.

BaadAsssss Cinema: A Bold Look at 70s Blaxploitation Films. Directed by Isaac Julien. Independent Film Channel, 2002.

Baraka, Amiri. "Malcolm as Ideology." In *Malcolm X in Our Own Image,* edited by Joe Wood, 18–35. New York: St. Martin's Press, 1992.

Bates, Karen Grigsby. "Interview with Sam Greenlee." *Day to Day.* National Public Radio. March 2, 2004.

Beale, Frances, "Double Jeopardy: To Be Black and Female." In *The Black Woman: An Anthology,* edited by Cade Bambara. New York: New American Library, 1970.

Beatty, Paul. *The White Boy Shuffle.* New York: Henry Holt, 1996.

Bederman, Gail. *Manliness and Civilization: A Cultural History of Gender and Race in the United States, 1880–1917.* Chicago: University of Chicago Press, 1995.

Bennett, Lerone, Jr. "The Emancipation Orgasm: Sweetback in Wonderland." *Ebony,* September 1971, 106–16.

Black, Louis. "New World Pioneer." Interview with Jack Hill. *Austin Chronicle,* March 15, 1999 <http:// www.auschron.com/issues/vol18/issue/28/screens.hill.tribute>.

Black Panthers. Directed by Agnès Varda. American Documentary Films, 1968.

Black Power: Music of a Revolution. Produced by Jonathan P. Fine. Shout! Factory, 2004.

Bobo, Jacqueline. *Black Women as Cultural Readers.* New York: Columbia University Press, 1995.

Bogle, Donald. *Toms, Coons, Mulattoes, Mammies, and Bucks: An Interpretive History of Blacks in American Films.* New York: Viking Press, 1973.

Britton, Akissi. "To Kim, with Love." *Essence,* October 2000, 115, 186.

Brody, Jennifer DeVere. "The Returns of Cleopatra Jones." *Signs* 25.1 (1999): 91–121.

Brown, Elaine. *A Taste of Power: A Black Woman's Story.* New York: Anchor Books, 1992.

Brown, Foxy. *Broken Silence.* Def Jam, 2001.

———. *Chyna Doll.* Def Jam, 1998.

———. *Ill Na Na.* Def Jam, 1996.

Burford, Michelle, and Christopher John Farley. "Foxy's Dilemma: Dignity or Dollars." *Essence,* August 1999, 72–76, 132–41.

Cameron, Sue. "Police Drama: Women are on the Case." *Ms.,* October 1974.

Canby, Vincent. Review of *Cleopatra Jones and the Casino of Gold,* directed by Charles Bail. *New York Times,* July 12, 1975.

———. Review of *The Spook Who Sat by the Door,* directed by Ivan Dixon. *New York Times,* September 21, 1973.

Carby, Hazel V. *Reconstructing Womanhood: The Emergence of the Afro-American Woman.* New York: Oxford University Press, 1987.

Carmichael, Stokely, and Charles Hamilton. *Black Power: The Politics of Liberation in America.* New York: Vintage Books, 1967.

Carmichael, Stokely, with Ekwueme Michael Thelwell. *Ready for Revolution: The Life and Struggles of Stokely Carmichael (Kwame Ture).* New York: Scribner, 2003.

Cleaver, Eldridge. *Soul on Ice.* New York: McGraw Hill, 1968.

Cleaver, Kathleen. "Interview with Asha Bandele." *Essence,* February 2004, 198.

Cleopatra Jones. Directed by Jack Starrett. Warner Brothers Studios, 1973.

Cleopatra Jones and the Casino of Gold. Directed by Charles Bail. Warner Brothers Studios, 1975.

Clover, Carol J. "High and Low: The Transformation of the Rape-Revenge Movie." In *Women and Film: A Sight and Sound Reader,* edited by Pam Cook and Philip Dodd, 77–84. Philadelphia: Temple University Press, 1993.

Coffy. Directed by Jack Hill. American International Pictures, 1973.

Collins, Patricia Hill. *Black Feminist Thought: Knowledge, Consciousness, and the Politics of Empowerment.* New York: Routledge, 1991.

———. *Black Sexual Politics: African Americans, Gender, and the New Racism.* New York: Routledge, 2004.

———. "Learning to Think for Ourselves: Malcolm X's Black Nationalism Reconsidered." In *Malcolm X in Our Own Image,* edited by Joe Wood, 59–85. New York: St. Martin's Press, 1992.

Combahee River Collective. "A Black Feminist Statement." In *Words of Fire: An Anthology of African-American Feminist Thought,* edited by Beverly Guy-Sheftall, 232–33. New York: New Press, 1995.

Cook, Pam. "Border Crossings: Women and Film in Context." In *Women and Film: A Sight and Sound Reader,* edited by Pam Cook and Philip Dodd, ix–xxiii. Philadelphia: Temple University Press, 1993.

Cripps, Thomas R. *Black Film as Genre.* Bloomington: Indiana University Press, 1978.

——. *Making Movies Black: The Hollywood Message Movie from World War II to the Civil Rights Era.* New York: Oxford University Press, 1993.

Davis, Angela. "Meditations on the Legacy of Malcolm X." In *Malcolm X in Our Own Image,* edited by Joe Wood, 36–47. New York: St. Martin's Press, 1992.

——. *Women, Race, and Class.* New York: Vintage Books, 1983.

Diawara, Manthia. "Spectatorship: Problems of Identification and Resistance." In *Black American Cinema,* edited by Manthia Diawara, 211–20. New York: Routledge, 1993.

Doane, Mary Ann. *Femmes Fatales: Feminism, Film Theory, Psychoanalysis.* New York: Routledge, 1991.

——. "Film and the Masquerade: Theorizing the Female Spectator." In *Issues in Feminist Film Criticism,* edited by Patricia Erens, 41–57. Bloomington: Indiana University Press, 1990.

Dunn, Stephane. "Foxy Brown on My Mind." In *Disco Divas: Women and Popular Culture in the 1970s,* edited by Sherrie Inness, 71–86. Philadelphia: University of Pennsylvania Press, 2003.

——. "The Primitive Speaks: The Politics of Race and Gender in Literary Modernism and the Modernist Imagination." Ph.D. diss., University of Notre Dame, 2000.

——. "Tamara Dobson: 'Cleopatra Jones' on My Mind." November 1, 2006 <www.newblackman.blogspot.com>.

Dyson, Michael Eric. *I May Not Get There with You.* New York: Free Press, 2000.

Everett, Anna. "The Other Pleasures: The Narrative Function of Race in the Cinema." In *Critical White Studies: Looking behind the Mirror,* edited by Richard Delgado and Jean Stefancic, 280–84. Philadelphia: Temple University Press, 1997.

Eyes on the Prize: The Time Has Come (1964–1966) / Two Societies (1965–1968). VHS. Directed by James A. DeVinney and Madison D. Lacy (*The Time Has Come*) and by Sheila Curran Bernard and Samuel D. Pollard (*Two Societies*). PBS Home Video, 1995.

Fanon, Franz. *Black Skin, White Masks.* New York: Grove Weidenfield, 1967.

Flowers, Sandra Hollin. *African American Nationalist Literature of the 1960s: Pens of Fire.* New York: Garland, 1996.

Foxy Brown. Director Jack Hill. American International Pictures, 1974.

Freeman, Jo. "The Bitch Manifesto." 1971. *CWLU Herstory.* June 2006 <http://www.uic.edu/orgs/cwluherstory>.

Gaines, Jane. "White Privilege and Looking Relations: Race and Gender in Feminist Film Theory." In *Feminism and Film,* edited by E. Ann Kaplan, 336–55. Oxford: Oxford University Press, 2000.

George, Nelson. *Hip Hop America.* New York: Viking Press, 1998.

Giddings, Paula. *When and Where I Enter: The Impact of Black Women on Race and Sex in America.* New York: Bantam Books, 1984.

Gilman, Sander. *Difference and Pathology.* Ithaca: Cornell University Press, 1985.

Giovanni, Nikki. "Woman Poem." In *The Black Woman,* edited by Toni Cade Bambara. New York: New American Library, 1970.

Golden, Thelma. "My Brother." In *Black Male: Representations of Masculinity in Contemporary American Art,* edited by Thelma Golden, 19–43. New York: Whitney Museum of American Art, 1994.

Greenlee, Sam. *The Spook Who Sat By the Door.* 1969. Reprint, Detroit: Wayne State University Press, 1990.

Griffin, Farah Jasmine. "Ironies of the Saint: Malcolm X, Black Women, and the Price of Protection." In *Sisters in the Struggle: African-American Women in the Civil Rights-Black Power Movement,* edited by Bettye Collier-Thomas and V. P. Franklin, 214–29. New York: New York University Press, 2001.

Guerrero, Ed. *Framing Blackness.* Philadelphia: Temple University Press, 1993.

Halberstam, Judith. *Female Masculinity.* Durham: Duke University Press, 1998.

Hall, Stuart. "What Is This 'Black' in Black Popular Culture?" In *Representing Blackness: Issues in Film and Video,* edited by Valerie Smith, 123–33. New Brunswick: Rutgers University Press, 1997.

Henry, Matthew. "He Is a Bad Mother*$%@." *Journal of Popular Film and Television* 30.2 (Summer 2002): 114–19.

Hernton, Calvin C. *Sex and Racism in America.* 1965; reprint, New York: Grove Press, 1988.

Hobson, Louis B. "Foxy as Ever." Interview with Pam Grier. *Calgary Sun,* December 21, 1997.

hooks, bell. *Ain't I a Woman: Black Women and Feminism.* Boston: South End Press, 1981.

———. *Black Looks: Race and Representation.* Boston: South End Press, 1992.

———. *Critical Thinking and Cultural Criticism.* VHS. Educational Foundation Media, 1997.

———. "Feminism Inside: Toward a Black Body Politic." In *Black Male: Representations of Masculinity in Contemporary American Art,* edited by Thelma Golden, 127–40. New York: Whitney Museum of American Art, 1994.

———. "The Oppositional Gaze: Black Female Spectators." In *Black American Cinema,* edited by Manthia Diawara, 288–302. New York: Routledge, 1993.

———. *Outlaw Culture: Resisting Representations.* New York: Routledge, 1994.

———. *Reel to Real: Race, Sex, and Class at the Movies.* New York: Routledge, 1996.

———. *We Real Cool: Black Men and Masculinity.* New York: Routledge, 2004.

———. *Yearning: Race, Gender, and Cultural Politics.* Boston: South End Press, 1990.

Hutch, Willie. *Foxy Brown.* Soundtrack. Motown, 1974.

Inness, Sherrie A. *Tough Girls: Women Warriors and Wonder Women in Popular Culture.* Philadelphia: University of Pennsylvania Press, 1999.

Jackson, Johnathan L., Jr. *Real Black: Adventures in Racial Sincerity.* Chicago: University of Chicago Press, 2005.

James, Darius. *That's Blaxploitation! Roots of the Baadasssss 'tude (Rated X by an All-Whyte Jury).* New York: St. Martin's Griffin, 1995.

Johnson, J. J. *Cleopatra Jones.* Soundtrack. Warner Brothers Music, 1973.

Jones, Steve. "Lil' Kim Clear on Big Plans." *USA Today,* June 30, 2000.

Kelley, Robin D. G. *Freedom Dreams: The Black Radical Imagination.* Boston: Beacon Press, 2002.

———. "The Riddle of the Zoot." In *Malcolm X in Our Own Image,* edited by Joe Wood, 155–82. New York: St. Martin's Press, 1992.

———. *Yo' Mama's Disfunktional! Fighting the Cultural Wars in Urban America.* Boston: Beacon Press, 1997.

Kincaid, Jamaica. "Pam Grier: The Mocha Mogul of Hollywood." *Ms.,* August 1975, 49–54.

Kitwana, Bukari. *The Rap on Gangsta Rap: Who Run It? Gangsta Rap and Visions of Black Violence.* Chicago: Third World Press, 1994.

Koven, Mikel J. *Blaxploitation Films.* Harpenden, Great Britain: Pocket Essentials, 2001.

Kuhn, Annette. *Power of the Image: Essays on Representations and Sexuality.* New York: Routledge, 1985.

———. *Women's Pictures: Feminism and the Cinema.* 2nd ed. New York: Verso, 1994.

Kuumba Workshop. *From a Black Perspective: A Searching and Critical Analysis of the Hit Film—Sweet Sweetback's Baadassss Song.* Chicago: Kuumba Workshop, 1978.

Lawrence, D. H. *Apropos to Lady Chatterley's Lover.* London: Mandrake Press, 1930.

———. *Lady Chatterley's Lover.* Garden City: Nelson Doubleday, 1928.

Leab, Daniel. *From Sambo to Superspade: The Black Experience in Motion Pictures.* Boston: Houghton Mifflin, 1975.

Lil' Kim. *Hardcore.* Atlantic, 1996.

———. *La Bella Mafia.* Atlantic, 2003.

Lindsay, Kay. "Poem." In *The Black Woman,* edited by Toni Cade Bambara. New York: New American Library, 1970.

Malcolm X. *The Autobiography of Malcolm X.* New York: Grove Press, 1965.

———. *Malcolm X: The Last Speeches.* Edited by Bruce Perry. New York: Pathfinder, 1989.

Manatu, Norma. *African American Women and Sexuality in the Cinema.* Jefferson: McFarland, 2003.

Mansbach, Adam. *Angry Black White Boy.* New York: Three Rivers Press, 2005.

Marable, Manning. *How Capitalism Underdeveloped Black America.* Boston: South End Press, 1983.

Martinez, Gerald, Diana Martinez, and Andres Chavez. *What It Is . . . What It Was! The Black Film Explosion of the '70s in Words and Pictures.* New York: Hyperion, 1998.

Massood, Paul J. *Black City Cinema: African American Urban Experiences in Film.* Philadelphia: Temple University Press, 2003.

Matthews, Trayce A. "No One Ever Asks What a Man's Role in the Revolution Is: Gender Politics and Leadership in the Black Panther Party, 1966–71." In *Sisters in the Struggle: African-American Women in the Civil Rights-Black Power Movement,* edited by Bettye Collier-Thomas and V. P. Franklin, 230–51. New York: New York University Press, 2001.

Mayne, Judith. "Paradoxes of Spectatorship." In *Viewing Positions: Ways of Seeing Film,* edited by Linda Williams, 155–83. New Brunswick: Rutgers University Press, 1994.

———. *The Woman at the Keyhole: Feminism and Women's Cinema.* Bloomington: Indiana University Press, 1990.

McKay, Claude. *Banjo.* New York: Harper, 1929.

———. *Home to Harlem.* 2nd ed. Boston: Northeastern University Press, 1987.

Mebane, Mary E. "Brother Caring for Brother." *New York Times Review,* Summer 1973, 104–5.

Mercer, Kobena, and Isaac Julien. "True Confessions." In *Black Male: Representations of Masculinity in Contemporary American Art,* edited by Thelma Golden, 193–99. New York: Whitney Museum of American Art, 1994.

———. *Welcome to the Jungle: New Positions in Black Cultural Studies.* New York: Routledge, 1994.

Morgan, Joan. *When Chickenheads Come Home to Roost: My Life as a Hip-Hop Feminist.* New York: Simon and Schuster, 1999.

Morrison, Toni. *Sula.* New York: Knopf, 1973.

Mulvey, Laura. "Afterthoughts on 'Visual Pleasure and Narrative Cinema' Inspired by King Vidor's *Duel in the Sun.*" In *Feminist Film Theory: A Classical Reader,* edited by Sue Thornton, 122–30. New York: New York University Press, 1999.

———. "Visual Pleasure and Narrative Cinema." In *Issues in Feminist Film Criticism,* edited by Patricia Erens, 28–40. Bloomington: Indiana University Press, 1990.

Murray, James P. *To Find an Image: Black Films from Uncle Tom to Superfly.* New York: Bobbs-Merrill, 1973.

Neal, Mark Anthony. *Soul Babies: Black Popular Culture and the Post-soul Aesthetic.* New York: Routledge, 2002.

Newton, Huey. *Revolutionary Suicide.* New York: Writers and Readers Publishing, 1995.

———. *To Die for the People.* New York: Random House, 1972.

Norton, Chris. "Cleopatra Jones 007: Blaxploitation, James Bond, and Reciprocal Co-option." *Images: A Journal of Popular Film and Culture,* July 1997 <http://imagesjournal.com/about.htm>.

Ogg, Alex, with David Upshal. *The Hip Hop Years: A History of Rap.* London: Channel 4 Books, 1999.

Pieterse, Jan Nederveen. *White on Black: Images of Africa and Blacks in Western Popular Culture.* New Haven: Yale University Press, 1992.

Pough, Gwendolyn D. *Check It While I Wreck It: Black Women, Hip Hop Culture, and the Public Sphere.* Boston: Northeastern University Press, 2004.

Powell, Kevin. *Who's Gonna Take the Weight? Manhood, Race, and Power.* New York: Three Rivers Press, 2003.

Read, Jacinda. *The New Avengers: Feminism, Femininity, and the Rape-Revenge Cycle.* Manchester: Manchester University Press, 2000.

Reid, Mark A. *Redefining Black Film.* Berkeley: University of California Press, 1993.

Rhines, Jesse Algernon. *Black Film/White Money.* New Brunswick: Rutgers University Press, 2000.

Rippy, Marguerite H. "Commodity, Tragedy, Desire: Female Sexuality and Blackness in the Iconography of Dorothy Dandridge." In *Classic Hollywood, Classic Whiteness,* edited by Daniel Bernardi, 178–209. Minneapolis: University of Minnesota Press, 2001.

Rose, Tricia. *Black Noise: Rap Music and Black Culture in Contemporary America.* Hanover: Wesleyan University Press, 1994.

———. "The Hip Hop Summit." *Crisis,* September 2001.

Royster, Francesca T. *Becoming Cleopatra: The Shifting Image of an Icon.* New York: Palgrave Macmillan, 2003.

Schiebinger, Londa. *Nature's Body: Gender in the Making of Modern Science:* Boston: Beacon Press, 1993.

Sloan, Margaret. "Keeping the Black Woman in Her Place." *Ms.,* January 1974, 30–31.

Souljah, Sister. *The Coldest Winter Ever.* New York: Pocket Books, 1999.

The Spook Who Sat by the Door. Directed by Ivan Dixon. United Artists, 1973.

Stewart, Jacqueline. "Negroes Laughing at Themselves? Black Spectatorship and the Performance of Urban Modernity." *Critical Inquiry* 29.4 (2003): 650–77.

Summers, Barbara. *Black and Beautiful: How Women of Color Changed the Fashion Industry* New York: HarperCollins, 2001.

Sweet Sweetback's Baadasssss Song. Directed by Melvin Van Peebles. Cinemation Industries, 1971. DVD distributed by Xenon Entertainment, 2003.

Tasker, Yvonne. *Spectacular Bodies: Gender, Genre and the Action Cinema*. London: Routledge, 1993.

Thompson, Nathaniel. Interview with Jack Hill. *Mondo Digital*. September 7, 2001 <http://www. mondo-digital.com/hilltalk.html>.

Van DeBurg, William L. *New Day in Babylon: The Black Power Movement and American Culture, 1965–1975*. Chicago: University of Chicago Press, 1992.

Van Peebles, Melvin. *The Making of "Sweet Sweetback's Baadasssss Song."* New York: Lancer Books, 1972.

Wallace, Michelle. *Black Macho and The Myth of the Superwoman*. London: Verso, 1990.

Weathers, Mary Ann. "An Argument for Black Women's Liberation as a Revolutionary Force." In *Words of Fire: An Anthology of African-American Feminist Thought*, edited by Beverly Guy-Sheftall, 158–61. New York: New Press, 1995.

Weems, Robert, Jr. *Desegregating the Dollar*. New York: New York University Press, 1998.

Williams, Linda. "Introduction." In *Viewing Positions: Ways of Seeing Film*, edited by Linda Williams, 1–22. New Brunswick: Rutgers University Press, 1994.

———. *Playing the Race Card: Melodramas of Black and White from Uncle Tom to O. J. Simpson*. Princeton: Princeton University Press, 2001.

Williams, Sadai. "Original Poem." Unpublished, 2006.

Willis, Sharon. *High Contrast: Race and Gender in Contemporary Hollywood Films*. Durham: Duke University Press, 1997.

Wurtzel, Elizabeth. *Bitch: In Praise of Difficult Women*. New York: Doubleday, 1998.

Yearwood, Gladstone. *Black Film as a Signifying Practice: Cinema, Narration, and the African American Aesthetic Tradition*. Trenton, N.J.: African World Press, 2000.

Index

Nation of Islam, 43
Nature's Body (Schiebinger), 111–12
NBFO (National Black Feminist Organization), 88, 144n8
Neal, Mark Anthony, 58–59
Negro Family, The (Moynihan), 44
New Jack City (movie), 22
Newton, Huey, 38, 58, 142n5
Nicholson, James H., 109
Norton, Chris, 95
"No Thing on Me" (song from *Super Fly*), 50
Notorious B.I.G. (Biggie Smalls), 29
Notorious K.I.M (album), 29

orgasm, and the making of *Sweetback*, 59–60
Owens, Dana. *See* Queen Latifah

Parks, Gordon, 49, 142n16
Parks, Gordon, Jr., 49
patriarchal structure: and the Black Power movement, 38–46; and black women, 2–3, 7, 104, 114–25; and blaxploitation movies, 5; in *Cleopatra Jones*, 101–2; and movie spectatorship, 143n17; and phallic empowerment, 6–7; and racial patriarchy, 7–8; in *Spook*, 74–76; in *Sweetback*, 56–73; threats to, 6–7, 104; and white supremacy, 8
Payne, Sheba (movie character), 131
Peck, Robert "Iceberg Slim," 51
Perry, Patricia, 45
phallic empowerment: and Bad Bitches, 29; and black female heroes, 108; and black men, 6–7, 56; and the Black Power movement, 39–40; in blaxploitation movies, 5–7, 17–18, 24, 50–53; in *Casino of Gold*, 103–5; challenges to, 28; and *Cleopatra Jones*, 86–90, 96–102, 144–45n19; and Coffy, 117; and *Foxy Brown*, 123–30; guns as symbol of, 113, 117; and patriarchal structure, 6–7; in *Spook*, 56, 74–76, 80–84; in *Sweetback*, 56–73. *See also* castration and emasculation imagery
"P.I.M.P." (50 Cent song), 28
Pimp: The Story of My Life Slim (Peck), 51

pimps, portrayal of, 2, 41–42, 50–53, 97–99, 129
Pirates of the Caribbean: Dead Man's Chest (movie), 135
Playing the Race Card (Williams), 10
"Poem" (Lindsay), 45
Poitier, Sidney, 48
polyphonic spectatorship, 19
Preston, J. A., 77
Priest (movie character), 49
primitive sex consciousness mythology, 60–61
Priscilla (movie character), 117
prostitutes and prostitution: and black women, 50–52, 64–65, 114–25; in *Coffy*, 111–25; in *Foxy Brown*, 111, 114–25; Malcolm X on, 42; in *Spook*, 80–82; and *Sweetback*, 64–65. *See also* sexual objectification of black women
Purdy (movie character), 97

Queen Bee. *See* Lil' Kim
"Queen Bitch" (Lil' Kim song), 28–29
Queen Latifah, 23, 28

racial patriarchy, 7–8
racial politics: in black action movies, 2–11; and the Black Power movement, 38–46; and blaxploitation movies, 131; and *Casino of Gold*, 103–5; and castration and emasculation imagery, 127–30; and Cleopatra Jones, 15; and *Cleopatra Jones*, 3, 86–90, 97, 101; and *Coffy*, 4, 86–87, 107–13, 123–30; and *Foxy Brown*, 4, 107–13, 123–30; and rape, 147–48n44; and sexuality of black women, 26–34, 114–25; in *Spook*, 57; in *Sweetback*, 57–73
Raisin in the Sun, A (Hansberry), 124
RAM (Revolutionary Action Movement), 37
rape: of a child, 62; in *Coffy* and *Foxy Brown*, 108, 121, 126–27; and race, 147–48n44; and slavery, 126–27; in *Sweetback*, 71. *See also* violence in blaxploitation movies
rap music, 24, 26–34, 138–39n25, 139n42
Read, Jacinda, 113

STEPHANE DUNN
is an assistant professor
of English at
Morehouse College.

The University of Illinois Press
is a founding member of the
Association of American University Presses.

_____

Composed in 10.5/13 Adobe Minion Pro
with FF Meta display
by Jim Proefrock
at the University of Illinois Press
Manufactured by Sheridan Books, Inc.

University of Illinois Press
1325 South Oak Street
Champaign, IL 61820-6903
www.press.uillinois.edu